Alienation After Derrida

Continuum Studies in Continental Philosophy
Series Editor: James Fieser, University of Tennessee at Martin, USA

Continuum Studies in Continental Philosophy is a major monograph series from Continuum. The series features first-class scholarly research monographs across the field of Continental philosophy. Each work makes a major contribution to the field of philosophical research.

Adorno's Concept of Life, Alastair Morgan
Badiou, Marion and St Paul, Adam Miller
Being and Number in Heidegger's Thought, Michael Roubach
Deleuze and Guattari, Fadi Abou-Rihan
Deleuze and the Genesis of Representation, Joe Hughes
Deleuze and the Unconscious, Christian Kerslake
Deleuze, Guattari and the Production of the New, edited by Simon O'Sullivan and Stephen Zepke
Derrida, Simon Morgan Wortham
Derrida and Disinterest, Sean Gaston
The Domestication of Derrida, Lorenzo Fabbri
Encountering Derrida, edited by Simon Morgan Wortham and Allison Weiner
Foucault's Heidegger, Timothy Rayner
Gadamer and the Question of the Divine, Walter Lammi
Heidegger and a Metaphysics of Feeling, Sharin N. Elkholy
Heidegger and Aristotle, Michael Bowler
Heidegger and Logic, Greg Shirley
Heidegger and Philosophical Atheology, Peter S. Dillard
Heidegger Beyond Deconstruction, Michael Lewis
Heidegger, Politics and Climate Change, Ruth Irwin
Heidegger's Early Philosophy, James Luchte
Levinas and Camus, Tal Sessler
Merleau-Ponty's Phenomenology, Kirk M. Besmer
Nietzsche, Nihilism and the Philosophy of the Future, edited by Jeffrey Metzger
Nietzsche's Ethical Theory, Craig Dove
Nietzsche's Thus Spoke Zarathustra, edited by James Luchte
The Philosophy of Exaggeration, Alexander Garcia Düttmann
Sartre's Phenomenology, David Reisman
Time and Becoming in Nietzsche's Thought, Robin Small
Who's Afraid of Deleuze and Guattari? Gregg Lambert
Žižek and Heidegger, Thomas Brockelman

Alienation After Derrida

Simon Skempton

continuum

Continuum International Publishing Group

The Tower Building	80 Maiden Lane
11 York Road	Suite 704
London SE1 7NX	New York, NY 10038

www.continuumbooks.com

British Library Cataloguing-in-Publication Data
A catalogue record for this book is available from the British Library.

ISBN: HB: 978-1-4411-0474-8

Library of Congress Cataloging-in-Publication Data
A catalog record for this book is available from the Library of Congress.

Typeset by Newgen Imaging Systems Pvt Ltd, Chennai, India
Printed in Great Britain by the MPG Books Group, Bodmin and King's Lynn

For Anna

Contents

Acknowledgements

I would like to thank Peter Osborne under whose supervision the first draft of this work was written. I would also like to thank Peter Hallward and Simon Glendinning for their useful and encouraging comments on the text.

Introduction: Derrida and Alienation

The concept of alienation initially appears to encapsulate what 'postmodern' and deconstructive thought claims to have laid to rest. With its theological origins and its use in Marxist social theory, the term suggests a teleological and eschatological grand 'meta-narrative' of fall and redemption, of the loss and hope for the restoration of a state of originary plenitude, a state of the fullness of presence and identity that would actually amount to a dangerous totalitarian form of metaphysical closure where difference and otherness are suppressed. Of course, this characterization of what the term 'alienation' suggests is provided by 'postmodern' and deconstructive thought itself. It is long established and entrenched, and for this very reason it demands a critical scrutiny that would itself be deconstructive.

The purpose of this book is to reassess and reinterpret the Hegelian-Marxist conceptions of alienation and de-alienation in the light of Derrida's deconstruction of the metaphysics of presence and 'the proper'. In so doing, the aim is to propose and outline an alternative interpretation of the relation between Derridian deconstruction and the theory of alienation to that which has hitherto been propounded by Derrida himself, his contemporaries, and his commentators.

The notion of alienation, along with the concepts of 'essence' and 'origin' which are purported to underpin it, has been long since discredited in anti-humanist currents of contemporary thought, particularly those associated with or deriving from French structuralism. The features of alienation have been determined there as constitutive of the human subject. When alienation is regarded as constitutive and insurmountable it becomes useless as a critical concept, and the promise of de-alienation becomes a pernicious myth.

While Derrida is a representative of such currents of thought, it could be argued that he does not address and is unconcerned with the theme of alienation. It is certainly the case that the word rarely appears in his writings. Nevertheless, one of the aims of this book is to demonstrate that the impetus of deconstruction is the unmasking and debunking of any notion of an unalienated condition that can be shown to be dependent on a metaphysics of presence and 'the proper'. What is in contention is the question of whether the unalienated condition is necessarily dependent on such 'metaphysical' conceptions.

Inalienable Alienation

Derrida's thought emerged in the 1960s within a wider theoretical context in which the critique of the concept of alienation was in the air. The idea of alienation to be found in the early Marx was held to involve the loss of something original and essential that could be regained in the future, entailing the belief in a lost and retrievable human 'essence', a belief that was identified with 'humanism'. Despite their diversity, Derrida and a number of his contemporaries reacted against 'humanism' as they saw it, and put forward non-humanist ideas loosely influenced by structuralism. The idea of a human 'essence' or authentic humanity became untenable in a theoretical universe of synchronic structures, differential relations, and discourse, in which the so-called human subject is but an effect and a function.

For example, Althusser's structuralist interpretation of Marxism starts from a critique of the early Marx's concept of alienation. He characterizes the concept of alienation to be found in the early Marx, Feuerbach and Hegel, as a 'myth of origins', a concept that presupposes the simple unity of an originary human essence. Alienation is an 'organic' concept dependent on the notion of an outgrowth from the unified simplicity of an originary essence, a concept that has no place in the anti-organic science of complex structurality. Althusser writes: '[O]rganic categories . . . cannot survive . . . particularly those categories that "cash" the theme of an original simple unity, that is, the "fission" of the simple whole, alienation.'[1]

Foucault is another example of a contemporary of Derrida who pitches his discourse against modern humanism. In his book, *The Order of Things*, Hegel, Marx, and the concept of alienation are all inextricably bound up with the anthropocentric *epis, tème*, the latter referring to the structural configuration of knowledge in the historical period of modernity. This *epistème* is centred on the notion of 'man' and his alienation. Foucault writes: '[T]he whole of modern thought is imbued with the necessity . . . of ending man's alienation by reconciling him with his own essence.'[2] Foucault identifies in Hegel and Marx, and in 'modern' thinking in general, the organic temporality of the loss of the plenitude of the origin and the promise of its eventual return.[3] For him, the concept of alienation and its attendant 'organic' concepts will disappear when the 'modern' anthropocentric *epistémè* is replaced by a different structural configuration of knowledge.

Derrida's thought emerged from a context where the French structuralist critique of the traditional concept of alienation held sway. This concept was identified with, and reduced to, an anthropocentric humanism, which itself was reduced to having an ultimate reference to the notion of a simple human essence. The concept of alienation was believed to be dependent on an organic temporality, a temporality based on the expressive development of a single unifying principle, manifesting itself in the retreat and promise of return of the origin. The ultimate reference to the simplicity of an essence was dismissed as a 'myth of origins'.

As with his contemporaries, Derrida postulates the constitutive permanence of alienation as opposed to the 'myth of origins'. An unalienated condition implies the originary simplicity of an essence, fully present to itself in the proprietary wholeness of an identity. This condition is a myth, because it is already marked by the trace of the other, always already alienated from the fullness of self-presence. In his later work, *Monolingualism of the Other*, he writes:

> This abiding 'alienation' [*aliénation à demeure*] appears, like 'lack,' to be constitutive. But it is neither a lack nor an alienation; it lacks nothing that precedes or follows it, it alienates no *ipseity*, no property, and no self . . . [This is a] structure of alienation without alienation, . . . [an] inalienable alienation[.][4]

If alienation is constitutive there is no alien*ation*, no making alien, because everything is always already alien.

For Derrida, the notions of origin, essence, and of what is proper to humanity, belong to 'metaphysics'. They are fundamental myths that govern the way we think. Derrida identifies metaphysics as logocentrism and onto-theology, the determination of being on the ultimate basis of a central governing principle, the presence to itself of the Word [*logos*] as manifested in the voice. While it is impossible simply to escape these fundamental myths, they can be undermined through a form of immanent critique called deconstruction. This involves analysing a text in order to make manifest the hierarchical binary oppositions underpinning it, and to demonstrate how they are undermined by the infinitizing polysemy of the operations of writing that they are constituted through, but which they have to suppress.

exupt when it's not

The notion of writing is important for Derrida, because it is traditionally seen as a derivative and alienated representation of speech, of the full presence of meaning in the voice. In his early work, *Of Grammatology* (1967), he describes the determination of writing by the metaphysical tradition in the following way: '[Writing] is a mediation and the departure of the logos from itself. Without writing the latter would remain in itself. Writing is the dissimulation of the natural, primary, and immediate presence of sense to the soul within the logos.'[5] Within this definition, writing is identical to what Hegel calls '*Entäußerung*' (translated as 'alienation' or 'externalization'). Derrida himself states the identity of writing and *Entäußerung* (alienation as exteriorization) in Hegel when he writes: 'Writing is . . . that exteriorization, the contrary of the interiorizing memory, of the *Erinnerung*.'[6] For Derrida, this derivative and alienated character of writing applies to meaning in general, which can never attain the fullness and immediacy of presence. Speech thus becomes merely a moment or a function of a generalized writing, an arche-writing, or an originary writing, which amounts to an originary non-originariness.

For Derrida, the fundamental metaphysical motif is that of presence, and he develops his notions of a generalized writing and *différance* to demonstrate the impossibility of its ever being achieved. *Différance*, spelt with an 'a', is a neologism which, in French, combines the meanings of difference, differing and deferral. Something can only be determined by its opposition to or difference from what it is not. The infinite chain of referrals that this sets off defers the presence of meaning. Something is never present in itself, it is always pervaded by the trace of what it is not; it is nothing more than a moment in an economy of traces. The trace is Derrida's term for what is neither present nor absent. The process of differentiation infinitely defers the reference to something present.

The myth of origins is the effacement of the originary non-originariness. The latter implies a generalized artificiality and inauthenticity, irreducible to any ultimate reference to the originariness of a natural authenticity. In *Of Grammatology*, Derrida casts Rousseau as a privileged example of the metaphysics of presence and the myth of origins. Rousseau decries the artificiality of civilization, claiming it corrupted the original natural innocence of humanity. He regards writing as an artificial aberration, a secondary distortion and corruption of the fullness and immediate presence of meaning in the voice. Writing is thus a 'supplement', an artificial prosthetic addition to something, external to its proper nature. However, Derrida argues, using evidence from Rousseau's own text marginalized from its main argument, that the original always already had the characteristic of prosthetic supplementarity, the voice already having the characteristics attributed to writing. The supplement, an addition to something that is apparently alien to its true nature, finds itself at the heart of that something, at the heart of its true essential nature, of what is proper and authentic to the self-presence of its own identity, thus problematizing the very notions of identity, the essential, and the proper.

For Derrida, the proper is inseparable from presence, and both are fundamental to his definition of metaphysics. His critique of metaphysics is thus a critique of the present and the proper. In order to elaborate further the implications of his critique of de-alienation it is necessary to investigate his treatment of these two concepts.

The Present

The metaphysics of presence is Derrida's term for the determination of the meaning of being as presence, that is, in terms of entities that are present. This is also his definition of metaphysics as such.[7] He derives this insight from Heidegger, who maintained that metaphysics as the determination of being in terms of what is, in terms of the present, is precisely the oblivion of the difference between presence and the present, and thus, more fundamentally, between being and entities, which is an oblivion of being as such.[8]

Despite the word's connotations of living concretion, presence, as the ultimate basis of metaphysics, as the constantly reiterated ultimate target of deconstruction, takes on the aspect of the emptiest of abstractions. While, as Derrida points out, the concept named by the Latin derived word for him involves an assimilation of various Greek and German words (*ousia, parousia, Gegenwartigheit, Anwesenheit,* etc.),[9] we will here concentrate on the determinations and associations that the single word *présence* ('presence') is subjected to in Derrida's writings, with particular focus on the first part of *Of Grammatology.* The word rarely appears there without being qualified and identified with other words.

One such qualification is the notion of fullness, or plenitude. For example, Derrida describes metaphysics as the 'subordination of the trace to the full presence summed up in the logos'.[10] There are also references to a writing that 'exiles us far from . . . the full presence of the signified in its truth',[11] and 'a full speech that was fully *present*'.[12] Is fullness intrinsic to presence, or is full presence a type of presence? Can there be a presence that is not full? Presence is defined as 'the trace of the erasure of the trace'.[13]

It may be the erasure of the trace, but it is still a trace, a trace that hides its tracelike nature. The neither present nor absent trace is the basis of presence, but presence effaces its basis. The concept of presence is of something that does not contain the trace of the other within itself, a something that is therefore full, fully itself. Derrida conceives the word 'presence' in terms of fullness. Presence is intrinsically full, but is fullness necessarily present? Fullness could be absent, but in this case absent would be conceived in terms of presence, a presence that is elsewhere, 'an *absence,* that is an other presence'.[14] Presence is thus identified with fullness and *vice versa*; it is fullness that is the target of deconstruction.

Derrida also qualifies the notion of presence with the notion of simplicity. For example, he refers to 'deconstructing the simplicity of presence',[15] and he defines the trace as 'that which does not let itself be summed up in the simplicity of a present'.[16] Presence and simplicity are identified; the present is simple and the simple is present. As presence is fullness, simplicity is fullness too. Complexity involves gaps, a lack of fullness. Simplicity can have no gaps and no lack. It does not contain any trace of the other within itself; it is fully itself and thus absolute and pure. Fullness is absolute and absolute is simple. Derrida writes of 'the plenitude of a present and an absolute presence'[17] and 'the concept of the simple absolute'.[18]

Presence as the basis of metaphysics involves the closure of an absolute identity, an identity uncontaminated by the trace of the other. Presence is a closure, a walling-in. Derrida claims that any thought founded on the *logos* is 'walled-in within presence'.[19] He maintains that retention and protention, both characteristics of the trace, 'sever the present . . . from its self-identity'.[20] The present in its presence is always an identity, and identity is always present. Presence and identity are identical.

Derrida describes the concepts of 'essence' and 'substance' as 'subdeterminations' of being that depend on the 'general form' of presence.[21] Essence is presence in that it effaces *différance* and the trace. Derrida defines *différance* in its opposition to essence as presence: 'There is no essence of *différance*, it (is) . . . that which threatens the authority of the *as such* in general, of the presence of the thing itself in its essence.'[22] Essence as the true nature of something, as what something is 'as such', involves a fullness and identity that excludes any trace of what it is not.

Derrida also equates presence with substance, in that the latter excludes the trace. He writes: '[T]hat which accommodates nonbeingness, cannot participate in presence, in substance, in *beingness* itself (*ousia*).'[23] Pure writing, writing that is not chained to the logocentrism of the phoneme and thus to the metaphysics of presence, undermines the notion of substance. Derrida writes:

> [Pure writing] menaces substantiality, that other metaphysical name of presence and of *ousia*. First in the form of the substantive. Nonphonetic writing breaks the noun apart. It describes relations and not appellations. The noun and the word, those unities of breath and concept, are effaced within pure writing.[24]

Substance is the opposite of relation. Difference is a relation and presence is the absence of relation. Derrida quotes Saussure's statement that 'language is a form and not a substance', and claims that this is based on Saussure's dictum that 'in language there are only differences'.[25] Whether substance is material, for example the phonic or graphic substance of expression, or immaterial, for example the meaning expressed, its essence lies in its non-relationality. Writing is constituted not by the graphic substance, but by the relationality between the graphemes, a relationality that amounts to a process of differentiation, a process that Derrida calls 'spacing'. Relationality as spacing is non-substantial and non-present. Derrida writes: 'Arche-writing as spacing cannot occur *as such* within the phenomenological experience of a *presence*. . . . No intuition can be realized in the place where "the 'whites' indeed take on an importance" (Preface to *Coup de dés*) [Mallarmé].'[26]

Derrida places the notions of consciousness and subjectivity firmly within the field of presence. He refers to 'the self-presence of the cogito, consciousness, subjectivity'.[27] Consciousness and subjectivity are particular forms of the metaphysics of presence, and they took hold through the Cartesian revolution in philosophy. Presence here becomes internalized as self-presence, which is identified with subjectivity. Derrida writes that, after Descartes, 'the determination of absolute presence is constituted as self-presence, as subjectivity.'[28] According to Derrida, subjectivity can only be thought in terms of presence and substance; the subject is self-present substantiality. He writes:

> [T]he category of the subject . . . however it is modified, however it is endowed with consciousness or unconsciousness, it will refer, by the entire thread of its history, to the substantiality of a presence unperturbed by accidents, or to the identity of the selfsame [*le propre*] in the presence of self-relationship.[29]

However, it is by no means certain that in the history of philosophy consciousness and subjectivity have always been conceived in terms of substantiality. Descartes' determination of the human mind as a 'thing that thinks'[30] involves the substantiality of thinghood. Derrida regards the Cartesian subject in substantial terms: 'Ideality and substantiality relate to themselves in the element of the *res cogitans*.'[31] However, Kant's inflection of the Cartesian subject in his conception of the 'transcendental unity of apperception' amounts to a desubstantialization of that subject. The subject of the 'I think' that must accompany all representations is transcendental and not empirical, a logical postulate and not a substantial being. Furthermore, Kant's 'noumenal' subject of moral action is unpresentable and non-phenomenalizable. It is thus insubstantial, as Kant places the notion of substance firmly in the phenomenal realm. For Kant, as for Derrida, substance and phenomenal presence are inextricably bound up. However, for Kant, the subject cannot be present, in contrast with Derrida's portrayal of the traditional philosophical conception of the subject as a self-present substantiality.

In the ensuing chapters of this investigation we will demonstrate the importance of an insubstantial conception of subjectivity to the development of the post-Kantian notion of alienation. Examples of such insubstantiality will include Hegel's notion of 'subject' as opposed to 'substance', of the subject as a disjuncture in the self-identity of substance, and Feuerbach's notion of the universality of the subject as an indeterminate determinable substitutability.

As we have seen, Derrida, in *Of Grammatology*, identifies the metaphysical concept of presence with fullness, simplicity and identity. He even reduces to presence the notion of 'infinite subjectivity'. However, does not infinity undermine presence? Infinity by definition cannot be de*fin*ed or de*termin*ed in terms of fullness and identity, which can only be finite. Infinity is a non-full, or rather unfulfillable, non-identity. Yet Derrida claims: 'The logos can be infinite and self-present.'[32] This contradicts Derrida's determination of presence as a 'walled-in' identity. The relationship between Derrida's thought and Hegel's distinction between the 'true' and 'spurious' infinities will be explored in the second chapter.

Derrida identifies presence with the fullness of life as the forgetting of death. He describes *différance* as 'the nonpresence of the other inscribed within the sense of the present, [and] the relationship with death as the concrete structure of the living present'.[33] The myth of the fullness of presence is thus the myth of the fullness of life, devoid of any relationship with death. Derrida describes his notion of the trace in terms of a relationship with death: '[T]he trace is the opening of . . . the enigmatic relationship of the living to its other.'[34] The erasure of the trace in the fullness of presence is the erasure of death. Conversely, Derrida also uses the word death to refer to the reified stasis of the fullness of life itself when he refers to 'being as presence, as parousia, as life without differance: another name for death'.[35] Derrida regards the fullness of life as a dangerous myth which he identifies with evil in his later writings, precisely because it involves the forgetting of death. In *Spectres of Marx*, he refers to 'absolute evil (which is, is it not, absolute life, fully present life, the one that does not know death and does not want to hear about it)'.[36]

Derrida often determines presence in terms of being a form, referring to the 'form of presence'.[37] He asserts that concepts such as essence, substance, consciousness, and subjectivity, are subdeterminations of the 'general form' of presence.[38] He goes further than this, though, claiming that form as such is nothing other than presence itself. He writes: 'Form is presence itself. Formality is whatever aspect of the thing in general presents itself, lets itself be seen, gives itself to be thought.'[39] Presence is also identified with form when Derrida claims that metaphysics assigns to being 'the closure of presence, the form-of-presence, presence-in-form, form-presence'.[40] The unformed or the amorphous are the non-present.

However, as we have seen, Derrida refers approvingly to Saussure's assertion that in language there are only differences, arguing that this is the basis of Saussure's view that 'language is a form and not a substance'. *Différance* is here linked to a certain understanding of form. Its opposition to substance implies that it involves a form of formalism, one that is different from form as presence. This indicates that it is only a certain conception of form that is reducible to the concept of presence. In fact, the later Derrida uses the word 'formality' to refer to non-presence as indeterminacy. He describes deconstructive thinking itself in terms of formality: 'In its pure formality, in the indetermination that it requires, one may find yet another essential affinity between it and a certain messianic spirit.'[41]

Pure form as the absence of determinate content is conceived by Derrida as the basis of a messianic, eschatological opening to the future. He writes: 'Apparently "formalist," this indifference to the content has perhaps the value of giving one to think the necessarily pure and purely necessary form of the future as such, in its being-necessarily-promised, prescribed, assigned, enjoined, in the necessarily formal necessity of its possibility.'[42] Here, the term 'future' does not refer, as it usually does, to a future present, but precisely to a lack within the present itself that disables it from being walled-in within the identity of the closure of its plenitude.

According to Derrida, time has traditionally been conceived on the basis of the present, as a spatial movement between presences. Derrida's conception of the future is a conception of time on the basis of non-presence. However, for the early Derrida, the notion of time is irredeemably soiled with the present. He writes: 'Time is that which is thought on the basis of Being as presence, and if something . . . is to be thought beyond the determination of Being as presence, it cannot be a question of something that still could be called *time*.'[43]

Despite this, Derrida makes a suggestive reference to the possibility of a 'delinearized temporality' that would involve a 'pluri-dimensionality' that would not be contained within the field of the present.[44] Linearity, time as a succession of presents, is the form of the organic temporality that Derrida, in *Of Grammatology*, calls 'history'. He writes: '[H]istory has no doubt always been associated with a linear scheme of the unfolding of presence, where the line relates the final presence to the originary presence according to the straight line or the circle.'[45] As we have seen, this linear 'history' of the loss and return of full presence describes the historicity of the concept of alienation as characterized by Derrida and his contemporaries.

Derrida identifies presence with fullness, simplicity, identity, closure, essence, substance and form. He identifies presence as the basis of consciousness, subjectivity, the fullness of life and linear temporality. What Derrida means by the term 'presence' is the fullness and closure of identity; identity without any trace of the other, any opening to non-identity.

The Proper

Derrida identifies 'the proper' with presence and identity. He claims that the notion of the subject involves 'the identity of the selfsame [*le propre*] in the presence of self-relationship'.[46] Presence is identical to the proper: '"[P]resence" (the proximate [*proche*], the own [*propre*] . . .)'.[47] He describes the erasure of the trace as being in 'the form of presence. In the form of the proper'.[48] The proper is identical to identity: '[I]ntegrity . . . *itself*, in its pure original self-identity, in its property.'[49]

The word 'alienation' principally refers to the loss of the proper, to ex-propriation. This can be a reference to the transference of property in the narrow sense of legally owned possessions, as in much of its pre-Hegelian usage, for example, in eighteenth-century political economy. It is also a reference to the loss of property in the wider and more fundamental sense of what is proper to the nature of something. The proper is the root of propriety, of the correct as in the appropriate. It ultimately entails the uncontaminated cleanliness of pure identity, uncontaminated by the other, by alienness. Alienation is expropriation; whatever particular loss is referred to, it is always the loss of something that belonged, that was at home, that had a place in the field of the proprietary totality of an identity.

Derrida himself defines alienation as expropriation. In *Spectres of Marx*, he describes the trace in the form of 'spectrality' as involving an 'expropriation or alienation'. He equates alienation as expropriation with his notion of supplementarity, referring to a 'supplementary dimension, one more simulacrum, alienation, or expropriation'.[50]

In his early essay, 'La Parole Soufflée' in *Writing and Difference*, Derrida uses the word *aliénation* to refer to an expropriation that he regards as originary and fundamental. He writes of an 'original alienation' that is not merely the loss of 'one of our innate attributes, but of our innateness itself, of the innateness proper to our being itself'.[51] He claims that the metaphysics of the proper, in this case a metaphysical lapse in the writings of Artaud, involves a conception of a primordial purity of identity that amounts to the belief in 'a place where property would not yet be theft'.[52] Derrida criticizes such a belief and argues that property is always already stolen, and thus that the proper is always already expropriated. The later Derrida, particularly in *Spectres of Marx*, uses the term 'ex-appropriation' to name the condition of being always already expropriated. Whereas the traditional term 'expropriation' implies the loss of the proper, the term 'ex-appropriation' is intended to imply that there was never anything proper in the first place.

Derrida regards all relationality, that is, difference and articulation, as involving expropriation. He writes: '[S]tructure is always a structure of expropriation.'[53] Here, 'structure' refers to differentiation and articulation, to relationality as such. It involves expropriation, because it renders impossible any ultimate reference to the proper as the substantiality of a pure identity that by definition eludes all relationality, all contamination by otherness.

For Derrida, the proper is the basis of the self-proximity of subjectivity. He writes: 'Proper is the name of the subject close to himself – who is what he is . . . the unity of the proper as the nonpollution of the subject absolutely close to himself.'[54] The proper is the basis of Derrida's concept of proximity because of an etymological association; he writes that '*proprius* [close] is attached to proper'.[55] Derrida claims that 'the metaphysics of a proper subjectivity' did not exist before 'the Latin era of philosophy'.[56] The notion of a proper subjectivity is a subjectivized inflection

of the metaphysics of presence, one that did not occur to the pre-Roman
Greeks.

The word 'alienation' also has Latin origins, and one of the meanings
it had in the Latin era, and has had since, is madness as the loss of
one's proper mind. According to Derrida, madness, as determined in the
metaphysical tradition, involves a fundamental expropriation, and is thus
a concept dependent on the metaphysics of the proper, on the notion of a
pre-alienated, pre-expropriated state. He writes: 'The concepts of madness,
alienation, or inalienation irreducibly belong to the history of metaphysics.
Or, more narrowly: they belong to the epoch of metaphysics that determines
Being as the life of a proper subjectivity.'[57]

Regarding human nature, one's essential property is that one's own
proper innateness is always already stolen, expropriated, alienated: 'By
definition, I have been robbed of my possessions, my worth, my value.'[58]
Derrida endorses Artaud's establishment of 'the proper departure from
that which is proper to oneself (the alienation of alienation) as the condition for the phenomenon of the proper'.[59] The phenomenon of the proper
is thus merely that improper phenomenon which effaces its own improper
nature, just as presence is the trace that hides its tracelike nature.

Derrida defines the word 'proper' in a particular way, and what he says
about it depends on this definition. In *Spectres of Marx*, Derrida writes,
explicating Marx: 'One must analyze the proper of property and how the
general property (*Eigentum*) of money neutralizes, disincarnates, deprives
of its difference all personal property (*Eigentümlichkeit*).'[60] Derrida here
translates *Eigentümlichkeit* as 'property', but it is usually translated as 'peculiarity', as it is in the quotation from Marx that follows in the same passage
from *Spectres of Marx*. Peculiarity suggests uniqueness and singularity.
Is it therefore the case that the deconstruction of the proper is also a
deconstruction of the singular?

As will be discussed in the first chapter, Max Stirner, in his book, *The
Unique and Its Own* [*Der Einzige und sein Eigentum*], conceptualizes the
singular in terms of the proper and *vice versa*. Derrida claims that Stirner's
thought involves 'the reappropriation of a living and unique body. The
living body, the "mine", "my property"'.[61] Therefore, according to Derrida,
Stirnerian singularity is embroiled in the metaphysics of the proper. However, Derrida's understanding of the proper is different to Stirner's. For
Derrida, the proper is identified with identity and presence, and refers to
what is proper to the nature of something; thus the proper is the essence,
or at least the notion of essence amounts to a form of the proper. In
contrast, Stirner radically detaches his concept of the proper, of ownness

[*Eigenheit*], from the notion of essence. Essence cannot be identified with the radical ownness of the unique individual, because it refers to the universally applicable attributes of something and not to its irreplaceable singularity. The proper is not the sum of the individual's attributes, or properties [*Eigenschaften*], despite the etymological connection. For Stirner, the notion of essence is itself an alienation of the individual's irreducible ownness, an expropriation of its ownmost singularity. Ownness, the proper, the peculiar and thus the particular, conceived radically and thus not on the basis of specificity as the classification of types, a specificity still chained to the general, refers to a singularity fundamentally opposed to the notion of essence, essence being the name of the formation of defining attributes that can be applied generally.

Stirnerian ownness [*Eigenheit*] prefigures, in a certain way, Heideggerian authenticity [*Eigentlichkeit*]. There is a concern with the proper, in various forms, throughout Heidegger's writings. The accuracy of Derrida's critique of the Heideggerian proper will be discussed in the fourth chapter.

Although Derrida equates singularity with the proper in his interpretation of Stirner, a notion of singularity detached from the proper is a prevalent theme of many of his later writings. In Derrida's writings there are two conceptions of singularity, one dependent on the proper and the other radically detached from it. In *Of Grammatology*, singularity is one of the targets of deconstruction; it is impossible because of an originary iterability. Derrida writes:

> A signifier is from the very beginning the possibility of its own repetition . . . It is the condition of its ideality, what identifies it as a signifier, and makes it function as such, relating it to a signified which, for the same reasons, could never be a 'unique and singular reality.' From the moment the sign appears, that is to say from the very beginning, there is no chance of encountering anywhere the purity of 'reality,' 'unicity,' 'singularity.'[62]

From the beginning there can be no singularity. In 'La Parole Soufflée', Derrida refers to Artaud's notion of the unique as that which 'eludes discourse and always will elude it'.[63] Language universalizes and so cannot apprehend the unique. Here, Derrida objects to the notion of an irreducible singularity that cannot be spoken of, and he wants to submit it to deconstruction. He writes: '[W]hen we appear to regret a silence or defeat before the unique, it is because we believe in the necessity of reducing the unique, of analyzing it and decomposing it by shattering it even further.'[64] To assert that there can be no irreducible singularity uncolonized by discourse is to assert that discourse, in its restricted economy of the selfsame [*le propre*], is all-powerful, extending its universalizing tentacles everywhere. Derrida is doing this to the extent to which he asserts that we are always already in the realm of discourse, of the sign, and that there is 'no chance of encountering' an uncolonized, unappropriated outside.

However, to make such an assertion is to be guilty of linguisticism, which Derrida himself identifies with logocentrism, the target of deconstruction. Derridian deconstruction is not a form of linguisticism. Derrida says, in an interview with Maurizio Ferraris, that, for him, deconstruction 'was a putting into question of the authority of linguistics, of logocentrism'.[65] There is a tension in Derrida's early work between a concern with radical alterity and a concern with the impossibility of apprehending an absolute outside. This tension is what is behind linguisticist misunderstandings of Derrida's work in the anglophone world. He laments the linguisticist reception of his work: 'Deconstruction was inscribed in the "linguistic turn", when it was in fact a protest against linguistics! . . . The paradox is that, even though I proposed to deconstruct the hegemony of linguistics, my work is often presented as a linguisticism.'[66]

Derrida's notion of *différance* undermines discourse, insofar as discourse constitutes a restricted economy of the selfsame [*le propre*], closed-off and walled-in from radical otherness. It names the instigation of a 'general economy', a paradoxical open-system, paradoxical because it undermines systematicity. The 'general economy' opens 'itself to nonmeaning',[67] non-meaning being the only possible discursive form of the radical alterity of irreducible singularity. For Derrida, singularity cannot be apprehended in an absolute outside of discourse. It can only come about through a disloca-tion within the functioning of discourse itself. Deconstruction involves a rigorous dislocation of the operativity of discourse, disabling the closure of self-identity, and preventing meaning from functioning *properly*. Identity is always already universalized; it is meaningfulness itself, and its meaningful-ness consists in it applicability to all cases with the same defining qualities. Non-identity, the dislocation of identity, is singular; it cannot be applied to cases of the same dislocation of the same identity, because then it would simply be another identity and not a non-identity at all. The unique eludes discourse within discourse, troubling its colonizing universality. Thus the unique is not lost and neutralized in an absolute outside; it intervenes, and is the name of intervention itself. A true event, a radical intervention, an occurrence that is not merely an effect of the calculable and predictable functioning of the systematic machine of the restricted economy of discourse, involves the absolute surprise of an irruption of irreducible incalculable singularity through a dislocation of systemic operativity.

Singularity is explicitly thematized in Derrida's later writings. In *Spectres of Marx*, he argues that singularity is always the singularity of the other and can only come about through the disjunction of systematicity. He writes:

> The lack of a system is not a fault . . . On the contrary, heterogeneity opens things up, lets itself be opened up by the very effraction of that which unfurls, comes, and remains to come – singularly from the other. There would be neither injunction nor promise without this disjunction.[68]

The disjunction allows the intrusion of the unassimilable singularity of the radically other within the identity of the present. This intrusion of a singularity that is always radically other is the true event, the irruptive event that liberates the 'now' from the present. Although *différance* is the infinite deferral of the present, it is the disjunctive condition of the 'now'. Derrida writes: 'In the incoercible differ*a*nce the here-now unfurls. Without lateness, without delay, but without presence, it is the precipitation of an absolute singularity, singular because differing, precisely [*justement*], and always other, binding itself to the form of the instant . . . No differ*a*nce without alterity, no alterity without singularity, no singularity without here-now.'[69]

Derrida describes singularity as 'an-economic',[70] meaning that it cannot occur within the confines of a restricted economy which by its nature reduces everything to the calculability of universal equivalence. The proper, as in property and ownership, operates within such a restricted economy and similarly reduces singularity. Singularity is incalculable; the unique is uncountable; it is not even the number one, despite the etymological connection. Derrida says, in an interview published in *A Taste for the Secret*: 'That which defies anticipation, reappropriation, calculation – any form of pre-determination – is *singularity*.'[71] In Derridian terms, singularity defies the proper.

Derrida's understanding of the proper in terms of presence and identity means that the proper is opposed to the singularity of radical otherness. Thus alienation as expropriation is the precondition of singularity, and not its loss. This conclusion is entirely dependent on an acceptance of Derrida's definition of 'the proper', as well as his inclusion of, within this same definition, the standard translation of this word into German and all the words etymologically connected to it as they occur in the writings of not only Stirner, but also Marx and Heidegger. The question of the validity or necessity of such an acceptance will be one of the guiding threads of this investigation.

The Human

Derrida conceives the personal on the basis of singularity, and thinghood on the basis of generality. He refers to the 'singular "who"' and 'the general "what"',[72] and 'the irreducibility of *who* to *what*'.[73] If 'who' signifies the singularity of radical alterity, and 'what' signifies an entity in the form of the substantial identity of presence, then deconstruction becomes a critique of reification. Reification, as understood by Lukács, is a condition of alienation where the proper singularity of humans is reduced to thinghood in the form of universal equivalence. The word 'who' refers to a unique person, whose singularity cannot be reduced to the general category of the human. What if the human, the 'proper' of humanity, the human 'essence', were simply defined as irreducibly singular alterity itself? If the essence is singularity then the essence is to not have an essence. As language can only refer to singularity in the form of paradox, there is nothing wrong with defining an essence as singularity, provided that the paradoxical nature of the statement is made clear. Derrida is issuing an ethical injunction to radically redefine the 'who'. The self must itself become an other in order to relate properly to the 'who' of the other, to its irreducible singularity. Self-othering engenders the 'singularity of an an-economic ex-position to others'.[74] The 'who' must always be other; the same could be said for the human.

Derrida himself does this when he explicates, endorses and radicalizes Kojève's view that the humanity of humanity is a pure form, undetermined, and not to be confused with any content, any particular determination. Derrida writes: 'There where man, a certain determined concept of man, is finished, there the pure humanity of man, of the *other man* and of man *as other* begins or has finally the chance of heralding itself – of promising itself.'[75] Here, Derrida is advocating the universal as the undetermined. This is the opposite of the essence as the universalization of particularity, the source of all false universalisms.

However it is defined, even if it is paradoxically defined in terms of irreducible singularity, the word 'human' is an answer to the question 'what?', not 'who?'. The answer to the question 'who?' is the meaningless of a proper name, meaningless precisely because it refers to irreducible singularity. The human is that strange paradoxical being whose truest nature is the loss of its nature, who, when residing in its proper element, is always other, other to all elements, property, residing, and to itself. As Derrida writes, in his early essay, 'The Ends of Man', playing on the twin meanings of the word 'end' as 'goal' and 'death', 'Man . . . is his proper end, that is, the end of his proper.'[76]

The Ensuing Investigation

Derrida's work arose out of a theoretical context where the concept of alienation was rejected on the basis of its supposed dependence on a humanist essentialism, a myth of origins, and an organic temporality. Derrida's writings themselves articulate a rejection of the concept of alienation in similar terms, but particularly on the basis of its supposed dependence on the notion of a lost and regainable unalienated condition that takes the form of a metaphysics of presence and the proper. Presence is false, because it is in reality a trace that hides its tracelike form. Presence is described as the basis of identity, plenitude, simplicity, substance and essence, which are in turn described as the bases of all notions of consciousness and subjectivity. However, consciousness and subjectivity can be and have been formulated in non-substantial terms. Derrida also defines the proper on the basis of presence, identity and essence. Alienation is expropriation, and this makes any notion of de-alienation or reappropriation dependent on a metaphysics of the proper. Derrida argues, in his earlier and later work respectively, that concepts of the unique in Artaud and Stirner are similarly dependent on the metaphysics of the proper. Despite this, Derrida develops his own concept of irreducible singularity on the basis of absolute alterity, a state by definition devoid of the proper. He even bases a notion of a universal humanity on an essential unessential indeterminacy and the irreducible singularity of the always other human.

If, as in Derrida's case, all conceptualizations of the proper, as well as closely associated notions, are understood in terms of the metaphysics of presence, identity and essence, then any notions of de-alienation as reappropriation are deconstructible. If the proper were conceived alternatively in terms of irreducible singularity itself, as it is in the writings of Stirner, then alienation, as expropriation and as the divestment of singularity, would itself be deconstructible, but de-alienation would then be an an-economic ex-position to singular alterity, the undeconstructible itself.

Hence, the guiding question of the ensuing investigation is whether the conceptualization of de-alienation necessarily depends on the 'metaphysical' conceptions of presence and the proper, and thus whether an alternative articulation of the notion of de-alienation is plausible. With this question in mind, the investigation will take the form of detailed critical analyses and discussions of the works of Hegel, Marx and Heidegger, focusing on the way in which their ideas relate to de-alienation and Derridian deconstruction. Hegel will be discussed both because a conception of alienation is central to his work and because Derrida's notion of *différance* is intimately bound up with Hegelian concepts and is put forward as a response to them. Marx will be considered because a conception of alienation is central to his critique of capitalism, and because his understanding of the overcoming of alienation is explicitly criticized by Derrida for being embroiled in the metaphysics of presence. Heidegger will be considered because he is of crucial importance to Derrida, who sees himself as continuing the Heideggerian project of a deconstruction of metaphysics, and because, it will be argued, Heidegger's writings constitute a critical response to the phenomena of alienation and reification.

Preceding the discussions of those three major thinkers, the first chapter will consider indicative examples from the history of the concept of alienation and concepts closely related to it. The concept's fall-redemption structure, as it manifests itself in a variety of philosophical forms over history, will be looked at with regard to Derrida's characterization of onto-theology, logocentrism, and the 'myth of origins' in terms of the departure and return of the *logos* to itself. However, the main emphasis will be on the vicissitudes of the concept in pre- and post-Hegelian German 'idealist' philosophy, for example Schiller, the Romantics, Schelling, Feuerbach and Stirner, with a view to ascertaining the extent to which such philosophy is restricted to or transcends the model of the historicity of logocentrism as the loss and return of the fullness of presence.

Following this, there will be an investigation into the role of alienation in Hegel's philosophy. The similarities and differences between Hegelian dialectic and Derridian deconstruction will be considered, as will Derrida's critique of Hegel's system as an exclusionary totality. Of particular importance will be the question of whether Derrida is right in describing Hegel's notion of the overcoming of alienation in 'absolute knowing' in terms of the '*parousia*' of metaphysical presence. Interpretations of Hegelianism in terms of an expressivist organic development of the *logos* will be submitted to critical scrutiny. The importance of Hegel's distinction between subject and substance will be discussed, with particular regard to the way in which his conception of the 'subject' affects his understanding of de-alienation, as well as the way in which it contrasts with Derrida's characterization of the notion of 'subject' in terms of a metaphysics of presence and substance. Hegel's understanding of de-alienation also involves a certain concept of infinity, and this will be discussed with regard to its relation to both Derridian *différance* and to the notion of an all-inclusive presence.

The third chapter will involve a discussion of Marx's concept of aliena- tion and its relation to Derrida's critique of metaphysics. The accuracy of Derrida's claim that the Marxian conception of de-alienation involves a desire to 'exorcise' the 'spectrality' and tracelike differential nature of exchange value and the commodity form will be investigated. The differ- ence between Marx and Hegel will be analysed regarding the relationship between the concepts of alienation and objectification. Marx asserts that alienation is merely one type of objectification, while, according to Marx, Hegel equates the two concepts. The supposed dependency of Marx's concepts on notions of human nature and appropriation will be looked at in the light of Derrida's critique of the metaphysics of presence and the proper. Marx's notion of unalienated 'free activity' will be analysed in its relation to Derrida's distinction between a 'restricted economy' of 'work' and the 'general economy' that exceeds it.

While the first three chapters will involve a reinterpretation, on the basis of Derrida's critical ideas, of the traditional conception of alienation to be found in the works of Hegel, Marx and others, the last two chapters will involve a reinterpretation of the implications of Heideggerian and post-Heideggerian (Derridian) deconstruction on the basis of the rethought conception of alienation itself. The fourth chapter will argue that Heidegger's writings are a response to the phenomenon of alienation, and are a deep- ening of the critique of the latter and of reification, Heidegger regarding 'alienation' as rooted in the abandonment of Being that manifests itself as 'homelessness'. The relationship between Heidegger and Derrida, as well the connections and distinctions between their respective deconstructive critiques of metaphysics, will be discussed as it relates to this theme. There will be discussions of Heidegger's treatment of the themes of objectification and finitude, which will be compared and contrasted with the relevant Marxian and Hegelian conceptions. The investigation will then deal with Heidegger's notions of appropriation and authenticity, and the nexus of concepts summed up by Derrida's term 'the proper'.

The final chapter will involve a rethinking of both Derridian deconstruc- tion and the notion of alienation on the basis of the preceding discussions. The relationship between deconstruction and conceptions of praxis and the political will be discussed. As will the question of the extent to which the notion of de-alienation necessarily entails a suppression of alterity, of alienness, which will be addressed by analysing the relationship between Derrida, Levinas, and the concept of alienation.

This investigation as a whole will strive to demonstrate the way in which Derrida's work can shed light on the nature, philosophical underpinnings, and implications of the concept of alienation, as well as to demonstrate the significance of alienation to understanding Derrida's work and its own implications. What is in question is whether taking on board Derrida's critique of the metaphysics of presence necessarily involves an acceptance of his rejection of the concept of alienation, and if not, what kind of reinterpretation of the traditional conception of alienation would be demanded by such a critique. The aim is to rethink, through thorough analyses of the relevant texts in the light of Derrida's critique of the metaphysics of presence, the Hegelian-Marxist notion of the overcoming of alienation. The results of these analyses will then be the basis for a reassessment of the nature and implications of deconstructive thought itself.

Chapter 1

Alienation and Presence: A Historical Sketch

Having established the relevance and importance of the concept of alienation to an understanding of Derrida's critique of metaphysics and the implications of this critique, it is now necessary to clarify the nature and implications of the concept itself in order to ascertain whether alienation is necessarily dependent on the metaphysics of presence. This will involve a brief overview of the thinkers whose writings provide pertinent contributions to the theme of alienation, followed by an exposition of the concept, its aspects, parameters and associations.

Origins: The Bible and Neo-Platonism

As we have seen, Derrida and his contemporaries regarded the concept of alienation as involving the 'myth of origins'. The notion of the loss of an original state of harmony and unity, and the promise of its future return, has religious origins which are most clearly represented by the story of the 'fall of man'. Adam and Eve were expelled from the paradise of the Garden of Eden, because they ate the forbidden fruit that gave them knowledge of good and evil and which thus destroyed their natural innocence and immediacy. Judeo-Christian redemption is a return to the divine on the basis of the very freedom and responsibility that came about through the fall, and thus is not a return to a state of prelapsarian ignorance. Derrida observes the fall motif at work in traditional conceptions of writing as a lapse from and corruption of the natural immediacy of speech. He writes:

> The epoch of the logos . . . debases writing considered as mediation of mediation and as a fall into the exteriority of meaning. . . . [T]he very idea of the sign . . . [retains] the reference to a signified able to 'take place' in its intelligibility, before its 'fall,' before any expulsion into the exteriority of the sensible here below. . . . [T]he intelligible face of the sign remains turned toward the word and the face of God.[1]

The historicity of logocentrism, the externalization of the *logos* from itself and its eventual return to itself, obeys a lapsarian logic.

The concept of alienation itself involves this fall–redemption structure. In the *New Testament*, Saint Paul uses the word '*apēllotriōmenoi*' (translated as 'alienated') to refer to a separation from God, the state of having 'fallen from grace'.[2] For example, in his 'Letter to the Ephesians', he writes regarding the unbelievers: '[T]hey are darkened in their understanding, alienated [απηλλοτριωμενοι [*apēllotriōmenoi*]] from the life of God.'[3] For Saint Paul, the terms '*apēllotriōmenoi*' and '*apokatallaxe̅* [αποκαταλλαξη]' (translated as 'might reconcile') refer to the state of fallenness (from grace) and the possibility of redemption respectively.[4]

Saint Paul's use of the term '*ekenōsen*' (translated as 'emptied') is a source of the Hegelian concept of *Entäußerung* (literally meaning 'externalization', but often translated as either 'alienation' or 'divestment'). In his 'Letter to the Philippians', Paul writes: 'Jesus, who, though he was in the form of God, . . . emptied [εκενωσεν [*ekenōsen*]] himself, taking the form of a servant, being born in the likeness of men.'[5] '*Ekenōsen*' here refers to the incarnation, whereby God 'empties' himself in order to become a human. In his translation of The Bible into German, Martin Luther renders '*ekenōsen*' as '*entäußerte*'.[6] '*Entäußerte*' is a verb form of '*Entäußerung*', and the notion of divine divestment in the incarnation at least formally resembles the Hegelian notion of the externalization and objectification of spirit. Derrida describes Hegelian *Entäußerung* as a broadening of the theological notion of *kenōsis* (the noun form of *ekenōsen*) into a philosophical theory of human subjectivity. He writes:

> The process which assures a 'mutual fashioning' . . . of the two instances of *kenosis*, the divine and the human, that of God and that of 'modern subjectivity', would be a process inherent to . . . a representation which *at the same time* exteriorizes and interiorizes (*Entäußerung/Erinnerung*). In exteriorizing, in extra-posing its object, it alienates and empties itself[.]'[7]

The Christian notion of the incarnation as the emptying externalization of the *logos* is later generalized in Hegel's philosophy as the self-externalization of the initially '*in*-itself' that is constitutive of a re-internalized self-conscious '*for*-itself' identity.

In the history of philosophy itself, the fall–redemption model is first used, independently of any Biblical influence, by the pre-Socratic philosopher, Empedocles. He put forward a cyclical theory of history where humanity falls from a harmonious 'Golden Age' into disharmonious times, and where history develops towards the Golden Age's eventual, but temporary, re-establishment. However, what is of interest here is the function of the fall–redemption model in an onto-theological metaphysics of presence, and Heidegger and Derrida, in their guise as historians of the latter, claim that such a metaphysics does not arise until the inception of what they call 'Platonism'.[8] Plato's philosophy contrasts the transitory empirical world with the unchanging realm of the ideal forms, the latter being the fundamental reality. But it is not until the rise of so-called 'neo-Platonism' that a redemptive metaphysics is systematically developed.

Plotinus, the principal neo-Platonist, claims that all being derives from a permanent primordial unity that he calls 'the One'. The circles of being emanate from the One, the outermost circle being the external material world, characterized by transitoriness, difference and fragmentation. The One can be apprehended by the human mind, but the mind must detach itself from its worldly material concerns in order to do this. Plotinus claims, in *The Enneads*, that people have forgotten their connection to the One, their origin in the divine unity; they have thus forgotten their own true nature by being fixated with ephemeral material things which are intrinsically alien to them. Plotinus's purpose is to recall people back to their origins in divine unity. He writes:

> The souls . . . no longer discern . . . the divinity of their own nature; . . . all their awe and admiration is for the alien, and, clinging to this, they have broken apart[;] . . . their regard for the mundane and their disregard of themselves bring about their utter ignoring of the divine. . . . A double discipline must be applied if human beings in this pass are to be reclaimed, and brought back to their origins, lifted once more towards the supreme and One and first.[9]

This early model of alienation and reconciliation involves an extreme rejection of the material world, a denial of the possibility that it might have any value or connection to the true nature of humanity, which is characterized in purely spiritual or intellectual terms. Later conceptions of alienation do not share this view of human nature, but some of the aspects of those conceptions, such as loss of the origin and dis-integration, are already discernible.

Augustine, influenced by neo-Platonism, similarly sees a choice between focusing on God as the unified centre of being and immersing himself in the fragmentation and multiplicity of the world. Neo-Platonist metaphysics also enabled him to see evil as separation and alienation from God, rather than as something that exists in itself.[10] In his book, *The City of God*, he uses the word '*alienatio*' (translated as 'alienation') to refer to such separation. For example, he writes: '[S]ince the soul . . . cannot . . . be without life of some kind, its utmost death is alienation [*alienatio*] from the life of God.'[11]

The neo-Platonist model of alienation is, in Derridian terms, metaphysical and logocentric; it is a thinking of difference that refers back (and forwards) to the orginary immutable eternal presence of the One. It is onto-theological in that it equates God with being *qua* being, conceiving of being as such as being a mode of being, the fundamental one. It is thus a prime case of the metaphysics of presence as described by Derrida in the following way: 'The subordination of the trace to the full presence summed up in the logos . . . [is] required by an onto-theology determining the archaeological and eschatological meaning of being as presence, as parousia, as life without difference.'[12] The understanding of difference and multiplicity in terms of being a fall and alienation from the unity and full presence of the *logos* is, for Derrida, definitive of logocentric metaphysics as such.

Despite this, Derrida regards some elements of Plotinus's 'mysticism' as exceeding what he calls the 'closure of metaphysics', particularly Plotinus's notion of the 'trace [ἴχνος [*ikhnos*]]'. Derrida quotes as an epigraph to his essay, 'Form and Meaning',[13] Plotinus's following statement: 'Form is the trace of the formless [Το γίφ ἴχνος του ἀμορφου μορφή [*To gar ikhnos tou amorphou morphē*]].'[14] As we have seen in the Introduction, according to Derrida, 'form' is one of the aspects of the metaphysical concept of presence. As the Plotinian One is indeterminate and formless it is not a case of presence as form. Derrida, in a footnote to his essay, 'Ousia and Grammē', claims that Plotinus's statement effectively means that 'presence . . . [is] the trace of nonpresence'.[15] Derrida argues that Plotinus's work is an example of metaphysics exceeding itself in its own text. He writes: 'An irreducible rupture and excess can always be produced within an era, at a certain point of its text (for example, in the "Platonic" fabric of "Plotinism").'[16] According to Derrida, Plotinus's text can be read as undermining the very logocentric Platonism that it presents. Whichever way it is read as regards the metaphysics of presence, it still involves a fall–redemption narrative of the loss and return of an originary union with the oneness that is at the foundation of being.

The Corruption of Nature: Rousseau

A secularized concept of alienation was developed during the eighteenth-century Enlightenment. In the writings of the Scottish political economists the term 'alienation' is used to refer to the transfer of property, a usage derived from one of its principal meanings in Latin. While the use of the word was restricted to this narrow meaning, it was clear that a society based on the activity of alienation, of selling and exchange, had lost the direct and unmediated relationship to its means of life that a more primitive society would have had. James Steuart writes: 'For as long as the earth nourishes directly those who are upon her surface, as long as she delivers her fruits into the very hand of him who consumes them, there is no alienation, no occasion for money.'[17]

Similarly, Rousseau uses the term '*aliéner*' (translated as 'to alienate') to refer to the transfer of property. He writes: 'To alienate [*aliéner*] is to give or to sell.'[18] However, the term is used only to demonstrate the inalienability of the right of freedom and of the sovereignty of the 'general will' of the people. He regards freedom as essential to being human; the alienation of freedom is the alienation of human nature. Inalienability means that something cannot be alienated, but, because it is here referring to the sphere of the right and just, it really means that something must not be alienated – it has the status of a moral imperative. Rousseau claims that people do not alienate their freedom in order to enter into the social contract; they give up their 'natural liberty' in order to gain 'civil liberty', a legally guaranteed freedom through property laws.[19] His notion of the social contract is put forward as a way of regaining the essential freedom of humanity within the realm of developed civilization, a freedom that had been curtailed by the loss of the primitive 'state of nature'.

Rousseau argues that humanity in its original natural state was free from war and exploitation. Rousseau saw in the development of civilization the corruption of humanity's original natural innocence. This viewpoint has clear parallels with the story of the 'fall of man', here 'civilization' taking the place of 'knowledge of good and evil'. For Rousseau, a return to prelapsarian innocence, based on pre-civilizational ignorance, is not possible. A society based on the social contract and civil liberty is the nearest that civilized humanity can get to the original freedom and innocence.

Inequality, hierarchy, property and exploitation were all effects of the artificial mediations of civilization imposed on natural humanity. Rousseau claims that civilization introduces 'from outside' all the vices of 'man' that are 'foreign to his constitution'.[20] The stated purpose of the second part of Rousseau's *Discourse on the Origin of Inequality* is to 'collect and consider the different accidents which may have improved the human understanding while depraving the species, and made man wicked while making him sociable'.[21] Society involves the depravation of 'the species', the corruption of human nature. Rousseau's first example of the 'accidents' that led to the development of civilization is the institution of property, an unnecessary artificial imposition upon humanity that is blamed for the worst crimes of civilization, such as wars and murders. He implies that this institution should not have been accepted: 'The first man who, having enclosed a piece of ground, bethought himself of saying "This is mine", and found people simple enough to believe him, was the real founder of civil society.' He adds: '[Y]ou are undone if you once forget that the fruits of the earth belong to us all, and the earth itself to nobody.'[22] The accidental and imposed nature of the institution of property indicates its unnaturalness, its artificiality. Thus, for Rousseau, property is not proper to humanity, but is a product of humanity's alienation from its natural condition.

As we have discussed in the introductory chapter, Rousseau's view that writing is a primary corruption of human nature, alienating humanity from the immediacy and self-presence of the voice, causes Derrida to regard him as a pivotal figure in the history of logocentrism.[23] Derrida claims that Rousseau's writings, while arguing that civilization and writing are corruptions of nature and speech, inadvertently demonstrate that there only ever existed the corrupt artificiality of writing. Derrida writes: '[W]e have read, *in the text*, that the absolute present, Nature . . . [has] never existed; that what opens meaning and language is writing as the disappearance of natural presence.'[24] Nature and presence have always already been corrupted, and can themselves be shown to bear the characteristics of artifice and *différance*.

Reintegration through the Aesthetic: Schiller

In response to humanity's corruption and alienation, Rousseau advocates not only a political system based on the social contract, but also a moral education that would turn a person into a mature and responsible citizen, relatively immune from the corruption and artificiality of civilization. However, a mere moral education was found by later thinkers to be inadequate to the task of rescuing humanity from increasing fragmentation. A more effective form of education would be one that addresses the whole person, not just her reason or her conscience. Education as cultivation of the whole person was known by the German word '*Bildung*'. Goethe was a pioneer of the novel of education, or *Bildungsroman*, which addresses the question of character formation through experience. The main character has to progress from the immaturity of one-sidedness and isolation to the maturity of a harmonized character and engagement with the world.

Goethe was opposed to the increasing social fragmentation of his age and the attendant increasing fragmentation of the human character into its specific faculties. Notions of wholeness and totality were crucial to him. He writes: 'All that man undertakes to perform . . . must proceed from all his powers united; everything isolated is worthless.'[25]

Schiller was similarly concerned with overcoming fragmentation, advocating an aesthetic education as one that would address the whole person. He operates with the familiar model of fall and redemption; fall from harmony through knowledge and return to harmony through knowledge: '[A]ny people caught up in the process of civilization . . . must fall away from nature by the abuse of reason before they can return to her by the use of reason.'[26] However, it is not the primitive state of nature that is the focus of his discourse, but the civilization of ancient Greece. The Greeks had a 'natural humanity' and a 'wholeness of being', in contrast to the fragmentariness of modern humanity. In his essay *On Naive and Sentimental Poetry* he argues that this originary natural wholeness should be regained: '[O]ur culture should lead us along the path of reason and freedom back to nature.'[27]

In his *Letters on the Aesthetic Education of Man*, Schiller provides a critique of the fragmentariness of modern humanity, and puts forward a notion of the aesthetic that would overcome it. He argues that the development of civilization has destroyed the wholeness of being that could be discerned in the ancient Greeks, a destruction that has been largely effected through the division of labour. The separate development of the human faculties, the full development of only one faculty in each person, leads to the stultification of humanity, the reduction of the human being to a particular function. People are reduced to 'developing but one part of their potentialities, while of the rest, as in stunted growths, only vestigial traces remain'.[28] Modern society and the modern human being cease to be organically unified wholes; living relations are reified into mechanical ones. Schiller describes modern society as 'an ingenious clockwork, in which, out of the piecing together of innumerable but lifeless parts, a mechanical kind of collective life ensued'.[29] The fragmentation of the individual is intrinsically bound up with the fragmentation of society, and Schiller sees this divisiveness as dehumanizing; the human is reduced to a specific function, to being a cog in the social machine:

Everlastingly chained to a single little fragment of the whole, man himself develops into nothing but a fragment; everlastingly in his ear the monotonous sound of the wheel that he turns, he never develops the harmony of his being, and instead of putting the stamp of humanity upon his own nature, he becomes nothing more than the imprint of his occupation or of his specialized knowledge.[30]

This de-totalization causes an alienated relationship between the individual and society:

> [T]he concrete life of the individual is destroyed in order that the abstract idea of the whole may drag out its sorry existence, and the state remains forever a stranger to its citizens since at no point does it ever make contact with their feeling.[31]

Despite his negative attitude to this fragmentation, Schiller concedes that it has been essential for human progress, for the development of civilization. He claims that the human species as a whole has benefited from this, but individual people have not. The point is not to reverse that progress and development, but to use it to reach a higher level where the lost wholeness is regained; not through nostalgic primitivism, but within the state of developed civilization itself. Schiller's stated aim is 'to restore by means of a higher art the totality of our nature that the arts themselves have destroyed'.[32]

The aim of the re-totalization of human nature is to be achieved through the aesthetic. The aesthetic can synthesize reason and the senses, and overcome any abstract one-sidedness. Schiller identifies two opposing forces at work within humanity, the 'sensuous drive' and the 'formal drive'. The former restricts humanity to its physical aspect, to the sensual world, the world of time and change. To be confined to the realm of sensation, to the flow of time and change, is to be confined to the 'limitations of the present'.[33] This confinement to the present involves self-alienation, a suspension of the personality: 'For this condition of self-loss under the dominion of feeling linguistic use has the very appropriate expression: *to be beside oneself*, i.e., to be outside of one's own self.'[34] In contrast, the other drive, the 'formal drive', restricts humanity to its rational aspect, to a realm of unchangeable timeless truths. This is a realm of universally applicable ideas, not restricted to the particularity of the present moment, where people are no longer 'individuals', but are 'species', or universal beings.[35] A confinement to the realm of form and reason would involve a loss of the personality through a negation of the possibility of its becoming manifest in the particularity of the world.

A union of these two opposing forces Schiller calls the '*Spieltrieb*' (translated as the 'play drive'). This involves reconciling change with identity, sensual life with rational form. The 'living form' that is the object of the 'play drive' is synonymous with beauty, or the aesthetic quality of things. The play drive overcomes the abstract one-sidedness of the other two drives, and instigates the concrete wholeness of the human being. It is only through aesthetic play that human nature is fully realized, or as Schiller puts it, '[M]an only plays when he is in the fullest sense of the word a human being, and *he is only fully a human being when he plays.*'[36]

The aesthetic relates to totality, because it is not bound to the one-sidedness of determination. It can relate to the whole person without constituting a determinate object for any particular aspect of that person. Schiller writes: 'A thing . . . can relate to the totality of our various functions without being a definite object for any single one of them: that is its *aesthetic* character.'[37] The sensuous and the rational are two opposing and exclusive determinations of humanity. When they are combined, and thus act simultaneously, they cease to be particular determinations, and the person enters a state of what Schiller terms '*Bestimmbarkeit*' (translated as 'determinability'). Determinability is a kind of productive indeterminacy, a freedom from determination that differs from indetermination in that it involves a limitless abundance rather than mere emptiness.[38]

This definition of the aesthetic as the 'free disposition' of limitless determinability, which is necessary for the full flourishing of human nature, puts into question the idea that totality, or wholeness, constitutes an overarching determination that subsumes difference under an exclusionary identity. Derridian *différance* is itself determinability in that it makes possible and undermines any particular determination. The opposition between determinacy and determinability is similar to Derrida's opposition between identity and the endless process of identification. The latter opposition is made explicit in *A Taste for the Secret*, where Derrida advocates identification as against identity. For examples, he advocates a political situation where 'there is no identity. There is identification'.[39] Similarly, in *Monolingualism of the Other*, he advocates an 'autobiographical anamnesis [that] presupposes *identification*. And precisely not identity. No, an identity is never given, received, or attained; only the interminable and indefinitely phantasmatic process of identification endures.'[40] Identification, *différance* and determinability involve a ceaselessly productive and destructive process that both makes possible and undermines identity, difference and determinacy.

For Schiller, aesthetic play is intrinsically linked to human freedom, because it both humanizes the world and is an activity free from external ends. Aesthetic contemplation domesticates nature, turning things into objects subjected to the human eye. Objectification *qua* domestication is necessary for human freedom *qua* power over nature. Schiller writes:

> That which hitherto merely dominated him as *force*, now stands before his eyes as *object*. Whatsoever is object for him has no power over him; for in order to be object at all, it must be subjected to the power that is his.[41]

Aesthetic play involves an interest and delight in superficial appearance, or semblance, rather than in reality; but in this case it is not the semblance of something real, but pure semblance itself. This is semblance as semblance, not semblance masquerading as reality. 'Reality' is alien to humanity whereas semblance is the work of humanity, its self-expression; humanity is at home in a world of semblance, a world of its own dominion:

> Since all actual existence derives from nature considered as alien force, whereas all semblance originates in man considered as perceiving subject, he is only availing himself of the undisputed rights of ownership when he reclaims semblance from substance, and deals with it according to laws of his own.[42]

This celebration of a semblance not anchored in reality resembles Derrida's 'affirmation of the play of a world . . . of signs . . . without truth, and without origin'.[43] However, there is one key difference; Derridian semblance does not 'originate in man considered as perceiving subject'.

Schiller describes aesthetic play as a kind of 'free activity', an activity which is an end in itself, which has no other purpose than itself, which is not appropriated as a means to any other end. It derives from play as such, which is facilitated by a superfluity of energy, beyond all necessity, that can be joyfully squandered.[44] This notion of play prefigures Derrida's notion of the play of *différance* as that which resists appropriation for any other purpose than itself, a nonproductive expenditure of energy that resists appropriation that would render it productive, a 'general economy' of 'sovereign' and free nonproductive play as opposed to a 'restricted economy' of productive work and dialectical reappropriation. Derrida describes such play as an 'affirmation [that] surrenders itself to *genetic* indetermination, to the *seminal* adventure of the trace'.[45] In its genetic indetermination and seminal adventurousness, Derridian *différance* is another name for the productive indeterminacy of Schillerian determinability.

Nostalgia for the Unity of Being:
The Early German Romantics

A lament over the irretrievable loss of an originary plenitude pervades the writings of the Romantics. Hölderlin's work involves the most acute thematization of this loss and yearning. Humanity's separation from nature through self-consciousness, reason, language and culture is experienced as the loss of an originary oneness with nature and being. Hölderlin expresses this explicitly in the unpublished penultimate preface to *Hyperion*: '[W]e have been dislocated from nature, and what appears to have once been *one* is now at odds with itself.'[46] The lost unity cannot be regained, but it is paradoxically present to humanity in the very form of its loss, a loss which is manifested in the aesthetics of tragedy.[47] In his essay, 'Being Judgement Possibility', he argues that the unity of being cannot appear to consciousness *qua* knowledge and reason, as the very nature of the latter is to separate through judgement. The best that philosophical knowledge can do is assert the identity of subject and object. But identity is not the same as unity; it is dependent on reflection and judgement [*Urteil*], and therefore merely constitutes the manifestation of a primordial separation [*Ur-Teilung*]. Unity means that no separation can take place without doing violence to what is to be separated, and this is not the case with identity. The unity of being cannot be apprehended by knowledge based on judgement, but only by intellectual intuition.[48] Hölderlin describes genuinely tragic poetry as 'founded on an intellectual intuition which cannot be any other one than that unity with everything living'.[49]

The writings of Novalis also involve the notion of the loss of an originary unity. In his poetry there is the figure of 'the stranger', someone who bears the memory of a lost golden age and hopes for its return. He characterizes philosophy itself in terms of a nostalgic longing: 'Philosophy is really homesickness, *the urge to be at home everywhere in the world.*'[50] The theme of homesickness also appears in his comments about childhood. Childhood is a time of naive immediacy that is always already lost in any state of conscious reflection, a golden age[51] that is still present in the memory of its loss. He writes: 'All fairy tales are only dreams of that home that is everywhere and nowhere. The higher powers in us that once, as genius, executed our will, are now muses that refreshen us with sweet memories during this dreary journey.'[52] What he means by 'genius' here is a naive openness to the external world, uninhibited by self-consciousness: '[T]he genius . . . is not involved in his representation and consequently the representation is not embroiled in him, but his observation chimes in free accord with the thing observed.'[53] The notion of childhood as an idyllic time of naive communion with nature that is corrupted and lost through adult consciousness and self-reflection, which reappears weakly in the form of nostalgic remembrance, is a recurrent theme in the poetry of Wordsworth, an English contemporary of the early German Romantics, for example, in his poem, 'Ode: Intimations of Immortality from Recollections of Early Childhood.' Childhood is another form of the prelapsarian state.

In his *Fichte Studies*, Novalis argues that consciousness is founded upon a primordial intuition of being that by its very nature it cannot apprehend. As with Hölderlin, the undivided oneness of being cannot be known, because it is in the very nature of knowledge to divide through predication. Consciousness is grounded on unknowable being, because self-consciousness depends on a subject recognizing an object as itself, which it would not be able to do if it did not already have an awareness of itself. This awareness, being prior to the differentiation between subject and object, is not in the register of consciousness *qua* knowledge, but rather of intuition, or what Novalis refers to as 'feeling'. Subjectification involves alienation from being, or the experience of being as loss. Novalis writes: 'I *am not* insofar as I posit myself, but rather insofar as I suspend [*aufhebe*] myself.'[54] The naive feeling of immediacy and oneness with nature and being, the experience of the child and the genius, the return to the 'homeland' of the golden age, would involve the suspension of the ego.

The inability of knowledge to apprehend being leads philosophy to become an unending task that can never achieve its goal. The self-consciousness of this inherent separation, irretrievable loss and the attendant philosophical scepticism takes on a more positive light in Schlegel's concept of irony, as opposed to the pathos of homesickness. Schlegelian transcendental irony, or what he calls 'the irony of irony',[55] involves an infinite regress of reflection which can never come to a stop at a basis of direct, non-ironic meaning. Schlegel celebrates such irony, linking it to freedom and the overcoming of any one-sided narrow-mindedness: 'Irony is the clear consciousness of eternal agility, of an infinitely teeming chaos.'[56]

Derrida similarly regards representation as involving an infinite chain of references, without the ultimate basis of an origin or a goal. He writes: 'In [the] play of representation, the point of origin becomes ungraspable. There are things like reflecting pools, and images, an infinite reference from one to the other, but no longer a source, a spring.'[57] Derrida's affirmation of the infinite play of *différance* resembles more the celebration of the infinite play of irony than any lament about the irretrievable loss of being.

Knowledge as Alienation: Schelling

Schelling's philosophy provides a more systematic expression of the Romantic concern with the retrieval of the primordial immediacy of being, an immediacy lost through consciousness and knowledge. He writes that the modern age is particularly 'alienated from that primordial feeling'.[58] Philosophy is conceived in terms of the fall–redemption model; a fall into freedom, and redemption through that very freedom. Knowledge destroys the originary unity between mind and nature, humanity and being, by setting up the distinction between subject and object. For Schelling, the aim of philosophy is to regain that primordial state of unity, to overcome the distinction between subject and object, and thus to overcome knowledge through knowledge, philosophy through philosophy. The aim of philosophy is its own destruction. Schelling says: '[Philosophy] proceeds from that original divorce to unite once more, through freedom, what was originally and *necessarily* united in the human mind . . . so it works in this respect for its own destruction.'[59]

As with Hölderlin, for Schelling, the only way the mind can apprehend the unity of being is through intellectual intuition. Knowledge cannot do this, because, by its very nature, it separates through reflection, judgement and the subject–object distinction, involving an estrangement between the freedom of the mind and the necessity of nature. Intuition is a form of awareness that does not separate itself from what it is intuiting, that does not turn it into an object. Mind and nature are united in intuition: 'In intuition the two are not to be distinguishable at all; there must be neither *before* nor *after*, but absolute simultaneity and reciprocity between them.'[60] As the intuition cannot be apprehended by knowledge based on judgement and reflection, Schelling associates it with the aesthetic imagination. He writes:

[T]he philosophy of mere reflection . . . sets out only to *separate* . . . whereas the pure intuition, or rather the creative imagination, long since discovered the symbolic language, which one has only to construe in order to discover that Nature speaks to us the more intelligibly the less we think of her in a merely reflective way.[61]

The aesthetic is the union of consciousness and nature, it completes philosophy's task of apprehending the originary unity of being, and thus 'the philosophy of art is the true organon of philosophy.'[62]

The absolute cannot be the absolute if it is posited as an object opposed to a subject, thus it can only be apprehended through a non-objectifying form of consciousness. Likewise, this form of consciousness cannot be that of a subject opposed to an object. The subject has to abandon itself in order to apprehend the absolute. This apprehension is a form of 'knowledge' without a subject or an object; it is thus not really knowledge at all, but could be more accurately described as a suspension of knowledge. Schelling calls this form of non-reflective consciouness '*Weißheit*' (translated as 'wisdom') or '*Denken*' (translated as 'thought'). He writes: 'Thought [*Denken*] means abandoning knowledge [*Wissen*].'[63] He equates wisdom with 'eternal freedom', or the absolute.[64] Eternal freedom is described in terms of being a productive indeterminacy, resembling Schillerian determinability: 'This freedom . . . is not mere independence from external determination. It is precisely the freedom to adopt a form.'[65] It is characterized as pure 'ability' and pure 'will', pure because ability and will are free of any object or intention which would restrict them; they are thus in a state of pure 'indifference'.[66] Despite the willful indifference and indeterminacy of pure will, wisdom *qua* eternal freedom is practical and active thinking, borne along by its productive determinability, thus 'belonging to life and action',[67] as opposed to mere contemplative reflection.

The intellectual intuition is renamed '*Ekstase*' (translated as 'ecstasy')[68] in Schelling's later work. The subject needs to stand outside itself, to abandon itself, in order to apprehend the necessarily non-objectified absolute. The self needs to alienate itself from itself in order to reconcile itself with its true basis in eternal freedom. The separation of freedom and nature through the objectification of nature is referred to as 'the *guilt* of man', and therefore as the legacy of the fall. This separation is phrased in terms of an alienation (estrangement) that can be overcome: 'Freedom estranged [*entfremdete*] from itself is nature, nature withdrawn back into itself is freedom.'[69]

The realm of the *logos*, of knowledge as the separation of mind from nature, of the self-presence of the subject of this knowledge, of the enclosure of metaphysics as the elision of fundamental difference in the name of the full presence of meaning, is the locus of alienation. The overcoming of alienation would involve the abandonment of the subject, of the logocentric enclosure of metaphysics, of meaning, knowledge and discourse, in order to apprehend, through a mystical un-knowledge, the unity of being, the absolute, the non-objectifiable absolute subject, which is itself nothing other than eternal freedom, the freedom of productive indeterminacy, or determinability, which, as we have seen, prefigures Derridian *différance*.

Knowledge as Reconciliation: Hegel

For Hegel, the overcoming of alienation is not, as in Schelling's system, the overcoming of philosophy; it is philosophy's full realization. The absolute is not a radical alterity to knowledge, but is immanent within knowledge. Hegel dismisses the notion of a primordial immediacy apprehended through intellectual intuition as an empty abstraction. The only way the absolute can manifest itself with concrete content is through the philosophical comprehension of the limits of all the forms of consciousness that attempted to grasp it.

Whereas for Schelling knowledge is the locus of alienation, because it separates the unity of being into subject and object, for Hegel knowledge is the locus of de-alienation which can itself ultimately overcome that separation. He writes: 'The I is at home in the world, when it knows it, and still more when it has conceived it.'[70] Absolute knowing is an unlimited form of consciousness, because it involves an awareness of the limited and one-sided nature of all forms of consciousness, of their inherent inability to grasp the absolute. The absolute thus manifests itself negatively, which it must do, because the positive is by definition that which is limited and therefore not absolute. The self-recognition of the constitutive limits of all forms of consciousness enables their overcoming, and absolute knowing is the philosophical comprehension of these self-negations and supersessions as a rational teleological progress, a progress whose result is absolute knowing itself, the overcoming of all limitation, an overcoming which knows itself as such. Subject and object are unified in the experience of absolute knowing, where all so-called externality is recognized as spirit's externalization [*Entäußerung*] and self-expression. The unity of absolute knowing is a unity full of content, a unity that contains all difference within itself, as opposed to the emptiness of abstract immediacy.

In Hegel's system all isolated particularity is ultimately overcome through the contradictions inherent in it. When he says, 'The True is the whole',[71] he means that the ultimate truth is the negative totality engendered by the dissolution of all isolated particularity. To see reality in terms of the isolated particularity of petrified facts unrelated to the wider totality is to be restricted to the analytical form of knowledge known as the understanding. This is a mechanistic form of knowledge which Hegel associates with a mechanistic reduction of humanity through the division of labour. This reduction involves alienation as reification and de-totalization. Hegel writes, regarding the division of labour:

> [T]his labor . . . is partitioned in itself and becomes a single laboring; and this single laboring becomes for this very reason more mechanical, because variety is excluded from it and so it becomes . . . more foreign to [the living] whole. . . . [T]he labor here is wholly quantitative without variety . . . something absolutely external, a thing[.][72]

While alienation and reconciliation are structural to Hegel's system, being necessary for the constitution and development of consciousness, speculative philosophy is put forward as a counter to the mechanistic reification of consciousness and life.

Derrida's notion of *différance*, of the trace of the other in the constitution of the selfsame, resembles Hegel's understanding of the self-othering involved in self-positing. Hegel writes: 'Only this self-*restoring* sameness, or this reflection in otherness within itself – not an *original* or *immediate* unity as such – is the True.'[73] However, Derrida claims that *différance* resists the Hegelian sublation [*Aufhebung*], the affirmative negation by which the self reappropriates itself at a higher level.[74] Derrida regards absolute knowing as the final arrival of the *parousia* of presence, that is, as a metaphysical mystification.[75] But, for Hegel, the absolute does not present itself in any figure, and is itself the dissolution of all figuration. Hegel sees the dissolution of all isolated particularity through the movement of differentiation as the negative manifestation of the absolute, whereas Derrida sees it as merely the infinite undermining of meaning.

The Projection of the Human Essence: Feuerbach

The post-Hegelian conception of alienation is initially developed in Feuerbach's philosophy of religion. The term '*entfremdet*' ('alienated') is here used to refer to the projection of the human essence onto something external and non-human. The argument put forward in Feuerbach's book, *The Essence of Christianity*, is that the notion of God amounts to nothing more than the characteristics of human nature attributed to an imaginary non-human, or divine, being, and not to humanity itself. He writes: '[The] differencing of God and man, with which religion begins, is a differencing of man with his own nature.'[76] Thus the essence of humanity is not recognized as the property of humanity, as humanity's own, but as belonging to an other, an alien entity; in this way the human essence is alienated. He writes: '[R]eligion alienates our own nature from us, and represents it as not ours.'[77]

For Feuerbach, it is human nature to have consciousness, and consciousness is, in its very nature, unlimited, infinite and universal. What distinguishes humans from animals is the ability to have an awareness that goes beyond immediate individuality, an awareness that is consciousness as opposed to mere instinct, that can apprehend the essential, that is, universal and ideal, nature of things. A human is therefore a being that can conceive of its own general, universal and essential nature – its genus [*Gattung*]. An individual can recognize her own limits, but this recognition can only come about through an awareness of the unlimited, and the unlimited is nothing other than the nature of this individual's own universalized essence, her 'genus' [*Gattung*], that is, humanity itself. Religious thought projects the unlimited onto an external imaginary being – God, whereas in reality the unlimited lies in humanity itself. He writes: '[I]f thou thinkest the infinite, thou perceivest and affirmest the infinitude of the power of thought; if thou feelest the infinite, thou feelest and affirmest the infinitude of the power of feeling.'[78]

Feuerbach criticizes the negativity and mediatedness of the Hegelian dialectic. He writes: 'Hegelian philosophy has *estranged* [*entfremdet*] the human being *from its very self*. It of course re-identifies what it separates, but only in a manner which is itself in turn *separable* and *intermediate*. Hegelian philosophy lacks *immediate unity*, *immediate certainty*, *immediate truth*.'[79] Feuerbach asserts that nature is where essence and existence are one, whereas humanity *qua* consciousness is where they are distinguished. Nature is the primordial reality, and is thus the foundation of humanity. For philosophy to be genuinely objective it must be grounded in intuition and not conceptual thinking. Thinking must be suspended for the object to assert its primacy. He says: 'True, objective thought, the true and objective philosophy, is generated only from thinking's *negation*, from *being determined* by an object . . . The intuition yields simply the essence *immediately identical with existence*.'[80] Alienation *qua* separation of essence and existence is reduced to being a mere epistemological error, but one constitutive of conceptual consciousness.

As we have seen, the notion of essence depends on the metaphysics of presence and is undermined by Derrida's notion of *différance* which 'threatens the authority of the *as such* in general, of the presence of the thing itself in its essence'.[81] Feuerbachian materialism would seem to be still in the thrall of the Platonic ideal, of logocentrism, insofar as it involves a notion of the universalizing nature of human consciousness as the ability to perceive the essence of things, their ideal and universal nature. However, Feuerbach maintains that it is only within consciousness that essence and existence are separated whereas in reality, in nature, they are one.[82] To say that essence and existence are one in reality is to abolish their distinction in reality. Their distinction is constitutive of consciousness, and is thus the way consciousness organizes its interpretation and understanding of the world. Feuerbach's essentialism is a mere epistemological, or even rhetorical, essentialism.

Furthermore, Feuerbach's understanding of the human essence is not so clearly reducible to the notion of presence. The human essence is the generic, universalizing nature of consciousness, the ability to see beyond all isolated immediacy. This ability is not the effect of any self-present substantiality; it is precisely the effect of emptiness and indeterminacy. Consciousness can be generic and universal because it is nothing in itself. A human being is free to assume any subject position, to be anyone, and this universality is the result of his insubstantiality. Feuerbach writes: 'Man is himself at once I and thou; he can put himself in the place of another, for this reason, that to him his species [*Gattung*], his essential nature, and not merely his individuality, is an object of thought.'[83] The emptiness that is the basis of universality is put forward as the freedom to adopt any determination, resembling Schillerian and Schellingian determinability. He writes: '[T]he *pantheistic* essence, which speculative philosophers or much more theologians have *separated* from the human being and objectified as an *abstract* essence, is nothing else but its *own* essence undetermined, but capable of *infinite determinations*.'[84] Emptiness and indeterminacy are the basis of the free determinability of universality.

Singularity and Authenticity: Stirner

According to Stirner, Feuerbach's notion of the human essence is merely another way in which the individual is alienated. In his book, *The Unique and Its Own* [*Der Einzige und sein Eigentum*], Stirner argues that Feuerbach, in returning the human essence from its religious projection to humanity itself, merely reproduces the religious division of the individual into an essential and unessential self. The generic human essence, or 'Man', is just as alien to the individual as God. The individual is unique and irreducible, and its identification with anything other than itself involves its alienation. All eternal, metaphysical ideals, such as God, truth, human nature, are alien to the ownness [*Eigenheit*] of the individual, to its peculiarity. Such ideals, along with any external determining forces, are referred to as 'sacred [*Heiligen*]'. The unalienated being is the genuine egoist at one with her ownness, to whom nothing is sacred. He writes: 'Alienness [*Fremdheit*] is a criterion of the "sacred". In everything sacred there lies something "uncanny", that is strange, such as we are not quite familiar and at home in. What is sacred to me is *not my own.*'[85] What is 'my own' is described in instrumental terms as that which is 'in my *power* or what I *control*.[86] The genuine egoist, to be authentically her own, must master herself, 'instead of being mastered . . . by anything else (God, man, authority, law, state, church)'.[87]

To be authentically its own the unique individual must not be reduced to any of its mere qualities. Qualities, such as humanity, are not what the individual is, but what it has. There is no essence to the unique individual, nothing beyond the naked fact of its existence. Its mortality is what distinguishes it, the possibility and imminent inevitability of its loss of existence, its death. Only the unique individual dies; humanity, 'man', the human essence does not: 'Ludwig dies, but the king remains; I die, but my spirit, man, remains.'[88] The terror of the French revolution is characterized in terms of the eternal abstraction, 'man', and its fatal effect on unique mortal individuals, 'men': 'Because the revolutionary priests or schoolmasters served *man*, they cut off the heads of *men*.'[89]

The ownness of the unique individual is defined negatively in terms of its refusal to attach itself to any external determinations, to believe in the sanctity of anything: '[D]oubt, which in practice becomes a *buffeting*, is what is most man's own.'[90] The unique individual has no essence, and so is a free nothingness, a productive indeterminacy or determinability *à la* Schiller *et al.* Stirner writes: 'I am not nothing in the sense of emptiness, but I am the creative nothing [*schopferische Nichts*], the nothing out of which I myself as creator create everything.'[91] He also writes regarding such 'creativity': '[O]wnness is the creator of everything, as genius (a definite ownness), which is always originality, has for a long time already been looked upon as the creator of new productions.'[92]

Stirner's writings appear to be radically anti-metaphysical and anti-essentialist. His notion of ownness [*Eigenheit*] as the irreducible singularity of mortal individuals prefigures Heidegger's account of authenticity [*Eigentlichkeit*]. However, the insubstantiality of ownness would not necessarily

free it from Derridian accusations of complicity in the metaphysics of presence, because Derrida's critique of Heidegger involves associating the
proper [*Eigentlich*] with the present. Stirner writes: 'I am not, like freedom,
extant only in the future and in hopes, but even as the most abject of slaves
I am – present.'[93]

Production and Commodification: Marx

For Marx, alienation is the manifestation of the mode of production of
capitalist society. Therefore its overcoming would involve a radical change
of that society. Communism is put forward as being the overcoming of
alienation, the 'reintegration and return of man to himself'.[94]

Alienation involves a loss of the control, mastery and self-determination
of human activity to an external, alien and hostile force. Properly human
activity is characterized as productive activity, or labour. The product
of labour is labour's own objectification, but this object is taken away,
expropriated by the alien force. The free productive activity of human
self-realization is distorted by the relations of production necessitated by a
society which has its basis in the commodity. The commodification of the
object of production affects the worker in a number of ways. She is alienated from the product of her labour, which becomes an alien object exercis-
ing power over her. A world of commodities comes about, produced by the
workers, but confronting them as something foreign, not their own. The
worker is also alienated from herself, from her own activity, which, instead
of being what it naturally should be, that is, the free development of her
'physical and mental energy', becomes something external that is not her
own, a deadening mechanical chore in which she feels outside herself,[95]
an activity that is a mere means to an external end. As a result of this,
the worker is alienated from her universal nature, her generic-being
[*Gattungswesen*]. This Feuerbachian notion involves the understanding
that humanity is, by its very nature, unlimited, universal, and therefore free,
that is, free from the restricted determinacy of isolated particularity. The
'free, conscious activity'[96] that is humanity's generic-character, an activity
that is an end in itself, is alienated, and distorted into a mere means to the
subsistence of the isolated individual. The worker is thus atomized and
thereby alienated from other people.

Fragmentation and de-totalization are the effects of the stringent division
of labour necessitated by commodity-based society. The human being is
alienated from its free and comprehensive nature by being reduced to a

particular function. The worker becomes commodified and reified, a thing for sale, with a particular function. Society is atomized, as the general social purpose of labour is lost and replaced by a functional 'homogeneous human labour'[97] that produces the alien realm of commodities that governs and controls the producers. This realm of commodities mystifies the social character of labour, in the form of the ideological distortion of reified consciousness: '[A] definite social relation between men . . . assumes here, for them, the fantastic form of a relation between things.'[98] The alienation of the worker from her products, her comprehensive nature and the social whole, causes in her consciousness an ideological misrecognition of the truly social basis of commodity society, a misrecognition that ultimately serves the reproduction of that society.

As we have seen, despite the fact that Derridian *différance* supposedly precludes any reference to a human essence, the notion of humanity's generic universality is based on indeterminacy, and not substance. However, the idea of overcoming the ghostly insubstantiality of the commodity form through the abolition of the mode of production it depends on is viewed by Derrida as an attempt at 'exorcism', the casting out of spectrality, *différance*, the trace, in favour of de-alienation as the return of full presence.[99]

Reification: Lukács

Marx's analysis of commodities provides the basis of Lukács's exposition of the phenomenon of reification [*Verdinglichung*]. Reification is the reduction of what is properly a living human relation into an ossified thing. It refers to the dehumanization caused by the commodification of all aspects of life. In a market economy the activity of humanity is commodified, and thus people are estranged or alienated from it: '[A] man's activity becomes estranged from himself, it turns into a commodity which, subject to the non-human objectivity of the natural laws of society, must go its way independently of man just like any consumer article.'[100] The increasing division of labour into specialized operations means that the worker has no contact with the final product and that the work itself loses all qualitative and human characteristics, becoming a mere mechanical repetition. Such work dehumanizes the worker into being a mere fragment of himself, a functional cog in a machine, the empty repetitiveness of the work measured in purely quantitative temporal terms where time itself loses its qualitative and variable nature. Lukács writes: '[Time] freezes into an exactly delimited, quantifiable continuum filled with quantifiable "things" (the reified, mechanically objectified "performance" of the worker, wholly separated from his total human personality): in short, it becomes space.'[101] This mechanized form of work also atomizes the workers, isolating them from each other and the social whole. While society is more unified than ever before, subject to a unified economic process, individual people experience this as increased atomization, because the mechanization of production separates people into different functions, breaking all human and communal bonds, replacing these with mere functional connections within the social machine.

Commodification effaces the qualitative nature of things in general, submitting them to pure quantitative calculability. Rational calculability destroys the authentic immediacy of substantiality. Lukács writes: 'This rational objectification conceals above all the immediate – qualitative and material – character of things as things. When use-values appear universally as commodities they acquire a new objectivity . . . which destroys their original and authentic substantiality.'[102] In this way the commodity society alienates humanity from nature.

The standpoint of the proletariat, of the workers as a class, when it can shed the reifying mystifications of bourgeois ideology, is oriented towards the social totality, and is not stuck in the isolated immediacy of empiricism. Seeing things in terms of isolated particularity is a product of the atomization of people through the mechanization of production. This is a false consciousness, because the reality of commodity society is that everything is ultimately interrelated. Capitalist society is a totality that hides itself from the consciousness of its subjects, who, in the thrall of reified ideology, experience their lives in the form of isolated particularity. If things are seen in terms of totality, the immediacy of empirical consciousness will be overcome, and the awareness of mediation will expose their inherent interconnectedness.[103] This will enable the overcoming of reification:

> Reification . . . can be overcome only *by constant and constantly renewed efforts to disrupt the reified structure of existence by concretely relating to the concretely manifested contradictions of the total development, by becoming conscious of the immanent meanings of these contradictions for the total development.*[104]

It is necessary to engage in areas of struggle with a consciousness of how they relate to the social totality.

Overcoming reification in this way involves an overcoming of humanity's alienation from the movement of time. Social praxis requires the present to be seen as a becoming, as a mediation between past and future, and not as the 'immediacy slipping away'[105] of empiricist reified consciousness. If either the past or the future are considered in the form of being external to their mutual mediation they become reified into existences that are alien to the human being, who in this case can only be a mere contemplator. The present as becoming is 'the focus of decision and of the birth of the new'.[106] De-alienation in this case involves taking control over the historical process. This involves people seeing the movement of time itself as their own. Lukács writes:

> Man must be able to comprehend the present as a becoming . . . by seeing in it the tendencies out of whose dialectical opposition he can *make* the future. Only when he does this will the present be a process of becoming, that belongs to *him*.[107]

As we have seen, Derrida dismisses the idea that the immediacy and qualitative authentic substantiality of things could be reawakened with the abolition of commodity society as a manifestation of the metaphysics of presence. However, Lukács's notion of authentic temporality involves an understanding of the present, not as immediacy, but as the mediation of the past and future through which humanity becomes part of a conscious and active becoming. Similarly, Derrida claims that the deconstruction of the present partly involves accounting for the 'dialectic' of 'protention' and 'retention' within it.[108] Derrida writes:

> [W]hat is anticipated in protention does not sever the present any less from its self-identity than does that which is retained in the trace. But if anticipation were privileged, the irreducibility of the always-already-there and the fundamental passivity that is called time would risk effacement.[109]

What Derrida is suggesting here is that the deconstruction of the self-identity of the present overcomes the reified givenness of the already-there and thus leads to the replacement of the contemplative passivity of 'time' by the activity and praxis of what Lukács calls 'becoming'. To this extent deconstruction is a form of the critique of reification. The active process of social change does not only not depend on a metaphysical notion of presence, it is itself furthered by the dissolution of the latter. The relationship between deconstruction and praxis will be discussed in more detail in the fifth chapter.

Derridian *différance* undermines all determinacy and the positivity of isolated particularity, overcoming the immediacy and self-presence of the objects of empiricist and positivist analytical consciousness, and thus the reified experience of atomization, by bringing to light the otherness that haunts any determined identity. However, it resists the dialectical reappropriation of this undermining, a reappropriation involving the positive consequence of an awareness of the broader picture, of the social totality, that would harness the dissolution of any isolated particularity in order to comprehend its mediation through the totality. For Derrida, the dissolution of identity does not have the Hegelian consequence that 'the True is the whole', but that all truth-claims should be replaced by the play of active interpretation. Such play would be dismissed by Lukács as a form of subjectivism, as the individual player experiences the dissolution of reified identity in social isolation, as with Rorty's 'private ironism', and in this way the experience itself remains reified. This argument is the basis of Hegel's critique of the subjectivism of the play of Romantic irony, as well as Lukács's own critique of the subjectivism of many of the features of modernist literature which portray the reified experience of the isolated individual as if it is a permanent metaphysical predicament of the human condition and not the concrete manifestation of a particular social formation.

Aspects of Alienation

Various manifestations of the concept of alienation and associated concepts within the history of philosophy have been discussed. The aspects of alienation that can be drawn from this discussion must now be recounted in order to clarify the concept's nature, associations and contradictory interpretations.

We began with the myth of the fall, a fall from the grace of primordial harmony into knowledge and responsibility, a separation from nature and God that was necessary for human freedom. The redemption of humanity and the return of paradise must be through the will and choice of humanity, through the very freedom and responsibility that originally constituted the loss of paradise. The fall–redemption motif can be found in the writings of thinkers as diverse as Rousseau, Schiller, Schelling, Hegel and Marx, but it refers to different ideas in the writings of each thinker. For example, redemption for Hegel is the philosophical comprehension of the dissolution of all one-sidedness, whereas for Schelling it is the overcoming of philosophy itself through a mystical 'wisdom' that reunites humanity with nature. The fall tends to be a fall from a state of immediacy, whether it be the immediacy of Rousseau's primitive man or Schiller's 'naive' ancient Greeks.

Prevalent in many accounts of alienation is the wish to regain an immediacy lost through the development of consciousness and knowledge. This is clear in Rousseau, Schiller, the notions of the lost golden age and lost unity of being in the Romantics and Schelling, the reawakening of the immediacy of things through the freeing of use-value from the mediacy of exchange-value in Marx and Lukács. However, immediacy is not always given such importance in theories of alienation. Hegel dismisses what he calls the 'indeterminate immediate' as an empty abstraction, exactly the opposite of the substantial concretion usually associated with immediacy. Marx may be opposed to the mediations of commodification, but he regards mere immediacy as the state in which animals live, human nature being constituted by conscious activity, where the person distinguishes himself from his life activity and thus is not immediately at one with it.[110] István Mészáros argues that in Marx there is no ultimate reference to immediacy, to an identity of subject and object, which he dismisses as mysticism. Instead of this there is what he calls the 'first order mediation' of unalienated conscious productive activity, which constitutes human nature, upon which is imposed the 'second order mediations', such as exchange value and division of labour, which constitute alienation.[111] However, for Schelling, a primordial immediacy, prior to the subject–object distinction, is no mere empty abstraction or descent to an animalistic vitalism; it is the locus of eternal freedom itself, the indeterminacy of immediacy as free determinability. For Lukács, while immediacy is the form of the unalienated qualitative authenticity of things, it is also the form of the alienated consciousness of a false atomism which can be overcome through a consciousness of mediation.

The concept of alienation implies the loss of the true nature of something, of its essence, such that its actual existence is divorced from its real nature. Alienation appears to depend on essentialism, the idea that there is a true nature to things; but what this nature is differs widely across the range of thinkers in question. For example, for Plotinus, it is a purely spiritual and intellectual oneness with divine permanence that is corrupted by a fixation with the ephemera of the external material world, whereas, for the likes of Rousseau it is a oneness with nature corrupted by civilization and intellectual knowledge. The notion of essence is a metaphysical concept to the extent that it refers to the ideal and universal nature of something. Derrida's notion of *différance* opposes the substantiality and presence of any notion of essence. However, essence merely refers to the definition of something, therefore it can signify anything. For Feuerbach and Marx, the human is a generic-being, meaning that the human essence is consciousness as the ability to universalize, an unlimitedness free from the restrictions of immediate isolated particularity, a universality that is only possible because of the emptiness, the lack of determinacy and substantiality, of the human being.

While essence refers to the properties of an entity without which it would not be what it is, it does not refer to its particular singularity, what is fundamentally its own , because the same properties can be applied to other entities of the same type. Therefore the essence of something is its universalized ideal, not the thing itself in its irreducible singularity. Essence refers to an entity's properties [*Eigenschaften*], that is, to the entity in the form of generality, not to the entity itself in its singular existence, its ownness [*Eigenheit*]. For Stirner, an entity's alienation is not alienation from its true nature, as it tends to be for other theorists of alienation, but alienation from its own uniterable being. Stirner regards the notion of the human essence as just another way in which the unique individual is alienated from itself.

Stirner's unalienated unique individual is a 'creative nothing', not externally determined, without any substance or essence, which would only entail a loss of its ownness, and is therefore free, that is, in a state of indeterminacy *qua* free determinability. This brings us to the question of the relationship between alienation and freedom. The loss of one's own true nature through external determinations is a loss of one's freedom. The idea that alienation involves a loss of freedom has many widely differing manifestations. Rousseau's primitive man has not yet lost his natural liberty through the chains of civilization. For Schiller, a person is only free when she is a whole, and wholeness is characterized by freedom from any *particular* determination, and thus as a state of free determinability. Free determinability is also the main characteristic of Schelling's pre-conceptual 'eternal freedom'. For Marx, free unalienated productive activity is free because it is an end in itself, not a means to anything else, such as mere physical subsistence, and it is not in the grip of an external hostile appropriating force. It may be argued that the idea of de-alienation as a return to freedom does not quite fit in with the usual content of the fall–redemption model in which freedom is regarded as an effect of the fall itself. Alienation from primordial immediacy is necessary for the existence and development of consciousness, of the mind, which is associated with freedom as opposed to the necessity of nature. However, for Hegel and Schelling, there are different types, or levels, of freedom. A one-sided and therefore restricted freedom, that is, a freedom opposed to necessity, is not true freedom. True freedom is the overcoming of the opposition between freedom and necessity, mind and nature, subject and object. However, this overcoming can itself take on a myriad of different forms, for example, Hegel's absolute knowing or Schelling's 'unknowable' absolute subject as eternal freedom.

The notion of de-alienation as a return to a state of freedom can manifest itself in opposing forms, depending on radically different interpretations of what freedom is. A major difference is whether de-alienation involves a oneness with being through a suspension of the subject, or an affirmation of the subject's own controlling mastery. Schiller's aesthetic de-alienation involves sharpening the subject–object distinction through the objectification of nature, where nature is domesticated into an object for a perceiving subject, an objectification that involves subjecting nature to the subject's power and dominion. Similarly, Marx's unalienated condition involves experiencing the world as humanity's own creation.[112] Stirner's state of unalienated ownness involves the self's mastery over itself and others, whether people or things, reducing them to instruments of utility. Conversely, Novalis and Schelling regard the subject–object distinction as the locus of alienation, and therefore de-alienation as the overcoming of this through the suspension of the subject, which enables the primordial oneness of being to manifest itself.

Many theories of alienation involve the notion that the loss of freedom and autonomy of the person involves a reifying dehumanization, the reduction of the human being to an object or a thing. In the writings of Schiller, Hegel, Marx and Lukács, this is connected to the fragmentation caused by the division of labour necessitated by the capitalist form of production, which reduces the human being to a particular function, a cog in a machine, usually involving dead and repetitive work. Reification is also demonstrated in Hegel's notion of the 'understanding' [*Verstand*], or analytical reason, as a way of thinking restricted to the form of the static isolated particularity of mere facts. It can be found in Marx's idea that the commodification of all aspects of life leads to the ideological misrecognition that human relations are relations between things.

Reification is usually said to involve a fixation with the petrified stasis of isolated particularity, a fragmentation of living wholeness into lifeless parts. De-totalization is a major aspect of many theories of alienation. Schiller's understanding of the aesthetic is that it restores to humanity its wholeness, a wholeness of personality undermined by the fragmentary nature of modern society and the modern individual. Hegel's notion of absolute knowing as the overcoming of alienation involves the idea that 'the True is the whole', as opposed to the alienated atomized one-sidedness of consciousness trapped in the realm of the 'understanding'. Marx's notion of the

alienation of humanity's 'generic-being', of its wholeness of character
produced by its universality in the form of freedom from specific determination, entails the atomization of the individual human from her fellow
humans, from the social whole. Lukács's account of reification involves
the atomization of individuals, and the reduction of consciousness to the
empirical immediacy of isolated particularity that is unable to recognize
the reality of interrelatedness that constitutes the mechanized social totality
of commodity based society.

At first it seems that alienation is simply a clear manifestation of Derrida's
metaphysics of presence, an interpretation of difference in terms of a
lost and ultimately regainable origin in a state of full presence devoid of
difference. This initial viewpoint on the matter is supported by a number
of the ideas that have been discussed. Rousseau's myth of origins, the primitive immediacy of presence corrupted by the artificiality of civilization and
writing, is explicitly addressed in those terms in Derrida's *Of Grammatology*.
It could be argued that Schillerian and Lukácsian notions of the wholeness of personality, not to mention the Marxian 'return of man to himself',
are a manifestation of self-presence. Derrida regards Hegel's de-alienated
'absolute knowing' as the '*parousia*' of full and infinite presence.

However, in many accounts of alienation it appears that the present itself
is the locus of alienation, not of de-alienation. The idea of the unalienated
wholeness of personality, to be found in the writings of Schiller, Feuerbach
and Marx, is dependent on humanity's universality, its indeterminacy as
lack of the immediate substantial fullness of presence of a specific determination, its free determinability and not its given presence. Schelling's
unalienated primordial immediacy is not a oneness with nature as fullness
of presence, but an apprehension of the non-objectifiable absolute subject,
which is not a substantial presence, but the insubstantial indeterminacy of
'eternal freedom', of free determinability. This concept of determinability,
prevalent in post-Kantian conceptions of de-alienation, is closer to the
productive indeterminacy of Derridian *différance* than to the determined
fullness and fixed exclusionary identity of the metaphysical notion of
presence.

Chapter 2

Difference and Alienation in Hegel

Derrida himself speaks of the 'relations of profound affinity with Hegelian discourse'[1] that his notion of *différance* maintains. Yet Hegelianism remains one of the principal targets of deconstruction, because it names a system of the ultimate reappropriation of difference. Derrida describes Hegel as 'the last philosopher of the book and the first thinker of writing'.[2] This means that Hegel is a thinker of irreducible difference (writing) at the same time as being a philosopher of metaphysical closure (the book), reappropriating difference in a speculative identity. Derrida emphasizes his proximity to Hegelian thought only in order to 'operate a kind of infinitesimal and radical displacement of it'.[3] The nature of this 'displacement' will be explored here with regard to its relation to the Hegelian concept of alienation. What is in question here is whether the notion of *différance* has more 'affinity' with Hegel's conception of alienation or his conception of the overcoming of alienation.

The Proximity of Derrida and Hegel

There are clear similarities between Derrida's notion of *différance* and certain Hegelian themes. The idea that something is never simply itself, but is always determined through what it is not, and the concomitant notion of infinite mediation are at the core of Hegel's philosophy. What Derrida objects to in Hegel is the notion of sublation, or *Aufhebung*. The German word *Aufhebung* combines the meanings of lift up, negate and retain. It refers to the moment in the Hegelian dialectic when consciousness is raised to a higher level through the process of the mediation of an idea by its other, a process that involves the idea's simultaneous negation, retention and supersession. For Derrida, the *Aufhebung* involves the recuperation of the self-presence of meaning through the suppression of *différance*. *Différance* is conceived as dialectical negativity, which means that it is harnessed and put to work in the service of the renewal and reconstitution of the positivity and self-presence of meaning. Derrida relates the operation of the *Aufhebung* to self-presence when he defines it in the following way: '[T]o *aufheben* [is] to deny while raising up, while idealizing, while sublimating into an anamnesic interiority (*Erinnerung*), while *interning* difference in a self-presence.'[4] Derrida's notion of *différance* is defined by its opposition to the *Aufhebung*. 'If there were a definition of *différance*, it would be precisely the limit, the interruption, the destruction of the Hegelian *relève* [*Aufhebung*] *wherever* it operates.'[5] He acknowledges the similarity of *différance* to Hegelian negativity, while again proclaiming its detachment from the *Aufhebung*. '*Différance* (at a point of almost absolute proximity to Hegel . . .) must sign the point at which one breaks with the system of the *Aufhebung* and with speculative dialectics.'[6] However, the *Aufhebung* does not merely bring the movement of the concept to rest in self-presence; it reinscribes it into a new dynamic of difference and contradiction. This restless temporal process only comes to an end in philosophical thinking, what Hegel calls 'absolute knowing'. The *Aufhebung* could be reinterpreted as the reconfiguration of discourse resulting from the undermining of binary oppositions, an operation resembling Derridian deconstruction. Derrida acknowledges this when he says: '*Aufhebung* could be written otherwise. Whence its proximity to all the operations conducted *against* Hegel's dialectical speculation.'[7] However, Hegel's rational comprehension of such reconfigurations as a teleological progress is unacceptable to Derrida, who sees it as a metaphysical reference to a future presence.

Alienation in Hegel is, at one stage, a manifestation of mediation, a process essential to and constitutive of human consciousness.[8] It refers to the self-othering involved in self-positing, which is the process of differentiation that constitutes identity; if the same is the same only insofar as it is not the other then the same contains the other within itself, it is itself at the same time as being other than itself. Hence the proximity of Hegelian alienation to the notion of a fundamental difference, or *différance*, that underlies and undermines the full self-presence of identity. However, as we have seen, for Hegel, alienation and difference are characterized as dialectical negativity, they are put to work in the service of the reconstitution of identity, sublated to a higher level. This higher level is a paradoxical mediated identity, an identity 'for itself', or a self-conscious identity. Derrida resists this recuperation of identity and strives to free *différance* from dialectical negativity, which would entail detaching alienation from its part in the process of the reconstitution of identity, rendering it absolute. In contrast, for Hegel, both alienation and its overcoming are necessary for the development of consciousness.

not logic

Two of the most suggestive manifestations of alienation in the narrative of the *Phenomenology of Spirit*, in terms of their prefiguring of Derridian themes, are the so-called 'unhappy consciousness' and the realm of 'culture' or 'self-alienated Spirit'. The unhappy consciousness arises out of scepticism. Hegel characterizes scepticism as self-contradictory. Through its negative attitude to the external world it confirms itself as a simple entity, which paradoxically maintains its stable determinacy by denying determinacy in general, while being nothing but the experience of indeterminacy.[9] Hegel uses the traditional argument against scepticism and relativism, asserting the contradictoriness inherent in the statement that nothing is true except the fact that nothing is true. He writes regarding scepticism: 'It pronounces an absolute vanishing, but the pronouncement *is*, and this consciousness is the vanishing that is pronounced.'[10]

Derrida's notion of *différance* can be seen as a form of scepticism insofar as truth and meaning are held to depend on the metaphysics of presence. Hegel includes in his description of scepticism a similar idea of difference:

[Determinacy] contains no permanent element, and must vanish before thought, because the 'different' is just this, not to be in possession of itself, but to have its essential being only in an other. Thinking, however, is the insight into this nature of the 'different', it is the negative essence, as simple.[11]

Sceptical thinking is the consciousness of fundamental difference. This consciousness is paradoxical and contradictory, because the difference that constitutes the possibility and impossibility of determinacy cannot be represented by a concept, as concepts are themselves determinate. It is for this reason that Derrida claims that *différance* is not a concept or a word, a paradox necessitated by the fact that the deconstruction of the metaphysics of presence can only be done using language and concepts that by their nature depend on such a metaphysics.

While scepticism involves consciousness experiencing itself as internally contradictory it is not actually aware of this state. When consciousness becomes aware of its contradictory condition it becomes what Hegel calls the unhappy consciousness. This form of consciousness is alienated from itself; it is split between the infinite changeableness of 'absolute vanishing', or fundamental difference, and the simple unchangeable determinacy that it necessarily is, being a *consciousness* of the changeable. Furthermore, being the self-consciousness of this split, or contradiction, it paradoxically identifies itself with the changeable, while being aware of its nature as an 'unchangeable' determinacy, yet also being unable to take this nature 'to be its own'.[12] Hegel identifies the unhappy consciousness with a religious yearning for an unattainable beyond. In not being able to grasp any stable self-presence, it yearns for a transcendent presence that is alien to it, and feels itself to be wretched and empty. However, the very feeling of alienation from the present being of the 'unchangeable' links consciousness to the 'unchangeable', bringing about an awareness of their, albeit negative and alienated, unity. Finally, in renouncing itself, consciousness embraces and identifies itself with the universal. It regains its self-presence by recognizing the unchangeable as intrinsic to its own nature, and not as an alien being, and becomes itself the reconciliation of the unchangeable universal and the changeable individual, a new form of consciousness that Hegel calls 'Reason'. However, the recovery of self-presence merely inscribes consciousness into a new set of differential relations.

Derrida refuses to accept that his own recognition of *différance* constitutes a higher form of consciousness or reason. Furthermore, he does not see the chain of referrals to an unattainable beyond as a melancholy and wretched yearning. On the contrary, he suggests a Nietzschean affirmation of the endless play of the world, liberated from any nostalgia or hope for a lost presence;[13] a 'happy' consciousness not envisaged in the *Phenomenology of Spirit*. This celebratory attitude precludes the use of the term alienation, with its unhappy connotations, to describe the self-othering involved in *différance*.

However, this affirmation of *différance*, of the play of changeable surfaces and masks, of the constant dissolution and reconfiguration of identities, with no anchor in a final self-presence, is described by Hegel as the 'nihilistic game'[14] of 'culture [*Bildung*]', a form of consciousness he terms '*der sich entfremdete Geist*' (translated as 'self-alienated Spirit'). This involves an absolute dissolution of identity and self-presence comparable to that of the unhappy consciousness, only this time in the more social realm of spirit. Hegel describes self-alienated spirit as a realm where all values are reversible, where everything is insubstantial and superficial, and where the individual is alienated into an empty universal, whose identity is unstable and constantly shifting, wearing many different masks and being nothing but those masks. He writes:

When the pure 'I' beholds itself outside of itself and rent asunder, then everything that is called law, good, and right, is at the same time rent asunder and is destroyed. All identity dissolves away, for the utmost disparity now occupies the scene; what is absolutely essential is now absolutely unessential, being-for-self is now external to itself: the pure 'I' itself is absolutely disrupted.[15]

Self-alienated spirit manifests itself in an ironic, 'clever and witty',[16] discourse. This is the product of the 'absolute perversion' of all values. The awareness of the absolute vanishing of all determinacy here takes the form of a playful, highly rhetorical and stylized use of language, where the play of form is everything and the self-presence of content is infinitely deferred, unattainable, and therefore provisional and substitutable.

At this stage Hegel's portrayal of alienation has clear parallels with the Derridian notion of the play of *différance*.

Externalization and Estrangement

Alienation is an aspect of Hegel's notions of mediation and negativity. Derrida regards the latter two concepts as involving a harnessing of difference that puts it to work towards the re-establishment of identity. Before proceeding further in our inquiry into the relationship between alienation and difference, it is necessary to clarify the distinctness of Hegel's use of the term, what makes it more specific than 'mediation' and 'negativity'. The establishment of such clarity requires critical engagement not only with Hegel's writings, but also with the arguments put forward on this question by certain of his interpreters.

Lukács, in his book, *The Young Hegel*, claims that the mature Hegel's concept of alienation is a development from the concept of 'positivity', a concept prevalent in his youthful early theological writings. 'Positivity' refers to the stolid thinghood of brute objectivity, external and alien to living subjectivity.[17] Lukács writes that 'positivity' is an 'alien, dead, "givenness"'.[18] Hegel's argument, at this time, is a critique of 'positive religion', religion that posits the moral law as something external and given. Lukács argues that in Hegel's first major work, the *Phenomenology of Spirit*, the concept of positivity is replaced by the concept of 'externalization [*Entäußerung* (alienation)]'. The word 'externalization' implies that the positivity of dead objectivity is itself the product of human activity, that positivity is the reification of living subjectivity through the latter's very actualization. Lukács writes:

Hegel came to believe that the positive spheres of modern society were also the products of human activity. . . . Hence they cease to appear as something ready-made. . . . [I]n the *Phenomenology of Mind* . . . the old concept 'positivity' is replaced by the new terms 'externalization' or 'alienation'. . . . 'Positivity' refers to a *quality* of social formations, objects, *things*. 'Externalization' is a specific mode of human *activity* as a result of which specific social institutions *come into being* and acquire the objective nature peculiar to them.[19]

The link between positivity and externalization can be clearly seen in the following extract from Hegel's *Phenomenology of Spirit*, where he describes the realm of abstract legal right, which is as stolidly external as the moral law of religious positivity:

> [T]he Spirit whose self is an absolutely discrete unit has its content as an equally hard and unyielding reality, and here the world has the character of being something external. . . . This world is . . . an alien reality already present and given, a reality which has a being of its own and in which it does not recognize itself. . . . But this external world . . . is not merely this elemental being confronting the self as something contingently given; on the contrary, it *is* his work. . . . It obtains its existence through self-consciousness's *own* externalization and separation of itself from its essence[.][20]

The term 'externalization' means that the reified world of 'absolutely discrete' isolated static positivities is itself the effect of the self, which is pure negative living activity positing itself in actuality.

It is important to note that Lukács claims that Hegel replaces the concept of 'positivity' not only with the concept of 'externalization', but also with another term: '"[P]ositivity" is replaced by the new terms "externalization" or "alienation" [*Entfremdung*].' There are two German words that Hegel uses that are usually translated into English as 'alienation'. These are *Entäußerung*, literally 'externalization', and *Entfremdung*, literally 'estrangement'. Lukács writes:

> In themselves there is nothing novel about the terms *Entäusserung* and *Entfremdung*. They are simply German translations of the English word 'alienation'. This was used in works on economic theory to betoken the sale of a commodity, and in works on natural law to refer to the loss of an aboriginal freedom[.][21]

While *Entäußerung* may refer to the divestment of property in economic theory, Lukács is here ignoring the influence of Luther's use of the verb '*entäußerte*' to translate the Pauline '*ekenōsen*', referring to the spiritual divestment (or '*kenōsis*') involved in the incarnation, a translation that we discussed in the previous chapter. Whether *Entäußerung* and *Entfremdung* are translations of one English word or not, what is in question here is whether or not these two terms are used interchangeably, with no distinction in meaning, in Hegel's writings.

Stanley Rosen argues that they have different meanings and should not be conflated. His claim is that alienation [*Entfremdung*], unlike externalization, can only be a characteristic of consciousness. He explains it thus:

'[E]xternalization' is the transition from the immediate to the mediate, in which the content latent in immediacy is rendered explicit. 'Alienation [*Entfremdung*]' takes place only when, or for so long as, the explicit content is separated from a source rendered self-conscious by the fact of separation.[22]

Rosen concedes that Hegel often uses the terms interchangeably, the main example of this being the use of the word *Entfremdung* to refer to what is usually called *Entäußerung* in the chapter on religion in the *Phenomenology of Spirit*, where God is said to be alienated in His creation and incarnation. Rosen, however, suggests that this terminological slippage only occurs, because, in this discussion of religion, the pre-philosophical language of religious representation is being used. He suggests elsewhere that *Entfremdung* is pre-philosophical and *Entäußerung* is logical.[23] He writes: '[E]xternalization is "alienation" in the pejorative sense, only for so long as spirit has not yet completely understood itself.'[24] Thus *Entfremdung* is a feature of the experience of consciousness, whereas *Entäußerung* is a logical term, a term used from the standpoint of philosophical comprehension, or absolute knowing.

Gillian Rose is another Hegel interpreter who asserts the difference in meaning between *Entäußerung* and *Entfremdung*, but for a different reason to that of Rosen. She writes: 'The idea that Hegel equated alienation [*Entfremdung*] with externalization in general is fundamentally mistaken. Alienated Spirit is a specific determination of spirit which does not characterize the modern period.'[25] She argues that Hegel's use of the term *Entfremdung* is restricted to his discussion of a particular, 'pre-bourgeois', historical period.[26]

However, it is debatable whether the section of the *Phenomenology of Spirit* entitled 'Self-alienated Spirit' is a description of a form of consciousness that only applies to one particular historical period, feudalism. The section itself alludes to the eighteenth-century transition from feudal courtly culture to the Enlightenment and ultimately the French revolution. But the problem is not the period itself; it is the reduction of a form of consciousness to a particular historical period. The narrative description of the development of forms of consciousness from sense-certainty to absolute knowing is not a social history. Phenomenology, or 'the Science of Knowing in the sphere of appearance', is sharply distinguished from history on the last page of the book, despite the fact that their combination is advocated.[27] The philosophical comprehension of forms of consciousness ordered into a logical narrative should not be confused with the contingent occurrences of empirical history. Historical periods are referred to in the *Phenomenology*, but as allusive examples. The forms of consciousness are not punctual; they could occur at various times in empirical history. Otherwise, for example, the abstract allegory of the 'master–slave dialectic' would have to be seen as a particular historical event, or 'scepticism', 'the unhappy consciousness', 'the beautiful soul', and 'religion' itself would have to be placed firmly in particular historical epochs. The section on 'Self-alienated Spirit' itself begins with a description of the abstract right of ancient Rome, before leaping into an extensive portrayal of eighteenth-century France.

The argument that *Entfremdung* names the conscious experience of *Entäußerung* in Hegel's work is put forward by Lukács himself in the following way: '[I]n the disintegrated consciousness [of self-alienated spirit], whose very essence lies in its self-knowledge, the subject attains an insight into the objective movement which had brought this externalized reality about.'[28] Self-alienated spirit is the conscious experience of externalization as estrangement in the social and collective realm of 'Spirit'. It is social ('spiritual') estrangement as the conscious realization of social ('spiritual') externalization. Lukács refers to this section in terms of 'the dawning realization that [the] societal world of objects has its foundation in "externalization"'.[29] Previous descriptions of estrangement, in earlier sections, such as 'the unhappy consciousness', are at the level of mere consciousness and self-consciousness, not yet at the level of objective social consciousness, or 'Spirit'.

Both terms, *Entfremdung* and *Entäußerung*, refer to the process of the constitution of identity through its own othering. They are often used interchangeably by Hegel. Despite this, Rosen's contention that the former is a specifically conscious form of the latter is useful and convincing, as *Entfremdung* most commonly occurs in Hegel's text in this regard. The English word 'alienation' is appropriate as a translation of both terms, to compliment the specific words 'externalization' and 'estrangement'. This is largely because 'externalization' is not itself adequate as a translation of some of the uses of '*Entäußerung*', for example, to refer to the divestment of property.

'Alienation', in *either* of its guises, names the process that Hegel calls 'experience'. (To comply with Rosen's distinction, *Entäußerung* describes the nature *of* experience, whereas *Entfremdung* describes that very nature manifest *within* experience.) 'Experience' is itself the process of self-othering and self-reappropriation that occurs throughout Hegel's narrative. Hegel defines it thus:

> Spirit becomes object because it is just this movement of becoming an *other to itself*, i.e. becoming an *object to itself*, and of suspending this otherness. And experience is the name we give to just this movement, in which the immediate, the unexperienced, . . . becomes alienated [*entfremdet*] from itself and then returns to itself from this alienation [*Entfremdung*], and is only then revealed for the first time in its actuality and truth, just as it then has become a property of consciousness also.[30]

The unexperienced abstract immediacy must become externalized to itself in order to manifest itself in actuality. This manifestation is its ex-position, its exposure to otherness, its leap out of unrelated immediacy into relationality, the dynamic relationality that Hegel calls 'spirit'. The manifest actualization occurs once the self returns to itself from its externalization. This so-called return is not a return to a new configuration of immediacy. It is the reconstitution of the self as 'revealed', as manifest in the openness of relationality. This actualization is an appropriation; it 'has become a *property* of consciousness'. That is to say, the self is a property of consciousness precisely because it has separated itself from itself. Thus its externalization, experienced as estrangement, becomes its self-appropriation and actualization.

This appropriation involves a certain de-alienation whereby the abstract immediacy is a positivity that is itself revealed to be an externalization of the subject's activity. While alienation (externalization) initially appears as the ex-position of this simple unmediated positivity, the point of de-alienation is not a return to the latter, a re-position. It is the effectivity [*Wirklichkeit*] of ex-position, the ex-posited rendered manifest and actual [*Wirklich*] in its very ex-position.

As Lukács points out, in Hegel's work, 'positivity' is an early name for the alienated condition. While the reified, unrelated, inanimate lifelessness of the simple positive initially appears to be an unalienated condition prior to its alienation (externalization), it is later revealed to be always already an externalized positedness, locked in its stasis, which the force of the negative then impels to undergo itself the experience of externalization, only this time the externalization does not end up locked in static positivity; it enters actuality, of which its externalization is itself the precondition, by doubling back on itself and subsisting in its mediatedness, thus subsisting in the open mediatedness of conscious relationality, of manifest actuality, whereby it for the first time appropriates itself, raises itself to the level of the proper, becomes a property of its own consciousness, a self-constitution and appropriation that subsists precisely in this very ex-position and self-differentiation.

Organicism or Critique

The idea that the immediacy of the simple positive is not an unalienated condition that is lost and regained through the work of the dialectic undermines certain interpretations of Hegel's system. These traditional interpretations regard Hegelianism as involving an organic temporality based on the expressive development of a single unifying principle manifesting itself in the retreat and the promise of return of the origin. As we discussed in the Introduction, this was the interpretation assumed by Derrida's early contemporaries, Althusser and Foucault. The organic and the dialectical are equated by a more recent commentator, Henry Sussman, who refers to 'the dialectical, organic, and consummate fate for the West that Hegel envisioned'.[31]

This is also the interpretation of Hegel's notion of alienation that Lukács adheres to. He writes:

> [T]he primal immediacy, the natural, . . . is replaced by a system of institutions created by man in the course of his own labours. . . . These labours . . . also transform the human subject since they annul his original immediacy, alienating the subject from itself.[32]

Lukács understands Hegel as saying that the original immediacy is lost through the dialectical process and is regained through a philosophical reconciliation of subject and object that is the immanent goal of that process.[33]

Such interpretations, ones that involve the notion of the loss and return of an original unity through an organic and expressive development, are, of course, suggested at certain points in Hegel's work. In *The Difference between Fichte's and Schelling's System of Philosophy*, Hegel claims that philosophy arises out of the need for the reconstitution of a lost unity, a reconstitution that can be achieved through dialectical reason.[34] He writes:

[T]he need of philosophy . . . is the attempt to suspend the rigidified opposition between subjectivity and objectivity; to comprehend the achieved existence of the intellectual and real world as a becoming. . . . [In this] Reason has united what was sundered and it has reduced the absolute dichotomy to a relative one, one that is conditioned by the original identity.[35]

In the *Phenomenology of Spirit*, Hegel uses organic metaphors to describe the development of forms of consciousness. Regarding such forms, he writes: '[T]heir fluid nature makes them moments of an organic unity in which they not only do not conflict, but in which each is as necessary as the other; and this mutual necessity alone constitutes the life of the whole.'[36] However, Hegel sharply distinguishes his dialectic from the notion of the organic dynamism of an expressive development in the form of natural necessity. The organicism of substantial necessity does not take into account the negativity of subjectivity. Hegel writes:

The circle that remains self-enclosed and, like substance, holds its moments together, is an immediate relationship, one therefore which has nothing astonishing about it. But that an accident as such, detached from what circumscribes it, what is bound and is actual only in its context with others, should attain an existence of its own and a separate freedom – this is the tremendous power of the negative; it is the energy of thought, of the pure 'I'.[37]

This contingent 'accident' that breaks free from the necessity of substance appears to contradict the non-conflictual mutuality of the organic unity referred to in the previous quotation. However, for Hegel, the relationality of the 'organic whole' to which he is referring is itself dependent on the dissolution of the isolated fixity of abstract positivity, an ex-position rendering fixed thoughts fluid through the negativity and self-ex-position of the pure 'I' that is their basis. Hegel writes:

Thoughts become fluid . . . when the pure certainty of self abstracts from itself . . . by giving up the *fixity* of its self-positing, by giving up not

only the fixity of the pure concrete, which the 'I' itself is, in contrast with
its differentiated content, but also the fixity of the differentiated moments
which, posited in the element of pure thinking, share the unconditioned
nature of the 'I'. Through this movement the pure thoughts become
Notions, and are only now what they are in truth, self-movements, circles,
spiritual essences. . . . This movement of pure essences constitutes the
nature of scientific method in general. Regarded as the connectedness
of their content it is the necessary expansion of that content into an
organic whole.[38]

Organic metaphors refer to the way in which Hegel's 'scientific method'
observes things in their relatedness, i.e. as a system. This method involves
regarding the (fluid) nature of the object of knowledge as inseparable from
the (fluid) nature of the subject; thus the subject of knowledge is part of the
field of scientific enquiry and not merely an untheorized presupposition.
This puts Hegel firmly in a post-Kantian paradigm; an organicism of the
necessity of an expressive development of substance would be pre-critical.

Hegel opposes the idea of a progressive expressive development without
the mediation of negativity. In *Glas*, Derrida points out that although Hegel
uses metaphors of organic circularity to describe the development of consciousness, he sharply distinguishes the latter from organic development
in nature, in the field of substantial necessity, because there is no negativity
in natural development. Derrida explains:

[L]ife as nature develops by itself without freedom insofar as its self-
mobility is finite. It does not go out of itself, it does nothing but develop
the germ: the quantitative increase without interruption, without relation
to the outside and the absolute other.[39]

In the *Lectures on the Philosophy of Religion*, Hegel writes critically of a 'development . . . [that] is only a positive bringing out of [natural] tendencies,
<unhindered within itself and not passing through negativity,> passing
[out of] possibility into actuality and activity without being mediated by a
negative moment'.[40]

One Hegel commentator, Charles Taylor, finds this notion of negativity
unacceptable. He writes:

[Hegel claims that] determinate reality . . . contains its own negation. . . .
But 'determinate being' is an indispensable concept; anything to be must
be determinate. If it also contains its own negation, then whatever meets

the conditions of existence also meets those of its own demise. . . . [It] cannot maintain itself in existence.[41]

Taylor, while finding Hegelian negativity 'incredible', wishes to retain what he sees as valuable in Hegel, i.e. the combination of 'expressive' organic unity with subjective autonomy.[42] However, for Hegel, negativity is the precondition of such a combination. The subject acts within substance as the latter's non-identity with itself, as negativity. The expressive development of self-identical substance, bereft of negativity, contains no place for subjective autonomy.

Such a notion of the development of substance as a purely objective process in the form of necessity is not only suggestive of a pre-critical dogmatism, but also contravenes Hegel's dictum that 'everything turns on grasping and expressing the True, not only as *Substance*, but equally as *Subject*'.[43] Despite this, Hegel's philosophical narrative appears to develop through dialectical logical necessity. Rodolphe Gasché regards Hegel's speculative system as 'preprogrammed and repetitive'.[44] There is certainly a teleological necessity operating in Hegel's narrative, of which Hegel's own system is the culmination. Lukács describes it thus: 'History . . . reaches its consummation, the goal immanent in it, the nature implicitly contained in it from the very beginning, only in philosophy, in a post-festum commentary on the path leading up to it.'[45] However, while teleological necessity is clearly discernible in Hegel's narrative 'commentary', this does not entail its immanence in 'history' itself, in the process which preceded the 'commentary'.

According to Žižek, in Hegel's system teleological necessity is something retroactively imposed on contingent events by the philosophical comprehension that is their result. Žižek writes:

> [W]hen, out of the contingent external conditions, their Result takes shape, these conditions are retroactively – from the viewpoint of the final Result itself – perceived as its necessary conditions. 'Dialectics' is ultimately a teaching on how necessity emerges out of contingency: on how a contingent *bricolage* produces a result which 'transcodes' its initial conditions into internal necessary moments of its self-reproduction.[46]

'*Bricolage*' is a term that refers to a piecing together of elements that are not internally related through any unifying expressive principle; it is the opposite of organicism. To regard Hegel's system in terms of the teleological necessity of an expressive organicism is not only to ignore the negativity of the subject, but also to ignore the backward-looking retroactivity of Hegelian necessity. Žižek maintains that, for Hegel, necessity is always a 'backwards-necessity', and he backs up this interpretation with a reference to Hegel's claim, in the *Philosophy of Right*, that philosophical comprehension only occurs after the event, as a belated backward-looking:[47] 'The owl of Minerva takes its flight only when the shades of night are gathering.'[48]

For Žižek, Hegel's dialectical sublation is a retroactive 'transcoding' of the preceding element in the development. As an example of this, he discusses the transition from being into essence in Hegel's *Science of Logic*. When 'being' passes into 'essence', 'being' is redefined as 'appearance'. 'Essence' itself is merely this redefinition. Žižek writes:

> [I]n the passage of 'being' into 'essence', the entire domain of 'being' is retroactively determined as that of the 'appearance', as the medium in which 'essence' becomes manifest . . . ('essence' is, as Hegel puts it, 'appearance *qua* appearance' – *nothing but* the principle of the transcoding of immediate being into a 'mere appearance': the illusion of Understanding is precisely that 'essence' is a positive entity *beyond* the negative movement of the appearance's self-sublation).[49]

Žižek identifies Hegel's circular 'self-relating of the Notion' with this retroactivity.

Derrida, at one point, concurs with this interpretation, in that he too relates Hegelian Reason with retroactivity. He writes: '[T]he truth of Hegelianism [is] conceived only at the end of the course, that philosophical narration be produced in the future.'[50] In other words, the teleological necessity that works towards the ultimate result of philosophical comprehension is merely a retroactive 'result' of that comprehension itself. Derrida also asserts that any reading of Hegel that involves a degree of biographical narration is un-Hegelian to the extent to which it avoids the circularity of the living unity of Hegel's discourse. A reading of Hegel using biographical narration is locked in the analytical divisiveness of the Understanding [*Verstand*], as opposed to the living unity of the circular retroactivity of Hegelian Reason [*Vernunft*]. Derrida writes:

> [O]ne applies a dissociating and formal analysis, the viewpoint of the understanding in a narration that risks missing the living unity of the discourse; how does one distinguish philosophically a before from an after, if the circularity of the movement makes the beginning the end of

the end? And reciprocally? The Hegelian tree is also turned over; the old Hegel is the young Hegel's father only in order to have been his son, his great-grandson.[51]

Hegel's circular retroactivity belies the idea that his is a philosophy of origins. In *Glas*, Derrida relates it to his own critique of origins. The manner of this 'relation' is, of course, one of 'proximity' and 'infinitesimal displacement', taking the form of a polygraphically parallel positioning of the following quotation about himself with the above extract about Hegel on the tri-columnar page in question. He writes:

[E]verything is always attacked *de dos, from the back*, written, described from behind. *A tergo.* I am *already* [*déjà*: also, D.J.] (dead) signifies that I am *behind* [*derrière*]. Absolutely behind, the *Derrière* that will have never been seen from the front, the *Déjà* that nothing will have preceded, which therefore conceived and gave birth to itself[.][52]

The Derridian critique of origins is based on the logic of the 'always already'; there is no origin from which we are alienated, we are always already alienated. This is parallel to the Hegelian notion that the *origin* is *derived* from the end result of the process that it is itself the inception of. The auto-productive '*Déjà*' (that 'gives birth to itself') has no origin, no positive given from which it derives; its 'inception', its constant self-conception, is the irruption of the pure negativity of the subject as decision, not origin.

Despite appearances to the contrary, there is no 'origin' in Hegel's system. There is no given source, positive and present, from which the Hegelian exposition emanates through its externalization. Hegel's is a philosophy without any presupposition [*Voraussetzung* (pre-ex-position)]. There is no originary foundation that precedes the exposition [*Aussetzung*]. In Hegel's system of circular retroactivity, the 'beginning' that is at the same time the 'end' is not an 'origin'; it is not even a beginning if a beginning must be something given. It is thus a decision, an irreducibly contingent irruption of subjective negativity within the objective positivity of the given. Charles Taylor writes of the Hegelian 'beginning' in these terms: '[B]ecause everything that is flows by rational necessity out of the first "decision", we cannot really say that *Geist* is faced with any givens.'[53] Jean-Luc Nancy agrees that the Hegelian 'decision' involves no given origin: '[E]very beginning in decision is not a beginning: it is an upsurge in the course of the given, a rupture, nothing that could be posited as such.'[54]

That the 'beginning' rests on a 'decision' is explained in Hegel's introduction to his *Encyclopaedia of the Philosophical Sciences*. He writes:

> With regard to the *beginning* that philosophy has to make . . . what we have here is the free act of thinking putting itself at the standpoint where it is for its own self, *producing its own object for itself*. . . . Within the Science this standpoint, which in this first act appears as *immediate*, must make itself into the *result* . . . in which it reaches its beginning again and returns into itself. In this way, philosophy shows itself as a circle that goes back into itself . . . so that the beginning only has a relation to the subject who takes the decision to philosophise, but not to the science as such. – Or, to put the same thing another way, the concept of the Science and therefore the first concept – which, since it is the first one, contains the severance that thinking is object for an (as it were external) philosophising subject – must be grasped by the Science itself. This is even its unique purpose, deed, and goal: to arrive at the Concept of its concept and so to arrive at its return [into itself] and contentment.[55]

The science has no beginning or end, but it is founded on an extra-scientific decision to philosophize, to make thinking the object of thought. The science, to be complete, must account for this particular founding decision, must include within itself its own meta-scientific principle, must theorize, within its own operation, the basis, the conditions of possibility of its operativity. It comprehends its non-scientific beginning within itself as an end, a result, through a retroactive reconfiguring, or 'transcoding', of its contingent starting-point into the end result of a rational and necessary teleological process. Hegel's system explicitly theorizes its own mode of operation. One of Derrida's common themes is that any rational system depends on an irrational decision to be rational, any system of meaning depends on a nonsensical decision to make sense, any system of law is founded through a non-legal moment of force. Hegel's system demonstrates an explicit awareness that this is precisely what it is doing, an awareness it includes within itself as a moment of its very systematicity. What Derrida terms the 'quasi-transcendental' nature of that which eludes and is necessarily suppressed by the system will be discussed in detail in a later section. For now, the point is that the Hegelian circle is not an expressivist organicism of a retreat and return of the origin. It is not a theory of the loss and return of an originary oneness, a theory that characterizes a pre-critical metaphysics. Rather, Hegelian circular retroactivity is a completion of Kant's critical revolution.

Hegel expresses this in the 'Introduction' to the *Phenomenology of Spirit*. He aims to radicalize Kant's critical project by superseding the latter's transcendental conditions of possibility of knowledge with an immanently self-critical approach. Hegel's critique of Kantian critique involves a questioning of the position from which knowledge can be known. The investigation into the nature and limits of knowledge itself involves a form of knowledge, the nature and limits of which in turn require examination. This leads to an infinite regress that demonstrates the ultimate incoherence of maintaining a presupposed position of meta-knowledge. Kant's philosophy is caught in a performative contradiction whereby his own critical approach to the study of knowledge is not itself submitted to critique, and the criteria applied by this approach are not applied to the approach itself, or to themselves, and are thus simply presupposed. Hegel wishes to investigate knowledge without such presupposed criteria. This is achieved by regarding knowledge as self-critical, as immanently engendering its own criteria of adequacy.

The distinction between knowledge and its object as an independently existing thing-in-itself is a distinction which lies within knowledge. It is a distinction within consciousness between consciousness of what appears to it to be the truth, or the *in-itself*, and consciousness of its knowledge of the truth. The distinction becomes a movement between two moments of consciousness, where there is a change in both knowledge and its object. That which was initially taken to be an *in-itself* is then recognized as being merely an in-itself for consciousness, and thus not an *in-itself* at all. In this way consciousness itself tests the adequacy of its knowledge, and the criterion of this test is itself tested and changed; thus both knowledge and its object undergo a transformation. Hegel writes:

> [I]t comes to pass for consciousness that what it previously took to be the *in-itself* is not an *in-itself*, or that it was only an in-itself *for consciousness*. Since consciousness thus finds that its knowledge does not correspond to its object, the object itself does not stand the test. . . . [T]he testing is not only a testing of what we know, but also a testing of the criterion of what knowing is.[56]

In this movement of consciousness the *in-itself* is not simply replaced by the *for-consciousness*, it is shown to have been always already a *for-consciousness*, through a retroactive reconfiguring. Consciousness is not aware that this is what is happening. This teleological progression of consciousness through circles of retroactive reconfigurations is itself a retroactive reconfiguring of the entire movement of the experience of consciousness, imposed from the

standpoint of philosophical comprehension, or 'absolute knowing', which
is the position of the narrator of the phenomenological discourse, referred
to in that discourse as 'us'. Hegel writes:

> [T]he new object shows itself to have come about through a *reversal of
> consciousness itself.* This way of looking at the matter is something contri-
> buted by *us*, by means of which the succession of experiences through
> which consciousness passes is raised into a scientific progression – but it
> is not known to the consciousness that we are observing.[57]

Hegel's circular retroactivity has certain implications for the meaning
of 'alienation' in his works. Žižek argues that 'de-alienation' in Hegel is
nothing more than a retroactive shift in perspective. He writes: '[T]he
Hegelian "loss of the loss" [consists] not in the annulment of the loss, not
in the reappropriation of the lost object in its full presence, but in the
experience of how we never had what we have lost.'[58] Žižek concurs with
the interpretation of Hegel that maintains that the de-alienating 'reconciliation' is effected through the recognition of inherent alienation, a
recognition that alters retroactively what was initially an alienating experience. He puts forward, as an example of this, the Pauline re-reading of the
death of Christ that founds Christianity:

> [T]he fundamental Hegelian motif[,] 'reconciliation'[,] does not convey
> any kind of miraculous healing of the wound of scission, it consists solely
> in a reversal of perspective by means of which we perceive how the
> scission is in itself already reconciliation – how, for example, Christ's
> defeat and infamous death are already in themselves reconciliation.[59]

For Hegel, there is no originary immediacy, or rather, what initially
appears to be originary immediacy is shown to be derived and mediated.
He writes: 'In the progression of the Idea the beginning proves itself to be
what it already is in-itself, namely, what is posited and mediated and not
what simply and immediately *is.*'[60] In the *Science of Logic*, Hegel argues that
the immediacy of the beginning is something grounded retroactively, and
thus derived, and that such immediacy is merely a provisional hypothesis.
He writes:

> [T]he retrogressive grounding of the beginning, and the *progressive
> further determining* of it, coincide and are the same. The method, which
> thus winds itself into a circle, cannot anticipate in a development in time
> that the beginning is, as such, already something derived; it is sufficient

for the beginning in its immediacy that it is simple universality. In being that, it has its complete condition; and there is no need to deprecate the fact that it may only be accepted *provisionally* and *hypothetically*.[61]

Originary immediacy is also derided in the opening chapter of the *Phenomenology*, on 'Sense-Certainty', where the immediate singularity of linguistic demonstratives is shown to be already mere abstraction and mediated universality.[62]

Hegel is opposed to any theory of the type exemplified by Rousseau that celebrates the primitive condition of natural immediacy. He is also opposed to any interpretation of the biblical fall myth on this basis. In his *Lectures on the Philosophy of Religion*, Hegel attributes to immediacy an ultimately evil self-seeking atomism.[63] He interprets the fall myth not as a fall *from* innocent immediacy, but as a fall *into* immediacy. It is a fall from the pure concept of the human, which is a divine idea in the image of God, into an actually existing initially sinful immediate self-consciousness.[64] Immediacy is not an unalienated condition that is later lost. It is itself, in its atomistic positivity, a state of alienation, alienation from the living unity of the concrete universal.

Hegel's system is not an expressivist organicism whereby the oneness of an originary immediacy externalizes itself and develops teleologically towards an eventual return to its oneness. The circular retroactivity of philosophical comprehension demonstrates that the originary immediacy is always already derived and mediated. Abstract immediacy, like positivity, is a form of alienation.

Substance and Subject

It is the power of the negative that overcomes the reified positivity of abstract immediacy, a power which is, as we have seen, identical to what Hegel calls subjectivity. Hegel writes:

> This power [of the negative] is identical with what we earlier called the Subject, which by giving determinateness an existence in its own element supersedes abstract immediacy, i.e. the immediacy which barely is, and thus is authentic substance: that being or immediacy whose mediation is not outside of it but which is this mediation itself.[65]

This 'authentic substance' is what Hegel calls '*Geist*' ('Spirit'), substance which is at the same time subject. It is a paradoxical unity of difference, a unity that subsists in its very mediatedness, a mediated immediacy. Hegel defines spirit thus: '[Spirit is] this absolute substance which is the unity of the different independent self-consciousnesses which, in their opposition, enjoy perfect freedom and independence: "I" that is "We" and "We" that is "I".'[66]

This implies a social unity founded on individualism, or at least on the freedom of the individual. In the *Science of Logic*, Hegel asserts the identity of negativity, subjectivity and freedom. He writes:

> [T]he negative of the negative . . . [is] the *innermost, most objective moment* of life and spirit, through which a *subject*, a *person*, a *free being*, exists. . . . [A]s absolute negativity the negative moment of absolute mediation is the unity which is subjectivity and soul.[67]

Stanley Rosen writes of Hegelian substance and subject in terms of social unity and individualism: '[S]ubstance (the ethical folk) and subjectivity (individualism)'.[68]

Substance transforming itself into subject is conceived as the overcoming of alienation. It is spirit knowing itself as spirit, and not as a limited figure, object or representation that is alien to itself. It is the absolute knowing that is the truth and overcoming of Christianity. For Hegel, the speculative meaning of the resurrection myth is the raising [*Aufhebung*] of the absolute in the form of representation into the absolute idea. He writes: 'This Knowing is the inbreathing of the Spirit, whereby Substance becomes Subject, by which its abstraction and lifelessness have died, and Substance therefore has become *actual* and simple and universal Self-consciousness. . . . In this way, therefore, Spirit is *self-knowing* Spirit.'[69] The transformation of substance into subject is the raising of the object, external and alien in its objectivity, into the Notion, paradoxically internalized *and* actualized in its spiritual comprehensibility, wherein there is no longer any distinction between subject and object. Hegel writes:

> [Spirit] is in itself the movement which is cognition – the transformation of that *in-itself* into that which is *for-itself*, of Substance into Subject, of the object of *consciousness* into an object of *self-consciousness*, i.e. into an object that is just as much superseded, or into the *Notion*.[70]

The overcoming of the religious representational form of reconciliation by the genuine form of reconciliation in the self-comprehending Notion is the entering into the actualized world of self-knowing spirit, a 'spiritual daylight of the present'[71] that spirit knows as its own self. Hegel writes:

Not until consciousness has given up hope of overcoming that alienation [*Fremdseyn*] in an external, i.e. alien, manner does it turn to itself, because the overcoming of that alienation is the return into self-consciousness; not until then does it turn to its own present world and discover it as its property[.][72]

Lukács bases his critique of Hegelian reconciliation on its subjectivism, its transformation of substance into subject. He recognizes that, for Hegel, the alienated realm of positivity is a realm of mere substance, devoid of the living activity of subjectivity, and that the overcoming of this realm necessitates an awakening of the subject within substance. He refers to alienation as 'subjectivity devoured by substance (positivity)' and reconciliation as the 'reintegration of substance in the newly-awakened subject'.[73] However, in his other formulations of Hegelian reconciliation he tends to ignore the role of substance, as if the awakening of the subject involves the abolition of substance. He interprets Hegelian de-alienation as the assertion of subjectivism at the expense of the abolition of objective reality. He writes that this de-alienation involves 'the abolition of the object-world along with "externalization"'.[74] For Lukács, de-alienation as absolute knowing is nothing but a subjectivist mysticism. He writes:

[T]he identical subject–object of absolute idealism, the return of absolute spirit from its total alienation in nature and its partial alienation in history to the perfected knowledge of itself, is ultimately nothing other than the absorption of all objectivity into the mystified subject which has allegedly created it: viz. the annulment of all objectivity.[75]

Lukács regards Hegelian de-alienation as an ultimate retreat into subjective idealism, a retreat from the objective idealism that led Hegel to take into account the importance of society and history in much of his system. According to Lukács, Hegel's absolute knowing is an 'attempt to abolish reality's character as real, to transmute objectivity into something posited by the subject and into an identity of subject and object, in short to complete the transformation of substance into subject'.[76]

Certainly, for Hegel, objectivity, which is the same as externality and positivity, is posited by the subject, is an externalization of the subject, is the subject's self-positing. But the subject itself, the subject to which Hegel refers, is not a positive being; it is not the individual. Hegel writes:

> [T]he living Substance is being which is in truth *Subject*, or, what is the same, is in truth actual only in so far as it is the movement of positing itself, or is the mediation of its self-othering with itself. This Substance is, as Subject, pure, *simple negativity*[.][77]

The Hegelian subject is the truth of substance, or, as we have seen, it is 'authentic substance'. Authentic substance is substance that is aware of its own self-positing nature, its non-pre-givenness. This is what Hegel means by its subjectivity. The subject is the negative activity of substance itself, what makes it 'living Substance'. The full awakening of the subject in absolute knowing is not therefore the abolition of substance. It is the abolition of the objectivity of substance, an objectivity which is nothing but substance posited as separate from and external to the positing subject. This abolition of objectivity means that substance itself *is* the subject, and *vice versa*. Thus the living authenticity of substance supersedes the dead positivity of pseudo-substance. The idea that the absolute cannot be absolute if it is an object opposed to a subject, that if it were such an object it would be merely partial and relative, and that it therefore must be apprehended directly as the absolute subject in order to be truly absolute, is the major theme of German Idealism, whether in its Schellingian or Hegelian form.

Living substance, substance that is at the same time subject, is precisely what Hegel calls *Geist* ('Spirit'). The de-alienated condition of absolute knowing is 'Spirit that knows itself as Spirit'.[78] Spirit [*Geist*] is a social and collective conception of the mind, therefore its 'subjectivity' is not that of the individual. Lukács, however, regards the Hegelian notion of absolute knowing as an 'internalization [*Erinnerung*]' of the objectivity that came about through the subject's 'externalization', a reintegration into the subject, conceived as the overcoming of all externality through an interiorizing reappropriation. He writes:

> According to Hegel, spirit has created the real objects of the world in the process of 'externalization'. It is only logical for the reverse process of 'internalization' to be nothing other than the supersession of the forms of objective reality so created, and their reintegration into the subject.
>
> The highest stage of spirit in the *Phenomenology* is designated absolute knowledge as opposed to religion because it alone clearly and unambiguously

expresses this principle, whereas religion . . . still retains a certain element of objectivity[.][79]

Lukács's interpretation of absolute knowing on the basis of internality is misleading. The absolute supersedes the opposition between inner and outer. It does not, therefore, make sense to describe it in terms of the abolition of the outer and the affirmation of the inner. As absolute knowing is 'Spirit that knows itself as Spirit', it is the self-knowing of a supra-individual collectivity. Hegel asserts that spirit must not be understood in terms of internality. He writes: 'Spirit . . . is not what is inner, but what is actual.'[80] Spirit is manifest relationality, relational because manifest; it subsists in its intrinsic relationality, and is thus both substance and subject, substance founded on negative activity, on the productive nothingness that is the subject.

Although it is a precondition for the differentiating unity of a society that respects the freedom of the individual, the Hegelian subject is not the self. Conflating the subject with the self involves ignoring Hegel's own definition of the subject as pure negative activity, and maintaining a non-Hegelian, even pre-philosophical use of the term. Jean-Luc Nancy writes:

> The Hegelian *subject* is not to be confused with subjectivity as a separate and one-sided agency for synthesizing representations, nor with subjectivity as the exclusive interiority of a personality. . . . In a word: the Hegelian subject is in no way the *self all to itself*. It is, to the contrary, . . . what . . . dissolves all substance – every instance already given, supposed first or last, founding or final, capable of coming to rest in itself. . . . The reader of Hegel who does not understand this . . . has surreptitiously presupposed an ideological notion of the 'subject' – a notion that is nonphilosophical, individualist, egoist, and 'liberal'[.][81]

The subject that is negative activity is not itself a self, is not itself substantial. It is the self-positing and self-dissolution of substance. However, it only 'dissolves all substance' if substance is conceived in terms of pre-given positivity. As we have seen, Hegel redefines substance at a higher level as 'authentic substance', manifest and living substance, manifest and living through the work of its own inherent subjectivity.

Thus Lukács's interpretation of absolute knowing in terms of a 'reintegration into the subject' of objectivity is also misleading. Nothing can be 'reintegrated' into the subject if the subject is the very principle of disintegration. The subject is the negativity of substance, therefore it is nothing but the inability of substance to remain identical to itself in a simple unity or immediacy. Hegel writes: '[The] negative . . . is . . . the disparity of the substance with itself. Thus what seems to happen outside of it . . . is really its own doing, and Substance shows itself to be essentially Subject.'[82] Žižek puts it in these words: 'The Subject is nothing but the gap in the Substance, the inadequacy of the Substance to itself.'[83] This self-division is what raises substance into spirit, an 'authentic substance', living and manifest, that subsists in its very division, its productive disintegration. Nancy writes:

> The subject is . . . the experience of its being-affected as the ordeal of what dissolves its subsistence. But . . . it is not 'some thing' . . . that undoes this subsistence from the exterior. It is not another subsistence that divides the subject; it is substance that divides itself – that enters into relation, or that opens itself to it, or that manifests itself. The subject is the experience of the power of division, of ex-position or the abandonment of self.[84]

The fact that the Hegelian subject is the negativity within substance that disables substance from being identical to itself undermines the claim of the early Derrida that the concept of the subject has always, in the history of philosophy, referred to a self-present substantial being.[85]

The transformation of substance into subject, the awakening of spirit in its self-knowing, is Hegel's conception of de-alienation. Through the subject, the productive negativity of the non-identical self-dissolution of substance, substance itself is actualized into the open, exposed, living, manifest relationality and collectivity of spirit, a unity in difference that is substance at the same time as it is subject. Authentic substance, manifest spirit, is the concrete universal, a genuine universality that depends on the productive indeterminacy, the free determinability that is the subject. The very contentlessness of the subject makes it both genuinely universal and irreducibly singular at the same time. The subject is negative universality in that it evades its own particularization in any determinate content. Such an evasion is also the basis of its irreducible singularity, as its particularization would involve the attribution of generally applicable predicates. In the *Science of Logic* Hegel writes:

> [T]he *I* is . . . pure self-related unity . . . only as making abstraction from all determinateness and content and withdrawing into the freedom of unrestricted equality with itself. As such it is *universality*; a unity that is unity with itself only through its *negative* attitude. . . . [T]he *I* as self-related

negativity is no less immediately *individuality* [Einzelheit] or is *absolutely determined*. . . . This absolute *universality* which is also immediately an absolute *individualization* [*Vereinzelung*] . . . constitutes the nature of the *I*[.][86]

The subject's absence of determination is the condition of both its 'absolute determination', the emptiness of its mere numerical identity, and its 'absolute universality', its unlimited non-specificity. Its universality depends on its bare singularity and *vice versa*. The two must be thought in their mediated unity. Žižek explains:

> On the one hand, subject is pure negative universality: an identity-with-itself which 'repels' . . . all its determinate content . . .; yet on the other hand, 'I' . . . is the very opposite of universal self-identity: a vanishing point, the 'other-of-itself' eluding every determination – in other words, a point of pure singularity.[87]

This mediated unity of supposed opposites is the basis of the concrete universal, the unity in difference of absolute spirit. The subject is the ex-position of substance that enables it to break free from the reified positivity of abstraction, whether particular or universal, and enter into a state of open and living relationality, a paradoxical unity of irreducible singularities, open and exposed to the singular otherness of each other.

in spirit at end of system as subject ?

Appropriation of the Other

However, the relation to otherness in Hegel's system often appears to take the form of a violent assimilative appropriation, a reduction and domestication of the other to a moment in the economy of the same. For example, Hegel conceives of self-consciousness as '*Desire* in general', the abolition of the otherness of what is other and the realization of itself as the other's underlying reality.[88] According to Derrida, Hegel's system is a 'restricted economy' where nothing can remain unassimilated by the appropriative logic of the dialectic; the other is always ultimately appropriated by the same and cannot subsist in its own irreducible alterity.[89] A primordial form of the relation to otherness is the dialectic of recognition. The '*re*' of *re*cognition suggests the abolition of the uniterable singular alterity of the other. Derrida writes: 'A pure singularity can recognize another singularity only in abolishing itself or in abolishing the other as singularity.'[90] Recognition involves an encounter with another self-consciousness. Only in such an encounter is self-consciousness actualized as self-consciousness. This is because in self-consciousness the object of the self is the self itself, a unity in difference of subject and object that can only genuinely occur through an encounter with an object that is at the same time a subject, i.e. another self-consciousness. Self-consciousness is actualized through the recognition of another self-consciousness; recognition of the other is at the same time recognition of the self. Hegel writes: 'A self-consciousness exists *for a self-consciousness*. Only so is it in fact self-consciousness; for only in this way does the unity of itself in its otherness become explicit for it.'[91] The self only recognizes itself through seeing itself in the other. Hegel writes: '[I]ts essential being is present to it in the form of an "other", it is outside of itself and must rid itself of its self-externality.'[92] The self is ultimately constituted in its proper element through the internalization and appropriation of the other.

This 'appropriation' of the other, however, is not a reduction of the other to the self; it is, rather, an awakening of the other as other within the self itself. Hegel writes that consciousness as reason 'seeks its "other", knowing that therein it possesses nothing else but itself: it seeks only its own infinitude'.[93] If the self is itself at the same time as being an other, it ceases to be enclosed within the simple static exclusionary positivity of an abstract finite identity. This is a reduction of the other to the self only insofar as it is also a reduction of the self to the other. Jean-Luc Nancy regards it one-sidedly in terms of the latter. He writes:

> [A]ppropriation *of* the other . . . is of the other as other. Which means that, in appropriating the other to myself, I do just the opposite of a taking of possession or an assimilation. I do not reduce the other to the same; it is, rather, the same – the one-sided, closed-off, and 'despotic' 'ego' – that makes itself other.[94]

Derrida concedes that Hegelian 'appropriation' can be read in both ways, as assimilation or loss. He writes: 'The logic of the *Aufhebung* (re)turns itself at each instant into its absolute other. Absolute appropriation is absolute expropriation. Onto-logic can always be reread or rewritten as the logic of loss or of spending without reserve.'[95]

The appropriation of the other involves the awakening of infinite alterity within the self itself, as well as the ex-position of both the self and the other, and their entering into the manifest relationality of actuality. Appropriation as the opening onto relationality is a necessary condition of the otherness of the other. The 'other' is an essentially relational concept. It would not be an 'other' if it were not the other *of* something that is not other, i.e. the self. Concomitantly, the self, to be properly itself in its relational actuality, must be, at the same time, an other. In the *Science of Logic*, Hegel writes:

> [T]he *mediating* determination . . . in its truth . . . is a *relation* or *relationship*; for it is the negative, *but the negative of the positive*, and includes the positive within itself. It is therefore the other, but not the other of something to which it is indifferent – in that case it would not be an other, nor a relation or relationship – rather it is the *other in its own self*, the *other of an other*, therefore it includes *its* own other within it and is consequently *as contradiction*, the *posited dialectic of itself.*[96]

The appropriation that the very otherness of the other involves is the exposition that is the condition of relationality. The occurrence of the other brings the abstract reified positivity of the self out into its relational actuality. For Hegel, self-recognition and self-consciousness only come about through the intervention of the other, through the self being at the same time an other. The other is this very intervention, not an abstract absolute externality.

Thus the phrase, 'its own other', indicates that the appropriation of the other is the occurrence of alterity in the constitution of the proper, the proper element of the self, its 'truth', being its actualization into the living relationality of spirit, a relationality dependent on the ex-position of the self through the infection of alterity. Appropriation is not then a violent assimilation of the other, but an opening to it. Nancy writes: 'The move out of self is . . . the appropriation of the other . . . which, as *my* other, is the infinite alterity, in me.'[97] This infusion of alterity enables the self to become truly itself in the 'spiritual daylight' of actuality, freed from the dead positivity of abstract givenness, alive in its 'truth', its proper element, which is the identity in difference that Hegel calls 'spirit', or what Nancy calls the 'community of negativity'.[98] For Hegel, the proper itself comes about only through the occurrence and appropriation of alterity. In *Glas*, Derrida explains it in this way: 'The "its other" is the very syntagm of the Hegelian proper.'[99]

The Transcendental Remainder

The main theme of Derrida's study of Hegel, *Glas*, is the 'remainder', which is that which cannot be assimilated into the system. He wishes to pay attention to that which cannot be domesticated by any system of thought, and to demonstrate that Hegel's all-inclusive totality depends on exclusion. The system understands itself as an all-inclusive infinite totality from which nothing can be excluded; all non-rational non-systemic singularities, alterities and diversities are regarded as negativity, and are thus co-opted as moments in the system and its self-reproduction. Derrida contends that not only is there an unassimilated remainder that is unconsciously repressed and excluded by the system, but also that this exclusion of the remainder is necessary for the system's very constitution. Derrida writes:

> Isn't there always an element excluded from the system that assures the system's space of possibility? The transcendental has always been, strictly, a transcategorial, what could be received, formed, terminated in none of the categories intrinsic to the system. The system's vomit.[100]

The exclusion of the remainder is the transcendental condition of possibility of the system.

As we have seen, Hegel's system is put forward as a supersession of the Kantian philosophy of the transcendental conditions of possibility of knowledge, replacing it with an immanently self-critical approach that avoids getting caught in the performative contradiction entailed by the transcendental position of meta-knowledge. For Derrida, however, the excluded remainder is the transcendental limit and condition of possibility of Hegelian knowledge. Hegel's critique of Kant involves the argument that it is self-contradictory to claim that there are ultimate limits to knowledge, because *knowledge* of a limit of knowledge is already the limit's overcoming.[101] However, the limit that the excluded remainder constitutes is not included within Hegelian knowledge; it is unknowingly repressed. The Hegelian systemic totality regards itself as unlimited, infinite and all-inclusive, whereas Derrida regards the system's self-knowledge as unconsciously repressing its own structural and textual operations that necessarily involve exclusion and restriction. Any systemic totality can only be constituted through what it excludes; an 'infinite totality' is thus a contradiction in terms. One of Derrida's commentators, Rodolphe Gasché, writes: 'For structural reasons, there is always more than totality; the extra valence added by the delegate of the asemic space of diacritical differentiation of the totality of semes always – infinitely – remains to be accounted for.'[102] *Train of Mind*

There is not always more than the Hegelian totality in that it is infinite, or rather, the 'always more than' is its very structure. However, Hegel's 'infinite' is the all-inclusivity of his system's meaningfulness, whereas

Gasché's Derridian 'infinite' is not of the order of meaning; it is 'asemic', and thus a structural category that necessarily undermines the operations of exclusion that occur in the formation of any meaningful closed totality and identity. A meaningful *open* totality and infinite identity, such as Hegel's speculative system, have to be demonstrated to be in reality closed and finite before the deconstructive infinite can undermine their closure. The notion of 'infinity' will be explored in detail in the next section. What is of concern here is the proximity of Hegel and Derrida in their treatment of the excluded remainder.

Gasché argues that the remainder must be conceived as a 'quasi-transcendental' condition of possibility and impossibility of the system, and not one of the system's dialectical moments. Its transcendentality is 'quasi-' because it is not semantic, but 'asemic' and 'infrastructural'. It is a condition of both possibility and impossibility, because the systemic totality not only comes to be through the exclusion of the unassimilable remainder, but also ultimately fails to operate as a systemic totality, fails to become identical with itself, because the unknowingly repressed remainder comes back to haunt the system as an undermining and disabling element. According to Gasché, this remainder cannot have the form of immediacy or mere being, as these do not elude the system, but constitute its first moment.[103] He also concedes that it makes no sense to speak of a remainder to the Hegelian absolute, as the absolute is by definition that which is without remainder, or as he puts it, 'the Absolute *is* sublated remainder, the remaining totality of all remains.'[104]

The remainder cannot remain as remainder if it is conceived as simply outside the system. A not yet systematized immediacy will always already have been integrated into the system as the system's starting point, whereupon it will immanently show itself to have always already been its own opposite. A simple outside of the system cannot help but become the system's speculative other, and thus one of the system's essential moments. A genuine non-assimilable remainder must therefore remain as that which *within* the system eludes the system. The system necessarily presents itself by means of a written text, and the materiality of the writing always exceeds the restricted economy of its idealization as system. The critical and analytical operation of deconstruction aims to highlight what, within the textual exposition of the system, both eludes the system and, in this very elusion, functions as central to the system's constitution, rendering the system possible and impossible at the same time. Deconstruction does not simply pinpoint, from an exterior standpoint, that which the system simultaneously excludes and depends on; it operates immanently and parasitically

within the text, with a strategy of repeating, doubling, re-marking and paro-
dying the moments of the system, so as to prevent the system from ossifying
into a closed totalized mechanism. Only in this way can the remainder
remain genuinely unassimilated, not as an abstract uncolonized non-
identity that will always already have been co-opted.

However, only a reductionist interpretation that overlooks Hegel's fundamental concepts of negativity and infinity could ever have regarded the
system as a closed totalized mechanism anyway. The notion of the excluded
remainder working as a condition of the institution of a positive system that
can never ultimately come to rest in an exclusionary positivity is remarkably
close to Hegel's depiction of negativity. As we have seen, Derrida concedes
that the proximity of deconstruction and Hegelianism is 'almost absolute',
and that the logic of the *Aufhebung* can always be read as a deconstructive
'logic of loss'. Indeed, the *Aufhebung* does constitute the loss of the positive
plenitude of abstract givenness and the founding of an identity in difference that maintains the infinity of living contradiction, the subsisting
effectivity of paradox and aporia.

In *Glas*, Derrida comments on the all-burning fire of the religion of light,
discussed by Hegel in the *Phenomenology of Spirit*, as a repressed and excluded
remainder that makes the system possible and impossible. It is a play of
light, without essence, self, identity or time. It thus cannot be a temporal
moment in the process of the constitution of self and the speculative identity of spirit that Hegel's system describes. But Hegel insists that it *must*
burn itself out and become 'for-itself'.[105] Derrida regards this Hegelian
'must' as 'the implacable force of sense, of mediation, of the hard-working
negative'.[106] For Derrida, this is the 'must' of force, not logical necessity.
The 'force of sense' is the senseless beginning of sense. This senseless force
is the senseless decision to make sense. However, as we have seen, Hegel
is fully aware that his system begins with a founding decision, not a given
origin. Nevertheless, for Hegel, the all-burning burns itself out due to its
own logic. The essenceless play of light is essenceless because in its all-
burning nature it constantly ceases to be what it is. The blaze itself must be
consumed and cease to be a blaze, or, as Derrida puts it, 'If you want to burn
all, you must also consume the blaze, avoid keeping [*garder*] it alive as a precious presence.'[107] For Hegel, this is the negation of the selfless from which
the self arises. He writes regarding the all-burning light: 'The *immediate
being* . . . is itself the *negative* power which dissolves its distinctions. It is thus
in truth the Self.'[108] The pre-systemic, essenceless flux will always already
have been negativity, the force which dissolves all distinct entities, but which
is the very motor of the system's development and self-reproduction. It is in

the nature of the Hegelian system that the pre-systemic be the not-yet-systemic, or the systemic-to-be, that will always already have been systemic. For the all-burning to be irreducibly what it is, it must, of necessity, burn itself out and become the first moment of the system; otherwise it would be reified as a sacred 'precious presence', thus losing its constantly changing essenceless nature. Gasché remarks: '[W]hat "jams it [the system] inconceivably" is also what confirms the implacable force of the hard-working negative.'[109] The remainder undermines and confirms the system at the same time. However, it is of the very nature of the Hegelian system to reaffirm through undermining, and for all confirmations to undermine themselves. A deconstructive parodic undermining through confirmation, a strategy not far removed from the dialectic of Socratic irony, barely differs from the operation of the Hegelian dialectic itself, the difference being infinitesimal, a rhetorical inflection that hardly 'jams the system'. The fact that Derrida describes the undialecticized all-burning remainder as a 'precious presence', a phrase that usually describes the principle target of deconstruction, indicates that the proximity of deconstruction and the Hegelian dialectic is such as to make them indistinguishable in this instance at least, the *Aufhebung* of the remainder here being the deconstruction of presence.

Another case of an 'excluded remainder' discussed in *Glas* is the nature of the relationship between sister and brother as portrayed in the *Phenomenology of Spirit*. For Hegel, this is a relationship of peace and equilibrium, devoid of the struggle for recognition and self-recognition, of the antagonistic mutual dependency characteristic of other human relationships, the archetype being the dialectic of master and slave. Hegel writes: '[Brother and sister] do not desire one another, nor have they given to, or received from, one another this independent being-for-self; on the contrary, they are free individualities in regard to each other.'[110] The conflictual mutual recognition that is the precondition of self-recognition is absent from the relationship of brother and sister. Derrida suggests that the uniqueness of this relationship contradicts the whole of the Hegelian system. Derrida writes: '[A] symmetrical relation that needs no reconciliation to appease itself, that does not know the horizon of war, the infinite wound, contradiction, negativity. Is that the inconceivable? What the greater logic cannot assimilate?'[111] It is an unalienated relationship, taking the form of diversity and immediacy, as opposed to contradiction and mediation, which cannot coherently participate in a system of alienation and reconciliation.

However, it does participate in Hegel's text, in his phenomenological, comprehensively rational description of the process of the development of spirit. In this narrative, it provides a prefiguration of the state of 'justice' in the realm of the ethical life [*Sittlichkeit*] of the community. Here the word 'justice' simply refers to balance and equilibrium, in this case a balance and equilibrium between the realms of 'divine law' and 'human law'. For Hegel, the term 'divine law' refers to the hidden realm of private life and singularity, which is the preserve of the feminine principle, and the term 'human law' refers to the outside realm of social life and universality, which is the preserve of the masculine principle. The brother–sister relationship is a figuration that symbolizes a relationship between feminine and masculine, of 'divine' and 'human', of singular and universal, devoid of a desire that has the form of the mutually antagonistic dependency of contradiction. It is thus a resolution of the conflict between feminine and masculine, an interpersonal *Aufhebung* that prefigures the social *Aufhebung* of the conflict between 'divine' and 'human' law in the harmony and equilibrium of the ethical social order of this stage of spirit. This ethical order is described by Hegel in the following way: 'The ethical realm is . . . an immaculate world, a world unsullied by any internal dissension.'[112] To suggest, as Derrida does, that the absence of contradiction in the brother–sister relationship itself contradicts the Hegelian system is to suggest the same of this harmonious ethical realm, as well as all other cases of non-contradictory harmony or diverse immediacy. However, the equilibrium of the ethical realm is temporary and new contradictions arise through the act of the individual insinuating its negativity. Neither non-contradictory harmony nor diverse immediacy lie outside the system; they are essential moments of the system, and as moments are inherently transient. Contradiction and the resolution of contradiction constitute change, the movement between these moments. Diverse immediacy, which is difference that does not enter into contradiction, cannot 'contradict the system' if it is to remain non-contradictory diversity. It must, however, be overcome, and become embroiled in contradiction and mediation, if it is to enter into the relationality of spiritual actuality, as opposed to the mere indifference of juxtaposition, devoid of the effectivity of intervention.

Žižek argues that the constitutive nature of the excluded remainder is fundamental to Hegel's system itself, and not merely a systemic oversight. His example is Hegel's portrayal of constitutional monarchy in the *Philosophy of Right*. This is a system in which the monarch is the irrational constitutive exception to a rational social totality. The monarch is excluded from the system of law, of equality before the law, of relations of exchange, of the restricted economy of meaningful mediation, and in her very exclusion she makes this system possible. She is an an-economic immediacy, in that her position is entirely based on biological lineage, on the natural and non-rational body, and in that she guarantees the system of law through the irreducibly decisionistic 'I will' behind the meaningless empty formality of the royal signature.[113] Žižek writes: '[The monarch] constitutes the Whole of the social fabric in its "organic articulation" [*organische Gliederung*] – the "irrational" surplus as a condition of the rational totality.'[114] This negative effectivity of the excluded remainder is a basic element of Hegelian logic. Žižek further writes:

for they know not what they do

The Monarch is a strange body within the fabric of the State; he remains 'unaccounted for' by rational mediation. However, precisely as such, he is the element through which rational totality constitutes itself. . . . In other words, what the Derridean 'deconstruction' brings out after a great struggle and declares to be the inherent limit of the dialectical mediation – the point at which the movement of the *Aufhebung* necessarily fails – Hegel posits directly as the crucial moment of this movement.[115]

Whatever the validity of Hegel's account of constitutional monarchy, it is clear that he regards the non-rational excluded remainder as constitutive of, and essential to, any rational totality. An-economic immediacy will always already have become the power of negativity within the system. He describes this effectivity of the remainder as 'truly speculative in its nature' and as belonging to 'logic'.[116]

It does not make sense to speak of an excluded remainder to the Hegelian system, because the system is not a closed mechanism. The word 'system' simply refers to a thinking together, a thinking of things in their interconnectedness and relationality. As we have seen, a closed system would involve the machinations of positive substance, without the dislocating power of negativity, the irruption of irreducible contingency and singular alterity that is the subject. Hegel's system is an attempt to think the effects of negativity within substance. There is nothing to say about the brute existence or mere being of indifferent diversity unless it comes to intervene in, and thus dislocate, a closed totality, unless, that is, it *acts* as negativity. Derrida himself is critical of thinkers, such as Georges Bataille, who make reference to an absolute outside of the restricted economy of discourse. For Derrida, the unassimilated remainder must intervene within discourse, dislocating and undermining it immanently. This is the very way that the Hegelian system 'assimilates', or rather, infects itself with,

cf. all the argument re. Incarnation

the so-called remainder. Of course, as we have seen, Derrida allows that Hegelianism can be interpreted in two ways, on the basis of a traditional notion of assimilation, or, alternatively, on a deconstructive basis. The claim that Hegel's system is exclusionary depends on the view that it is ultimately closed and finite.

Actual Infinity

Hegel's system is a critique of all limitation and finitude. The form of a teleological narrative that reaches completion implies closure, but in this case the 'completion' is the knowing of the absolute that dissolves all finitude and closure. Hegel's system, and the meaning of its very systematicity, rests on the idea stated in the preface to the *Phenomenology* that 'the True is the Whole'.[117] This statement means that the true, or the absolute, is nothing particular or finite. The 'whole' is not an exclusive totality that could be compared to other exclusive totalities, which would just be a big particular finitude. It is the dissolution and overcoming of all finitude. The absolute manifests itself negatively; it cannot be represented in the positivity of a finite figure. Thus all determinate claims to absolute truth are demonstrated to be false, or mere transient moments. Hegel's system is a critique of false absolutism. It differs from any critical relativism in that its critique is based on the insinuation and manifestation of the absolute within the finite, effecting the latter's dissolution. Jean-Luc Nancy writes: 'What is asked of thought . . . is . . . to not give up on the inscription of the absolute in the present, such that no present . . . is absolutized.'[118] The absolute is the force of the negative that overcomes all finitude. The absolute, to be absolute and unconditional, cannot be defined in opposition to anything else, cannot be bounded or finite. For Hegel, the form of the absolute, and of his speculative system in general, is the infinite. This is the infinite not as something abstract and unattainable, but as concrete, living, actual and effective.

Hegel distinguishes between two types of infinity, the 'bad', or 'spurious', infinite and the 'true' infinite. The 'bad infinite' refers to an endless progress, or regress, that implies completion in an unattainable beyond; a merely potential infinite that Hegel characterizes as the perennial and ultimately unrealizable 'ought' of a religious yearning.[119] In Hegel's work, the word *schlechte* (translated as 'bad' or 'spurious') means the same as 'abstract', or something that is one-sided, that is not mediated through its other, and thus remains trapped in its own finitude. This infinite stands in opposition to its other, the finite. It is thus limited and therefore itself finite. Hegel writes:

> The finite reappears *in the infinite itself* as its other, because it is only in its *connection* with its other, the finite, that the infinite is. . . . The infinity of the infinite progress remains burdened with the finite as such, is thereby limited and is itself *finite*.[120]

The 'bad infinite', abstract and one-sided in its absolute opposition to the finite, is implicated in an equally abstract and one-sided treatment of finitude. Hegel writes: '[T]he spurious [*schlechte*] infinite, held fast as only negative . . . is supposed to be unattainable . . . which is at bottom the result of holding fast to the *finite* as such as a *merely affirmative being.*'[121] Abstract infinity and abstract finitude are two sides of the same coin; the former, whether a religious yearning for an unattainable beyond or the endless slippage and deferral of literal meaning of a Romantic or 'postmodern' irony, is implicated in the latter, a positivist empiricism that restricts knowledge to isolated facts that are not regarded as inherently related in a wider whole.

What Hegel calls '*die wahrhafte Unendlichkeit*' ('the true infinite') is the self-overcoming of all finitude and one-sidedness. It is not opposed to the finite, but is the self-mediation and interpenetration of the finite and infinite. It contains the finite within itself and is itself contained within the finite. It is truly infinite and unlimited, because it is not opposed to anything other than itself, but is beyond all opposition, containing the whole process of opposition and limitation within itself. In the 'true infinite' the finite does not subsist as the isolated entity of positivism, but is a self-negating and dissolving moment in a relational totality. Hegel writes that in the 'true infinite' the finite 'is not an *independent, self-subsistent* being, but only a *moment*'.[122] The 'true infinite' is the self-ex-position of the finite. Hegel describes it as the very nature of his speculative dialectic, which immanently overcomes finitude and enables the manifestation of a wider whole. He writes:

> [T]he specific nature of speculative thought . . . consists solely in grasping the opposed moments in their unity. Each moment actually shows that it contains its opposite within itself and that in this opposite it is united with itself; thus the affirmative truth is this immanently active unity, the taking together of both thoughts, their infinity – the relation to self which is not immediate but infinite.[123]

It is this form of comprehension, one which overcomes the limits of a thought and sees its immanent and infinitely mediated unity with its other and in this way sees beyond the one-sidedness of any finite dogmatic assertion, that is Hegel's conception of 'Reason [*Vernunft*]'. The immanently active unity of opposites goes beyond the finite decidability of the law of non-contradiction, affirming the infinite undecidability of intrinsically exposed and manifest relationality, which takes the form of impossible paradox only to the limited consciousness of the chained-to-finitude analytical 'Understanding [*Verstand*]'.

For Hegel, the infinite is the true nature of the finite. The finite is only finite through being opposed to an other, the other thus being intrinsic to the finite's very subsistence; its limit, the absolute otherness of its other, is thus overcome in its very constitution. Hegel writes regarding the finite:

> [I]t is its nature to be related to itself as limitation . . . and to transcend the same, or rather, as self-relation to have negated the limitation and to be beyond it. . . . [T]he finite is only this, through its own nature to become itself the infinite. . . . Thus the finite has vanished in the infinite and what *is*, is only the *infinite*.[124]

The finite will always already have been the infinite. It is ultimately false, a reified atomistic abstraction, the abstraction of dead positivity. The genuine infinite, the infinite restlessness that is the essential nature of the finite, is identified with 'Life' in the *Phenomenology of Spirit*. Hegel writes: '[In] [t]he determination of Life . . . *[e]ssence* is infinity as the *supersession* of all distinctions . . . its self-repose being an absolutely restless infinity.'[125]

The 'true infinite' is infinite in that it has no other, and it has no other precisely because it is itself the opening to the other. Hegel writes: '[T]he genuine Infinite . . . consists . . . in remaining at home with itself in its other, or . . . in coming to itself in its other.'[126] He further comments: '[I]n its passing into another, something only comes together *with itself*, and this relation to itself in the passing and in the other is *genuine Infinity*.'[127] The 'true infinite' thus involves openness to alterity, and not the annihilation of all the remains of otherness through its appropriating all-inclusiveness.

Derrida, however, maintains that the latter is the true nature of the Hegelian infinite. He regards it as the abolition of all alterity and the absolute dominion of the metaphysics of presence. Interpreting Hegel, Derrida writes: 'The destruction of singularity must leave no remain(s), no empiric or singular remain(s). It must be total and infinite.'[128] The 'true infinite' is thus the name of the destruction of all singular alterity *qua* singular alterity

is this living?

through the active actuality of the all-encompassing, limitlessly appropriating, speculative identity. Actual infinity is absolute presence, the annihilation of all trace of singular alterity. According to Derrida, Hegelian absolute spirit is infinite in that it is a self-knowing and self-presence without exteriority. He describes it as 'the infinite of a knowing that, as infinite, no longer has any exteriority, thus knows itself, becomes present to itself. Presence (*Dasein*) that knows itself since it is infinite and has no outside'.[129] Thus Derrida regards the Hegelian manifestation of the absolute in absolute knowing in the form of genuine infinity as involving the arrival of *parousia*, the absolute presence of the fullness of being.[130] In the *Science of Logic*, Hegel himself appears to characterize the 'true infinite' in terms of full presence and absolute closure. He writes: '[T]he image of the true infinity, bent back into itself, becomes the *circle*, the line which has reached itself, which is closed and wholly present, without *beginning* and *end*.'[131]

Derrida claims that the 'true infinity' of absolute knowing involves the abolition of all exteriority and thus an infinite internalization. As we have seen, Lukács makes the same claim, arguing that absolute knowing is the ultimate internalization [*Erinnerung*], an integration of all external objectivity into the subject. We argued that at this point the notion of internalization is misleading as the absolute overcomes the distinction between inner and outer, it being Hegel's view that spirit is 'actual' and not 'inner'. The circle image demonstrates that the 'true infinite' constitutes the self-relation of speculative identity, an identity that returns to itself through the other, and is only constituted through this return. Without the return, the circular bending back to the self, the infinite would entail the ultimate loss of identity. The circle demonstrates that the infinite is actual and not an unattainable beyond. The latter is the 'bad infinite' and is represented by a straight line that goes on forever. As the end of the line can never be reached, it is a potential infinite. The circle thus represents the actuality of the 'true infinite', hence its 'presence'. The non-presence of the 'bad infinite' involves the supposition of an absolute distinction between the infinite as unattainable, as non-actual non-identity, and the finite as a simply positive exclusionary identity. In contrast, the speculative identity is infinite, in that it maintains itself while containing its other within itself. This is the infinite intervening in the finite, actual and effective, as opposed to the non-actual and ineffectual subjectivist neutrality of the spurious infinite. The circle image makes sense only if it is understood as an image of genuine infinity as opposed to the unending straight line of spurious infinity. Its 'closure' indicates nothing other than that the self returns to itself in its otherness, enacting a speculative identity, a paradoxical infinite identity, an identity in

difference that is actually an open identity. If it represented a closed identity, exclusive of alterity, it would be a representation of abstract finitude.

Derrida's notion of 'presence', set up as the ultimate target of all decon-
structions, refers to both the exclusionary finitude of the full simplicity of a
'walled-in' identity and the all-inclusive infinity of the total manifestation of
absolute being, the *parousia*. The deconstructive critique of the former, the
demonstration of the trace of the other within the selfsame, in itself does
not conflict with Hegelianism. However, Hegel would agree with this critique precisely on the basis of the all-inclusive 'true infinite', which he conceives of as the infinite within the finite. The stasis of an absolute fullness
and completion is a misleading portrayal of the 'true infinite'. The circle
image does not represent completion, but endlessness, incompletion, infinity; it is 'without beginning or end'. It represents the movement of turning,
of self-othering and return, the effectivity of the other within the same,
the infinite within the finite. The infinite is the restlessness of the finite.
Jean-Luc Nancy writes:

> The form that Hegel privileges is indeed the circle, but this circle is a
> 'circle of circles'; not the simple disposition of the same that always comes
> down to the identical, but much rather, at the same time, both the ground
> of all circles, the pure movement of the point that turns . . . and the
> ceaseless movement that leaves nothing at rest.[132]

The unending turning of the circle of circles represents the self, not as the
completion of a simple identity, but as a ceaseless process of identification
and determination, of self-othering and return, where an open transformative identity is exposed to the constant intervention of irreducible alterity.
The infinite within the finite is the intervention of the other within the
selfsame. Actual infinity is active alterity. It is not the *parousia* of absolute
presence, if absolute presence means the annihilation of all alterity. Nancy
writes:

> [For Hegel,] there is, explicitly, neither beginning nor end, but only
> the full and complete actuality of the infinite that traverses, works, and
> transforms the finite. Which means: negativity, hollow, gap, the difference
> of being that relates to itself through this very difference, and which *is*
> thus . . . the infinite act of relating itself to itself, and thus the power of
> the negative. It is this power of the negative that inhabits the gap where
> relation opens, and that hollows out the passage from presence to presence:
> the infinite negativity of the present.[133]

The 'true infinite' can be convincingly read as the undermining of the metaphysics of presence, rather than its ultimate expression.

Derrida, however, reads it as the latter. This raises the question of the relation between deconstruction and what Hegel calls the 'bad infinity'. The notion of *différance* refers to an infinite deferral of the presence of meaning through the perpetual process of differentiating determination, whereby the same is constituted purely by the negation of its other, this trace of the other rendering the same simultaneously possible and impossible, being that which constitutes and dislocates any determinate self-present identity, the latter being merely a momentary illusory effect and effacement of the perpetual dislocating chain of the movement of the trace, a play of presence and absence that never comes to rest in the pure presence of an origin or an end. *Différance* is thus an infinite regress, like the effect of mirrors reflecting each other, like the 'endless succession of mirrors'[134] of the infinity of Romantic irony, the Schlegelian 'irony of irony'. Derrida himself depicts the play of the trace in terms of such an infinity. In *Of Grammatology* he refers to it as an 'infinite reference' from mirror to mirror,[135] and to the 'indefinitely multiplied structure – *en abyme*' of 'textuality'.[136] This is an infinity that resists totalization, its endlessness meaning that it is unfulfillable and non-identical. It is opposed to the Hegelian 'true infinite' in that the latter refers to the all-encompassing nature of the absolute totality. It would thus appear that the deconstructive infinite is an affirmation of what Hegel dismissed as a spurious 'bad infinite'.

However, Rodolphe Gasché argues that Derrida is as much opposed to the 'bad infinite' as he is to the 'true infinite'. This argument involves the claim that the deconstructive infinite is a 'structural infinity', one which is of a different order to the Hegelian distinction between a spurious potential infinite and a genuine actual infinite. Deconstruction involves the endless undermining, through the infinitizing movement of the trace, of the stability of presence, the latter always being a closed, and thus finite, totality or identity. Derrida himself refers to 'the structural necessity of the abyss'.[137] Gasché interprets this statement as meaning that the Derridian infinite is structural and necessary, as opposed to semantic and empirical. He writes: '[Structural infinity's] structurality . . . is in contraposition to the semantic. . . . In many ways similar to spurious infinity, structural infinity . . . is different from it because it is a nonsemantic concept and is distinguished by . . . necessity.'[138] The structural necessity of the Derridian infinite distinguishes it from the 'bad infinite', which is semantic and empirically contingent. Gasché's interpretation of Derrida's notion of *différance* in terms of infinity as a structural necessity is an expression of his reading of Derridian concepts as 'infrastructural' 'quasi-transcendental' conditions of the possibility and impossibility of meaning. This differs from the Kantian transcendental philosophy that asserts that *finitude* is constitutive, that the *limits* of knowledge are the conditions of its possibility. The quasi-transcendentality of the structural infinity of *différance* indicates that meaning is constituted by that which makes it ultimately impossible, the infinity whose chain of differentiation produces the effect of meaning while endlessly preventing and deferring its stabilization in the closure of a finite identity. The constitutive necessity of the Derridian infinite suggests that it is closer to the Hegelian genuine infinite than to the empirically contingent 'bad infinite'. As we have seen, for Hegel, the infinite is the truth of the finite, because the latter's very constitutive limit, the otherness of its other, is overcome in the very act of constitution, whereby the other is essential to the identity of the same. Thus both the Derridian and Hegelian infinites are conditions of both the possibility and impossibility of any finite determinacy. Despite this, Gasché wishes to maintain a distance between his Derridian structural infinity and the Hegelian genuine infinity, which he does by holding to Derrida's interpretation of the latter as the ultimate destruction of alterity. He writes: '[Structural infinity] opens up the possibility of genuine infinity, of the dream of totalization, but in such a manner that it remains essentially limited by its indelible reference to its Other.'[139] However, as we have seen, the genuine infinite has no other, because it is itself the opening to the other. The same can be said regarding structural infinity or *différance*. The structural infinite may describe the opening and reference to the other inscribed within finite identity, but it does not make sense to refer to it as limited by *its* other, otherwise it would itself be finite. *Différance* is more fundamental than the logic of opposition, therefore it should not be inscribed within that logic; it is not, for example, the opposite of presence. *Différance*, like genuine infinity, has no other, but is itself the trace and intervening effectivity of the other within the same.

'True infinity' and '*différance*' also have in common the fact that they are put forward as resisting or evading all forms of mastery and servitude. In 'Ousia and Grammē', Derrida writes: '[The trace] (is) that which must elude mastery. Only presence is mastered.'[140] Similarly, for Hegel, only the finite can be mastered, while the infinite is unmasterable. In *Glas*, Derrida paraphrases Hegel's ideas on this matter: 'One masters only finite life'.[141] Hegel himself states, in his early essay, 'On the Scientific Ways of Treating Natural Law', that it is only the limited and finite that can be coerced. He writes: '[N]othing is external to [freedom], so that no coercion is possible for it. . . . By virtue of singularity [*Einzelheit*], the individual is [placed] directly among determinacies, so that something external is present for him, and coercion is accordingly possible.'[142] Only the finitude of determinacy can be coerced; the infinity of indeterminate determinability evades all coercion.

Despite all this, as we have seen, Derrida reads the Hegelian infinite as the *parousia* of full presence, the ultimate effacement of alterity, *différance*, and the trace. He regards Hegel as effectively equating finite servility with the notion of the trace. In *Glas*, he writes: 'Seen since *Sa* [*savoir absolu* (absolute knowing)], thought of the trace will then be a jealous (finite . . . servile . . .) thought.'[143] This equation of the trace with finitude only makes sense if one accepts that the Hegelian infinite involves full presence, in which case the trace, which is neither present nor absent, would be finite in Hegelian terms. However, the 'presence' of the genuine infinite refers to an 'actuality [*Wirklichkeit*]' different from the stasis of the absolute (abstract) fullness of completion, the latter being an ultimately exclusionary and thus finite totality. The 'actuality' of the genuine infinite is its activity and effectivity [*Wirklichkeit*], such that it is not an abstraction separated from the finite, but concretely intervenes within the latter, enacting its ex-position from its dead positivity into living relationality, through the infiltration of the negativity of the absolute that prevents the abstract absolutization of any determinate finitude. The 'presence' of the genuine infinite refers to the active infinity of difference, of active difference, differentiation, *différance*. In the 'Natural Law' essay, Hegel writes: '[T]he absence of difference . . . presents the totality as something enclosed and undeveloped [*unentfaltet*], in which movement and infinity are not present in their reality.'[144] The 'presence' of genuine infinity works against the 'presence' of enclosure and exclusion. Likewise, the Derridian trace enacts the exposition of the static closure of self-present determinacy into the openness of infinite determinability, enacting the intervention of alterity as opposed to the indifference of juxtaposition. The trace is the trace of the other in the self-same that prevents the latter's closure within the presence of a simple finite identity. It is thus an infinitization of the finite, the self-overcoming of the finite that Hegel characterizes as the genuine infinite.

The 'true infinite' is the form of the absolute idea and its actuality is the de-alienated condition. In the *Lectures on the Philosophy of Religion*, Hegel refers to 'the sublation of natural finitude, of immediate existence, the overcoming of divestment [*Entäußerung* (alienation as externalization)], the dissolution of limitation'.[145] Here the overcoming of externalization is equated with the overcoming of finitude, de-alienation with the actual infinite.

Unalienated Mind

It has been demonstrated that Derrida's concept of *différance* can be seen as involving, in Hegelian terms, either a 'spurious infinite' or a 'genuine infinite', depending on how it is interpreted and the implications that are drawn from it. We have already discussed the 'almost absolute proximity' of certain Derridian and Hegelian concepts. We have also discussed the proximity of *différance* to the infinity of Schlegelian Romantic irony. It is significant that Hegel places Romantic irony at a point of proximity to his notion of 'absolute knowing', the culmination and self-theorization of his system of philosophy. Irony is invoked towards the end of last volume of the *Encyclopaedia of the Philosophical Sciences*, immediately before the final chapter on absolute knowing entitled 'Philosophy'. Here, irony is compared and contrasted with absolute knowing, and argued to be the subjectivistic empty form of the latter. Hegel writes:

> If the result – the realized Spirit in which all mediation has superseded itself – is taken in a merely formal, contentless sense, so that the spirit is not also at the same time known as *implicitly* existent and objectively self-unfolding; – then that infinite subjectivity is the merely formal self-consciousness, knowing itself in itself as absolute – Irony. Irony, which can make every objective reality nought and vain, is itself the emptiness and vanity, which from itself, and therefore by chance and its own good pleasure, gives itself direction and content, remains master over it, is not bound by it – and with the assumption that it stands on the very summit of religion and philosophy, falls back rather into the vanity of wilfulness. It is only in proportion as the pure infinite form, the self-centred manifestation, throws off the one-sidedness of subjectivity in which it is the vanity of thought, that it is the free thought which has its infinite characteristic at the same time as essential and actual content as an object in which it is also free.[146]

Irony and absolute knowing occupy the same position, that of the result and self-consciousness of the process of the mediations and reconfigurations of the forms of consciousness. Spirit, when reaching this position of self-awareness, is faced with a choice between the two. Both irony and absolute knowing involve the self-consciousness of the necessary failure of the absolute to be represented in any figure of consciousness. However, irony restricts this self-consciousness to being a mere empty play of subjectivity. In this play of irony the subject provides its own content which it can dissolve

at will. It overcomes all one-sidedness except the one-sidedness o
subjectivity, and thus remains a spurious infinity, one that is u
limited. In contrast, absolute knowing is truly free and unlimited, ın ɯnat
it is spirit that knows itself as spirit in its 'objective self-unfolding', which
comprehends the activity of the absolute in the logic of the dissolution of
all the figures of intelligibility.

To the extent that Derridian deconstruction involves merely an affirmation of the freeplay of the signifier and of active interpretation it remains
locked in what Hegel would dismiss as the empty subjectivism of irony.
Rorty reads Derrida in this way and calls deconstruction an example of
'private ironism'. However, deconstruction that intervenes, ethically and
institutionally, that enacts the ex-position of reified positivity and the opening to alterity, is closer to the genuine infinity of an absolute knowing.
Close, but not identical, for Derrida does not explicitly theorize his deconstructive praxis as a higher form of knowledge and reason. Unlike Hegel
with his notion of absolute knowing, Derrida does not account for the
possibility and standpoint of the deconstructive operation as a form of
conscious activity.

Absolute knowing is not a mysterious arrival of the *parousia* of absolute
being, manifest and illuminated in its fullness of presence. It is but a self-
description of the necessary nature of the standpoint of Hegelian philosophy, the conditions under which it is possible to observe and describe, in
a rationally comprehensive, therefore purposive and teleological, manner,
the process of configuration and de-figuration of forms of consciousness
and intelligibility. The chapter on the 'Absolute Idea' at the end of the
Science of Logic is not a revelatory consummation of the fullness of being, but
is merely a brief discussion of method, describing the method and standpoint of philosophy as Hegel conceives it. He writes, regarding the absolute
idea: '[W]hat remains to be considered here is not a content as such, but
the universal aspect of its form – that is, the *method*.'[147] The absolute idea
cannot be separated from the dialectical process leading up to it, and
consists of nothing but that process, it being the unity of theory and practice, the 'unity of the theoretical and the practical Idea'.[148] It is the self-
description of the narrator of this comprehensive process. Žižek describes the
Hegelian absolute thus: '[*T*]*he true Absolute is nothing but the logical disposition
of* [*the*] *previous failed attempts to conceive the Absolute.*'[149] The absolute can only
ever manifest itself as negativity, and absolute knowing is the self-consciousness
of the negative power that is the dialectical method of thought.

Absolute knowing is a looking-back on the dialectical temporal process
leading up to itself. Hegel writes: 'This movement, which philosophy is,

finds itself already accomplished, when at the close it seizes its own notion – i.e. only *looks back* on its knowledge.'[150] The 'annulment of time'[151] referred to in Hegel's characterization of absolute knowing does not mean that the latter is a supra-temporal or supra-historical form of knowledge whose content applies to all time, including the future. Absolute knowing is only a looking-back, and is inseparable from the temporal process it looks back on. It is not itself within time, as it is formally unlimited; it is the self-consciousness of the temporal dialectical process, a self-consciousness that only comes about retrospectively when the process reaches the unlimited consciousness that is the self-knowing of the dialectic itself. This absolute knowing is beyond time in the sense that the self-knowing of the dialectic cannot itself be dialecticized, simply because it is itself the name of the process of dialecticization. That is to say, the absolute, the true infinite, the self-overcoming of finitude, cannot itself be overcome, precisely because it *is* the act of overcoming itself.

The dialectical comprehension of history, i.e. Hegel's system, may be the 'end' of history, but this does not mean there will be no more history in the future. Absolute knowing is a comprehension of the past, and is beyond time in the sense that such comprehension can only occur when the past is finished, that is, from the standpoint of the present. Lukács writes: 'Hegel is neither ahistorical nor supra-historical, but instead he provides a *recapitulation* of the entire process from his present vantage-point.'[152] The 'annulment of time' is merely the necessary standpoint of the present. In the *Philosophy of Right*, Hegel, writes:

> Philosophy, as the thought of the world, does not appear until reality has completed its formative process, and made itself ready. . . . When philosophy paints its grey in grey, one form of life has become old, and by means of grey it cannot be rejuvenated, but only known.[153]

Systematic rational knowledge is retroactive; the future is contingently open, and does not obey the laws of necessity. Žižek writes:

> For Hegel, . . . there is no contradiction between our absorption into the historical process and the fact that we not only can but are obliged to speak from the standpoint of the 'end of history'. . . . And 'absolute knowledge' is nothing other than the explication of this historically specified field that *absolutely limits our horizon*: as such, it is 'finite'[.][154]

The standpoint of the present, of the end of the process leading up to it, is a necessity for philosophical comprehension, but future periods of history will have other 'ends'. However, Žižek's use of the word 'finite' to describe the 'horizon' of absolute knowing involves a different understanding of 'infinity' to that of Hegel. The Hegelian infinite is the self-overcoming of finitude, and thus an opening to alterity, not an all-encompassing knowledge irrespective of time or place. The latter would entail omniscience, or at least a pre-critical metaphysics. The retrospectivity of absolute knowing, its status as the standpoint of the present looking back, means that only the past can be philosophically comprehended, implying that the future is ungraspable by systematic thought. Nancy interprets the Hegelian characterization of the philosophical standpoint of the 'present' in the following way:

> [T]he present [is] . . . the restlessness opened between the twilight of a fulfillment and the imminence of an upsurge. . . . It is not the time of an apotheosis outside of time and of a parousia of the absolute. It is what each time is for itself: the grasping of its passage, which means at the same time self-affirmation *and* the restlessness of the other.[155]

The past is knowable as spirit's knowing of itself, of its own unfolding and development. The future is something undetermined and unknowable.

For Hegel, the 'standpoint' of the absolute is an unalienated consciousness. It is spirit that knows itself as spirit, that recognizes all its positive externalizations as moments of its own self, but is itself liberated from the limited positivity of figuration and determinacy, being in a state of infinite determinability, and thus independent and free. In its state of genuine infinity it is grounded on nothing but itself, itself being nothing other than the negativity of the conscious overcoming of determinacy. In absolute knowing there is no distinction between subject and object, as it is a self-knowing, the self-knowing of the absolute idea that knows itself as such. This identity of subject and object gives absolute knowing the quality of simple immediacy, formally resembling in this respect the simple indeterminate immediacy of sense-consciousness that the system begins with, only this time consciousness is actual, effective, concrete and living, a universality that intervenes and contains all particularity within itself in the identity-in-difference of a living oneness, unlike the alienated abstraction of universality that the purported particularity of sense-consciousness proved itself to be.

Hegel writes:

> [T]he self-knowing Spirit, just because it grasps its Notion, is the immediate identity with itself which, in its difference, is the *certainty of immediacy*,

or *sense-consciousness* – the beginning from which we started. This release of itself from the form of its Self is the supreme freedom and assurance of its self-knowledge.[156]

The freedom and self-knowing of the absolute involves the liberation of the self from the form of the self, from form itself, from the determinacy of figuration. The self-othering and overcoming that is the opening to alterity is the genuine infinity of absolute knowing. For Hegel, absolute knowing is the pure negativity of indeterminate singularity that is the condition of genuine universality, a universality involving indeterminate determinability, not the false universality of a hypostatized determinacy. He writes:

> [Absolute knowing] is 'I', that is *this* and no other 'I', and which is no less immediately a *mediated* or superseded *universal* 'I'. It has a *content* which it *differentiates* from itself; for it is pure negativity or the dividing of itself, it is *consciousness*. This content is, in its difference, itself the 'I', for it is the movement of superseding itself, or the same pure negativity that the 'I' is. . . . [I]t is only when the 'I' communes with itself in its otherness that the content is *comprehended*.[157]

The self that is liberated from the self, that is always other, exposed to alterity in its negative indeterminacy, the point of pure singularity and haecceity, that in the negativity of its singularity is universality, the negative unity of all singularities, that is the '"we" that is "I"' of the identity-in-difference of spirit, knows itself to be all its content, all reality, the actual infinity of the othering of the same, the absolute.

Hegel's conceptualization of de-alienating appropriation does not necessarily depend on a metaphysics of presence. The authentic proper comes about in the actuality of spiritual relationality, which itself comes about through the ex-position and deconstruction of abstract, reified, positive givenness. By taking seriously Derrida's assertion of the proximity of deconstruction and Hegelianism, the latter can be convincingly interpreted as a rational philosophical system based on the same premises as the former, the *Aufhebung* being read as the reconfiguration of discourse through the intervening power of negativity, or active difference, which dislocates the one-sided identity, and given positivity, of a walled-in presence. Hegelianism is not a philosophy of origins and an expressive organicism whereby an originary plenitude of immediacy is lost and regained at a higher level through an immanent teleological development, as the originary immediacy is shown to be a false, reified and alienated abstraction. The development occurs through the negative intervention of infinite alterity, and the recon-figurations are given the form of teleological necessity retroactively from the philosophical standpoint that occurs when spirit overcomes the limitation of figuration and subsists in the self-awareness of the genuine infinity of its proper element. This de-alienated condition of absolute spirit occurs when the reified abstraction of 'substance' is transformed into the 'authentic substance' of spirit, a substance which is at the same time 'subject', the subject being the negativity of the irruption of irreducibly singular alterity within the self-identity of substance. Appropriation of the other is not a violent reduction of alterity, but the liberation of the self from itself through the intervention and infinite act of the other. Hegel's system is not an exclusionary totality, as it attempts to think the absolute as an actual infinity, which is itself to think the intervening effectivity of the excluded remainder of any closed configuration. The Hegelian infinite is not the all-inclusive fullness of presence of the *parousia*, but the infinite within the finite which is the opening to alterity. Actual infinity is the form of Hegel's system and the unalienated mind wherein absolute spirit knows itself as such in all its manifestations. De-alienation is not an exclusionary completion in the fullness of presence, but is the state of freedom that is the opening to the other, the conscious experience of the actuality of infinity.

Chapter 3

Determinability and Objectification in Marx

According to Derrida, Marx's concern with the overcoming of alienation is a case of the metaphysics of presence, involving a desire for the suppression of *différance* and the 'exorcism' of the spectrality of the trace. The concern here will be to ascertain the extent to which Marx's writings support an alternative interpretation of the relationship between deconstruction and de-alienation.

This investigation will involve an inquiry into the relationship between Derrida and Marx, with particular emphasis on the way in which *différance* inheres within phenomena which Marx regards as manifestations of the capitalist mode of production. The fundamental role that social relationality plays in Marx's conception of the human 'essence' will be discussed with regard to its implications for any notion of essence based on substantial presence. Marx's concept of 'objectification' will be analysed with regard to its relationship to alienation and de-alienation, and attention will be given to the extent to which the latter furthers a narcissistic appropriation. The relationship between Marxian de-alienation and the Derridian notions of restricted and general economy will then be discussed. The question here is not only the accuracy of Derrida's critique of Marx, but also how the aspects of Marx's conception of the overcoming of alienation may be interpreted anew in the light of Derrida's critique of the metaphysics of presence in general.

Capitalist *Différance*

For Derrida, Marx's critique of capitalism exhibits an aversion to *différance* and a desire for the establishment of the fullness of presence. In the terms used in Derrida's *Spectres of Marx*, Marx objects to the spectral quality of capitalist social relations and wishes to 'exorcise' this in order to restore the reality of a living presence. This spectrality is that of the trace, of *différance*, of that which is neither fully present nor fully absent, nor *fully* anything.

Marx's dislike of this spectrality, and his concomitant desire for the overcoming of the capitalism and alienation that it manifests, involve a prejudice in favour of the spurious, and ultimately dangerous, metaphysical myth of a fully integrated life, free from the disjuncture of otherness and death. In the *1844 Manuscripts*, Marx writes that '[C]ommunism . . . [is] the complete return of man to himself . . . the true resolution of the strife between existence and essence'.[1] For Derrida, this reintegration of 'man with himself' in the abolition of alienation involves the elision of alterity, and thus of the possibility of a 'justice' understood as the opening to the other. He writes:

> Is not disjuncture the very possibility of the other? How to distinguish between two disadjustments, between the disjuncture of the unjust and the one that opens up the infinite asymmetry of the relation to the other, that is to say, the place for justice?[2]

The question indicates the possibility of a distinction between two types of 'alienation', one bad and unjust, and the other good and just, the badness of the first and the goodness of the second both having their basis in 'disjuncture'. The disjuncture in question is that of alienation, as Derrida explicitly identifies alienation with his deconstructive concepts, for example, when he writes that the 'ghost effect' of spectrality amounts to 'a supplementary dimension, one more simulacrum, alienation, or expropriation'.[3] It is Marx's notion of the overcoming of capitalism's alienating disjuncture that Derrida equates with a 'pre-deconstructive ontology of presence',[4] as opposed to the 'hauntology' of deconstructive and capitalist *différance*, a 'hauntology' of the spectrality of the commodity form.[5]

Derrida claims that Marx effectively determines the commodity form in terms of the 'spectrality' of exchange value as opposed to the 'real presence' of use value. In the *Grundrisse* Marx writes: '[E]xchange value is present, exists, only in use value.'[6] The use value of a thing is that which within its qualitative presence responds to human needs. Exchange value is thus an insubstantial, phantom-like non-presence, detached from the specific qualities of the thing upon which it rests. Marx writes that exchange value is the 'pure *form* of value – in which the traces of its becoming, as well as its specific presence in use value, have been extinguished'.[7] It is the illusory phantom that provides the 'basis' of the capitalist system of production and circulation.

Conversely, Derrida argues that the 'presence' of use value is an illusory effacement of the movement of *différance*, a *différance* that he detects in

Marx's characterization of exchange value. The presence of use value is always already 'haunted' by the spectral, phantasmatic *différance* of exchange value. Derrida writes: 'The commodity . . . haunts the thing, its specter is at work in use value.'[8] Derrida identifies exchange value with the fundamental difference of the trace. He writes:

> Just as there is no pure use, there is no *use-value* which the possibility of exchange and commerce (by whatever name one calls it, meaning itself, value, culture, spirit [!], signification, the world, the relation to the other, and first of all the simple form and trace of the other) has not in advance inscribed in an *out-of-use* – an excessive signification.[9]

Capitalism is a manifestation of this excessive 'possibility', an open system, or 'general economy' of *différance*, whereby the limitless circulation of exchange value is set in motion by the extraction of excess value, surplus-value. One commentator on the relation between Derrida and Marx, Michael Ryan, puts it in the following way:

> The structure that initiates this interminable process without closure [of exchange value] is the extraction of surplus value from labor. . . . There is . . . a skidding inscribed in the very rationality . . . of the capitalist system which situates the system in an interminable seriality it cannot arrest or close off.[10]

Although Ryan goes on to suggest that it is this excess that contains the potential for the system's immanent deconstruction, a more apposite inference from what he and Derrida have to say about the infinite excess of exchange and surplus value is that capitalism is itself deconstruction.

Indeed, money itself has the emptily formal, insubstantial and excessive quality of *différance*. Marx notes, with horror, the menace it does to the properness of meaning. He writes: '[Money is] the transformation of all human and natural properties into their contraries, the universal confounding and distorting of things.'[11] In effacing the qualitative presence of anything, money enacts an infinite play of distortion and reversal. Its infinite excess disrupts the 'restricted economy' of the proper, of the *oikos*, the home. In *Given Time*, Derrida identifies money with the 'general economy' of *différance*. 'As soon as there is monetary sign – and first of all sign – that is, differance and credit, the *oikos* is opened and cannot dominate its limit.'[12] Simon Critchley concludes from this that 'money is a kind of decon-struction, it opens the closure of the *oikos* to the unrestricted "economy" of desire where money circulates and where wealth is accumulated or squandered – the nomadic and quasi-automatic flows of capital.'[13]

However, money, and thus *différance* as money, is, according to Marx, in its formal universality, an alienated projection of humanity's own universal character, its generic nature. He writes: '[T]he *divine* power of money – lies in its *character* as men's estranged, alienating and self-disposing *species-nature*. Money is the alienated *ability of mankind*.'[14] The universal character, or generic-being [*Gattungswesen* ('species-being')], of humanity rests on the latter's sociality and relationality. Derrida links the spectrality and *différance* of the commodity form to relationality and sociality when he writes: '[T]he spectral effect of the commodity . . . is born of a *relation* (ferance, difference, reference and differ*ance*), as double relation, one should say as double social bond.'[15] For Marx, this empty spectral relationality of exchange value and the commodity form is merely the alienated projection of humanity's essential relationality.

Essential Relationality

A spectral, emptily formal, insubstantial relationality is what for Marx characterizes humanity. This insubstantiality is the basis not only of sociality, but also of the formal universality definitive of consciousness. In his early works, particularly the *1844 Manuscripts*, Marx uses the term *Gattung-swesen* to refer to the conscious universality intrinsic to humanity. *Gattung-swesen* can be translated into English as 'genus-essence', 'genus-being' or 'generic-being', but has usually been misleadingly rendered as 'species-being', a disastrous translation given that it is generality and not specificity that is being emphasized. The term *Gattung* ('genus') refers to generality and universality, and to say that a human is a *Gattungswesen* is to say that it is a living universality, that is, a conscious being. Consciousness involves apprehending universals as objects, and is not the mere awareness of phenomena in their immediate sensuous particularity, an awareness that animals are limited to. Marx writes:

> Man is a species-being [*Gattungswesen*], not only because in practice and in theory he adopts the species [*Gattung*] (his own as well as those of other things) as his object, but . . . also because he treats himself as the actual, living species [*Gattung*]; because he treats himself as a *universal* and therefore a free being.[16]

Unlike an animal, a human is not confined to the immediacy of its individual life activity. The ability to separate itself from its individuality and apprehend generality is what makes a being conscious. Marx writes:

> Man makes his life activity itself the object of his will and of his consciousness. . . . It is not a determination with which he directly merges. . . . It is just because of this that he is a species-being. Or it is only because he is a species-being that he is a conscious being[.][17]

Awareness of genera depends on not being bound to a specific determination.

As Marx's notion of *Gattungswesen* derives from the works of Feuerbach and Hegel, its meaning and implications can be clarified by looking at the use of the concept of 'genus' by these thinkers. In Feuerbach's *The Essence of Christianity*, awareness of generality is the basis of consciousness. Feuerbach writes:

> Consciousness in the strictest sense is present only in a being to whom his species [*Gattung*], his essential nature, is an object of thought. . . . Where there is this higher consciousness there is a capability of science. Science is the cognizance of species [*Gattungen*].[18]

It is the understanding of generality as such that is important here. For Feuerbach, an animal is directly at one with its immediate individuality, whereas a conscious being distinguishes itself from its individuality, having a 'twofold life'; an outer life of particularity and an inner life of universality, of thought, of the apprehension of genera. This universality is only possible because of an insubstantial indeterminate determinability and substitutability. Feuerbach writes:

> Man thinks – that is, he converses with himself. . . . Man is himself at once I and thou; he can put himself in the place of another, for this reason, that to him his species [*Gattung*], his essential nature, and not merely his individuality, is an object of thought.[19]

Thought and consciousness are possible because human 'nature' is not substantial, but relational. The universality of consciousness is an effect of the insubstantial indeterminacy of an infinite determinability that is essentially relational. Thought and consciousness are essentially a conversation, a relation.

This emptiness of consciousness, its lack of a permanently limiting determinacy, makes possible its infinitely flexible ability to assume any determination. Feuerbach writes: '[C]onsciousness is essentially infinite in its nature.'[20] As consciousness is what distinguishes humans from animals, human 'nature' is precisely this unlimited creative nothingness. Feuerbach claims that 'human nature' is 'infinitely varied, infinitely modifiable'.[21] In other words, the human 'essence' is not to have a substantive essence; the distinguishing feature of humans is not to have a distinguishing feature. It is this that makes possible the free conscious universality and limitless modifiability of humanity.

Of course, each actual instantiation of this limitless universality, each living conscious being, is, in its individuality, limited and finite. Feuerbach writes: '[T]he human being, as an individual, can and must . . . feel and recognize himself to be limited; but he can become conscious of his limits, his finiteness, only because the perfection, the infinitude of his species, is perceived by him.'[22] Therein lies the human's 'twofold life'; a finite living being that is also free and conscious, conscious in that the limitless universality of the genus, as a determinable nothingness, is manifest within it. It is this infinitude of humanity, of general consciousness as opposed to the finitude of the individual, that Feuerbach argues is falsely projected onto an alien theological being.

Feuerbach's notion of living genus, or general consciousness, is, despite its purported 'anthropological' concretization, merely a more abstract version of Hegel's concept of 'spirit'. It is significant that in the *Phenomenology of Spirit* the term '*Gattung*' ('genus') is only used at the point of the inception of 'spirit' in the narrative of the development of consciousness. Just prior to the exposition of the experience of mutual recognition (the 'master–slave dialectic'), the term 'genus' is used to refer to an iterable universality characteristic of genuine consciousness that comes about through the self-othering relationality of nascent sociality. The genus is the negative unity of the general relationality, or sociality, that constitutes consciousness. Hegel writes:

[The genus] is the *universal* unity which contains all [its] moments as superseded within itself. It is the simple genus which, in the movement of Life itself. . . . Life points to something other than itself, viz. to consciousness, for which life exists as this unity, or as genus. . . . The simple 'I' is this genus or the simple universal, for which differences are *not* differences only by its being the *negative essence* of the shaped independent moments. . . . [The] universal independent nature in which negation is present as absolute negation, is the genus as such, or the genus as *self-consciousness. Self-consciousness achieves its satisfaction only in another self-consciousness.*[23]

The term 'genus' occurs at the point of transformation from sensuous particularity to the negative universality of spirit, of consciousness as social being, and names that negative universality in its initial abstractly formal aspect.

For Marx, as for his predecessors, the term *Gattungswesen* refers to the negative universality that constitutes consciousness, a universality stemming from the lack of any specific determination, an insubstantial intrinsic relationality. To say that a human is a *Gattungswesen* is simply to say that a human is a conscious being, having the indeterminacy productive of universal awareness. It is *not* to say that a human is a being who has an identification with its biological 'species', with humanity. Marx writes:

> An animal forms objects only in accordance with the standard and the need of the species to which it belongs, whilst man knows how to produce in accordance with the standard of every species, and knows how to apply everywhere the inherent standard to the object.[24]

A human *qua* conscious being is a 'species-being [*Gattungswesen*]' precisely because it does not 'belong' to a 'species', because it is free from specific determination and is hence able to perceive generality. A human *qua* sensuous bodily individual finite being is a type of animal, and 'belongs' to the 'human' biological species. The point is that *Gattungswesen* involves freedom from specific determination.

Misunderstandings of the term *Gattungswesen* have tended to involve regarding it as referring to a human 'essence', a set of qualities distinguishing humans from other 'species'. For example, Allen Wood writes that *Gattungswesen* refers to 'humanity as a single collective entity or else to the essential property which characterizes this entity and makes it a single distinctive thing in its own right'.[25] *Gattungswesen* is actually not a distinguishing property, but an absence of properties enabling an awareness of universality, which paradoxically 'distinguishes' a conscious being from an animal. Wood goes on to state:

> Feuerbach believes that it is our consciousness of our own species nature which makes it possible for us to be conscious of the species nature of other things, and hence that our species being is the foundation of our

ability to form universal concepts. There are some passages in Marx which may be read as endorsing this thesis. Neither philosopher, however, presents any real arguments in favor of the thesis . . . in fact, the truth would seem to be just the opposite, that it is the human ability to form universal concepts which makes it possible for people to know themselves as members of a species.[26]

Wood's error is to regard 'species being [*Gattungswesen*]' as consciousness of being a member of a species. It is nothing of the sort, but rather the awareness of universality as such, being itself 'the ability to form universal concepts', an ability founded on an inherent indeterminacy, on not belonging to a species.

The infinitude of the genus also involves freedom from the finitude of need. Marx writes: '[M]an produces universally. [An animal] produces only under the dominion of immediate physical need, whilst man produces even when he is free from physical need and only truly produces in freedom therefrom.'[27] The alienation of the *Gattungswesen* of the worker under capitalism turns her productive activity into a mere means to her physical subsistence; the free universal productive ability is harnessed, expropriated, and becomes for her a mere means to the maintenance of the bare subsistence of her finite particularity. Marx writes: '[I]n degrading spontaneous, free activity to a means, estranged labour makes man's species-life a means to his physical existence. . . . Estranged labour turns thus . . . [*m*]*an's species-being* . . . into a being *alien* to him, into a *means* for his *individual existence*.'[28] The infinitude of genus-ability is distorted into being the means for an enslavement to finitude.

According to Marx, human *Gattungswesen* is alienated through the division of labour. He writes: '[T]he *division of labour* . . . is nothing else but the *estranged* [*entfremdete*], *alienated* [*entäußerte*] positing of human activity as a *real activity of the species* or as *activity of man as a species-being* [*Gattungswesen*].'[29] This means that under the division of labour the universality of humanity, its lack of restriction to specific determinacy, is a feature of humanity in general that is alienated from individual human beings. The latter are restricted to particular one-sided activities that stifle their multi-faceted potential. Division of labour and exchange are both expressions of human universality and the way in which that universality is alienated from individuals in capitalism.[30]

In Marx's later works the term *Gattungswesen* is abandoned, but his concern with human universality is not. In *Capital* he asserts that the one-sided determinate particularity of the individual enslaved to partiality through the division of labour must be replaced by the unrestricted universality of a multi-faceted individual. He writes: '[T]he partially developed individual, who is merely the bearer of one specialized social function, must be replaced by the totally developed individual.'[31] In the *Grundrisse* he argues that human universality is made possible by capitalist exchange and that capitalism simultaneously alienates it from individuals. He writes:

> Universally developed individuals . . . are no product of nature, but of history. The degree and the universality of the development of wealth where *this* individuality becomes possible supposes production on the basis of exchange value as a prior condition, whose universality produces not only the alienation of the individual from himself and from others, but also the universality and the comprehensiveness of his relations and capacities. In earlier stages of development the single individual seems to be developed more fully, because he has not yet worked out his relationships in their fullness, or erected them as independent social powers and relations opposite himself. It is as ridiculous to yearn for a return to that original fullness as it is to believe that with this complete emptiness history has come to a standstill.[32]

As we have seen, Derrida argues that Marx wishes to 'exorcize' the insubstantial spectrality of exchange value. Yet here Marx argues that it is the very 'emptiness' of exchange value that makes possible the universal comprehensiveness of the individual, while at the same time alienating her from this universality. The purported fullness of the pre-capitalist individual of a 'Romantic' conservatism is the fullness of an immediacy that is ultimately one-sidedly determined, which contrasts with the suggested post-capitalist comprehensive individual who has the mediated 'fullness' of an infinite determinability. The latter is not the fullness of a final, i.e. finite, fulfilment, but is the fulfilling freedom of an absolute becoming. This is clear when Marx refers to 'the universal development of the individual . . . as a constant suspension of its *barrier*, which is recognized as a barrier, not taken for a *sacred limit*'.[33]

The spectrality of exchange value is precisely its negative universality, devoid of the particularity of use value. This spectrality is the precondition of both alienation and the realization of human universality. In the *Grundrisse* Marx writes:

> [W]hen the limited bourgeois form is stripped away, what is wealth other than the universality of individual needs, capacities, pleasures, productive

forces etc., created through universal exchange? . . . The absolute working-out of his creative potentialities . . . [w]here he does not reproduce himself in one specificity, but produces his totality? Strives not to remain something he has become, but is in the absolute movement of becoming? In bourgeois economics – and in the epoch of production to which it corresponds – this complete working-out of the human content appears as a complete emptying-out, this universal objectification as total alienation, and the tearing-down of all limited, one-sided aims as sacrifice of the human end-in-itself to an entirely external end.[34]

Thus the universality of exchange value, and hence the system of production resting on the commodity form, brings about the absolute becoming of infinite determinability of humanity in general, while at the same time alienating it from the human individual, who is in the process reduced to the most limiting one-sided specificity, a repetitive, mechanistic, quantitative labour, an isolated cog in the machine of human universality. It is the individual who is alienated, from the freedom of the productive nothingness of infinite malleability, from the negative universality of her *Gattungswesen*, by a capitalism that brought it about in the first place.

The spectrality of the commodity form, of exchange value, its trace-like nature, its non-presence, its *différance*, is the precondition of the free determinability of the universally developed individual, but it is alienated from the individual through the capitalist relations of production. This means that the *différance* that is brought into the open by capitalism is itself alienated through the latter from the human individual. This individual, because of the essential nothingness and non-presence that underpin its nature as a conscious being, is itself the source of the *différance* from which it is alienated. It is not the lack of a determinate essence itself that is a product of capitalism, but the manifestation of this indeterminacy. The fact that humans differ in their specificity across history and geography, unlike any other species of animal, is testament to the essential unessential indeterminate emptiness of their 'nature'. Capitalist modernity enables this free universality to become consciously manifest. This is a Hegelian view of modernity as the awakening of reason *qua* the unbounded consciousness of freedom. In *Spectres of Marx*, Derrida, interpreting and advocating Kojève's quasi-Hegelian thesis on 'post-historical Man', writes:

There where man, a certain determined concept of man, is finished, there the pure humanity of man, of the *other man* and of man *as other* begins or has finally the chance of heralding itself – of promising itself. In an apparently inhuman or else a-human fashion.[35]

The negative universality of form frees humanity from being tied to the positive specificity of a particular content. What Derrida is advocating here is identical to Marx's conception of *Gattungswesen*.

For Marx, as for Hegel, the universality of humanity is inherently bound up with its sociality. Marx writes:

> My *general* consciousness is only the *theoretical* shape of that of which the *living* shape is the *real* community, the social fabric. . . . In his *consciousness of species* [*Gattung*] man confirms his real *social life* and simply repeats his real existence in thought[.][36]

Conscious universality is an expression of sociality. A human is not bound to its immediate sensuous existence, and is hence a conscious generic being, because of its intrinsic insubstantial relationality.

The notion of essential relationality is most clearly expressed in Marx's 'Sixth Thesis on Feuerbach'. He writes: '[T]he human essence is no abstraction inherent in each single individual. In its reality it is the ensemble of social relations.'[37] Traditionally, the term 'essence' has referred to the set of qualities which are shared by all things of a certain type, without all of which a thing would not be a member of that type. Thus the notion of a human essence refers to the qualities that make a human what it is and distinguishes it from non-humans. If a human's 'nature' as a conscious being is to have no fixed determinate qualities then there is no human essence. However, as the term refers to *what* something is, it is involved in the linguistic function of defining, and a *linguistic* definition need not refer to something *ontologically* qualitative and substantive. Hence the term 'essence' can itself be redefined, or at least its meaning can be displaced. Étienne Balibar writes: 'To say that . . . the human essence is the ensemble of social relations . . . is to attempt radically to *displace* the way in which it has until now been understood, not only where "man" is concerned, but also as regards "essence".'[38] 'Essence' is displaced here, because traditional ontologies in which the term operated were unable to account for relationality. Balibar continues:

> At bottom, the words 'ensemble', 'social' and 'relations' all say the same thing. The point is to reject both of the positions (the *realist* and the *nominalist*) . . . the one arguing that the genus or essence precedes the

existence of individuals; the other that individuals are the primary reality, from which universals are 'abstracted'. For, amazingly, neither of these two positions is capable of thinking precisely what is essential in human existence: the multiple and active *relations* which individuals establish with each other . . . and the fact that it is these relations which define what they have in common, the 'genus'.[39]

An essential relationality, a relationality that makes humans what they are, does not inhere *within* humans, but occurs *between* them. Humans are beings for whom nothing is intrinsic other than, paradoxically, this very betweenness. Balibar uses the term 'transindividual' to name the '*constitutive relation* which displaces the question of the human essence', and explains that it is '[n]ot what is ideally "in" each individual (as a form or a substance), or what would serve, from outside, to classify that individual, but what exists *between individuals* by dint of their multiple interactions.'[40] As the '*Gattungswesen*' is the contentless negative universality that constitutes the necessary non-essence of the social, or relational, individual, it is itself nothing other than this 'transindividual'.

Allen Wood argues that the 'Sixth Thesis on Feuerbach' merely means that the human essence is embroiled in social relations, not that it is displaced or replaced by a notion of relationality. He writes: 'The sixth thesis on Feuerbach does not deny that there is a "human essence" shared by individuals, but only asserts that this essence is inextricably bound up with the social relationships in which those individuals stand.'[41] However, for Marx, the 'human essence' is not *bound up* in social relations; it *is* nothing other than those relations. Michael Ryan argues that radical relationality is indeed a fundamental feature of Marx's 'ontology', and he identifies relationality with Derridian *différance*. He writes: 'To say that what appears to be a simple "thing" is in fact a "relation" is to say that alterity precedes and produces identity.'[42] He goes on to claim that Marxian social relationality and Derridean *différance* are analogous:

Marx describes the relationality that becomes congealed in 'things' like property as social. Derrida confines to philosophical terms the differential relations that produce entities and things without themselves being reducible to an ontology of 'being.' But the general pattern . . . is analogous.[43]

Just as, for Marx, the proletariat is the 'universal class', the class that represents not only specific interests but the interests of humanity as a whole, precisely because it *has* nothing, no *property*, the universal relationality of humanity is based on its essential lack of determinacy, its lack of essential *properties*. A free universal consciousness becomes manifest due to the universalization of exchange, the modern, capitalist rendering paradigmatic of the 'spectral' indeterminacy of the commodity form, of exchange value, a universality that is at the same time alienated from the individual through the capitalist relations of production.

Types of Objectification

As we have seen, Marx claims that the empty universality of money, and thus of the exchange value of commodities, is an alienation, projection and objectification of the emptily determinable universality of humanity. Alienation and objectification are related but not synonymous terms. A rigorous distinction between the two concepts is the basis of Marx's critique of Hegel's notion of alienation. Marx regards Hegel as falsely equating the two terms. For Marx, alienation is a type of objectification; there can be an unalienated objectification. This distinction is also the basis of Lukács's critique of both Hegel and his own earlier work, a critique of the equation of the overcoming of alienation with the overcoming of objectivity.

Marx regards all production as objectification, which means that a product is the result of the transformation of productive activity, or labour, into an object. Marx writes: 'The product of labour is labour which has been embodied in an object. . . . Labour's realization is its objectification. Under these economic conditions this . . . appears as loss of realization for the workers; objectification as *loss of the object*.'[44] All production involves objectification, but it is under the economic conditions of capitalism that this objectification takes the form of alienation.

Allen Wood explains the meaning of Marx's use of the term 'objectification' in the following way: 'All labor does . . . display or embody itself in an "object" if that term is understood broadly as any result or state of affairs in the external world which labor has brought about.'[45] The term 'brought about' implies a simple cause and effect relation between labour and its 'object', which suggests far less than the term 'embody'. In the *Grundrisse* Marx elaborates:

Products . . . are objectified labour. As objects they assume forms in which their being as labour may certainly be apparent in their form (as a purposiveness posited in them from outside; . . . this is not at all apparent with e.g. the ox, or with reproduced natural products generally) [.][46]

The products of purposive activity, or labour, express, embody and objectify that purposiveness.

For Marx, objectification as such is a necessary aspect of being a conscious being, it being the creative expression and realization of the conscious being's generic abilities. The living generic being, i.e. the human individual, is only able to be creative because she is an infinitely determinable nothingness. Marx writes in the *1844 Manuscripts*: '[I]t is only when the objective world becomes everywhere for man in society the world of man's essential powers . . . that all *objects* become for him the *objectification* of himself, become objects which confirm and realise his individuality.'[47] This objectification occurs through the activity of labour, the activity of positive freedom. Marx writes in the *Grundrisse* that with free labour 'the external aims become stripped of the semblance of merely external natural urgencies, and become posited as aims which the individual himself posits – hence as self-realization, objectification of the subject, hence real freedom, whose action is, precisely, labour.'[48] Labour involves objectification, and when it is freed from need it becomes creative self-realization, an actualization of the limitlessly malleable potential of the indeterminate nothingness of the human 'essence'.

Objectification takes the form of alienation under historically specific social and economic conditions. Alienation is a type of objectification. Marx writes that under capitalism '[t]he *alienation* [*Entäußerung*] of the worker in his product means not only that his labour becomes an object, an *external* existence, but that . . . the life which he has conferred on the object confronts him as something hostile and alien.'[49] The term '*Entäußerung*' ['alienation', 'externalization'] does not simply mean 'externalization', this English word being neutral and non-judgemental; it can also be translated as 'dispossession' and 'divestment'. It entails not only an externalizing objectification, but also the loss and estrangement of the object. Here, objectification is not experienced as self-realization, but as loss of the self in the product and the production process. Marx writes:

> [F]rom the standpoint of capital . . . [t]he emphasis comes to be placed not on the state of being *objectified*, but on the state of being *alienated*, dispossessed, sold [Der Ton wird gelegt nicht auf das *Vergegenständlichtsein*, sondern das *Entfremdet-*, Entäussert-, Veräussertsein]. . . . [T]his process of objectification . . . appears as a process of dispossession [*Entäußerung*] from the standpoint of labour[.][50]

We argued in the previous chapter that in the interpretation of Hegel's writings the meanings of the two terms for 'alienation', *Entäußerung* and

Entfremdung [estrangement], can be clearly distinguished, the latter naming the conscious experience of the former, the former being a purely formal and logical term. For Marx, in contrast, the two terms are inextricably bound up, the very meaning of *Entäußerung* entailing *Entfremdung*.

Objectification under capitalism is formal and quantitative, in contrast to the qualitative and determinate objectification characteristic of pre-capitalist modes of production. Marx writes:

> Before it is replaced by exchange value, every form of natural wealth presupposes an essential relation between the individual and the objects, in which the individual in one of his aspects objectifies [*vergegenständlicht*] himself in the thing, so that his possession of the thing appears at the same time as a certain development of his individuality: wealth in sheep, the development of the individual as shepherd. . . . *Money, however, as the individual* of general wealth . . . as a *merely social result*, does not at all pre-suppose an individual relation to its owner; possession of it is not the development of any particular essential aspect of his individuality; but rather possession of what lacks individuality, since this social [relation] exists at the same time as a sensuous, external object which can be mechanically seized, and lost in the same manner.[51]

The pre-capitalist qualitative objectification involves an individual tied to a particular determination, such that 'one of his aspects' metonymically constitutes his entire being. The quantitative generality of capitalist pro-duction is unrestricted by primitive determinacy, but this unrestrictedness is a 'merely social result' in that it is alienated from the individual. Marx writes: 'All production is an objectification [*Vergegenständlichung*] of the individual. In money (exchange value), however, the individual is not objectified in his natural quality, but in a social quality (relation) which is, at the same time, external to him.'[52] Capitalist objectification is a socializa-tion, but an alienated one as regards the individual. What is socially realized is general social labour, not the worker in her living individuality. Marx writes that, for bourgeois economists, 'the necessity of the *objectification* of the powers of social labour appears to them as inseparable from the necessity of their *alienation vis-à-vis* living labour.'[53] The worker *qua* social labour is realized in the multi-faceted sociality of modernity, but the worker *qua* living individual is alienated from her social product. There can thus be found three types of objectification in Marx's writings: the pre-capitalist qualitative objectification, particular labour producing a particular use value; the capitalist quantitative objectification of abstract social labour into the universal substitutability of exchange value; and the post-capitalist free manifold objectification as the realization of the universal determinability of the human.

General quantitative labour produces the sociality of exchange value, as opposed to the particular qualitative labour that produces use value. Exchange value only comes about if the labour that produced it is measured in purely quantitative terms, regardless of the particular nature of the work itself. In *Capital*, Marx writes that the labour that produces exchange value is 'undifferentiated, *socially necessary general* labour, utterly indifferent to any particular content'.[54] The exchange values, or commodities, are an objectification of labour as a quantitative homogeneity. Marx writes:

> There is nothing left of them [the products of labour] in each case but the same phantom-like objectivity; they are merely congealed quantities of homogeneous human labour, i.e. of human labour-power expended without regard to the form of its expenditure.[55]

Commodities *qua* commodities are insubstantial, substitutable, non-things; they are social relations that are produced by formal quantitative labour, relations that take the form of insubstantial things, things that are not things and are thus 'phantom-like'. The separated, isolated, thingly appearance of the social relations produced by labour is an expression of the worker's alienation from sociality. These 'things' masquerade as a power independent of their producers. In his essay 'Results of the Immediate Process of Production' (1865) Marx writes: 'The objective conditions essential to the realization of labour are *alienated* [*entfremdet*] from the worker and become manifest as *fetishes*.'[56] This fetishism disguises the fact that commodities, or exchange values, are not things but social relations, which are themselves the objectification of social labour taken as a purely quantitative amount of human labour. Commodities are thus an alienated form of social relations, specifically an alienation of individual workers from social labour, from the totality of labour. In *Capital* Marx writes:

> [T]he commodity reflects the social characteristics of men's own labour as objective characteristics of the products of labour themselves. . . . Hence it also reflects the social relation of the producers to the sum total of labour as a social relation between objects, a relation that exists apart from and outside the producers. Through this substitution, the products of labour become commodities, sensuous things which are at the same time suprasensible or social. . . . [The commodity-form] is nothing but

the definite relation between men themselves which assumes here, for them, the fantastic form of a relation between things.[57]

Commodities are a disguised manifestation of the comprehensive sociality that capitalism produces. A radicalized and mechanized division of labour produces general social labour, but this sociality is alienated from the individual workers in that it is experienced by them as homogeneous, abstract, quantitative labour activity, whose products they experience as autonomous, separate, and entirely independent from the labour that produced them.

A commodity is the objectification of abstract quantitative labour. The formal, quantitative, insubstantial substitutability of exchange value is the product of a mechanically quantitative abstract labour. The value of a commodity is understood by Marx to be determined by the quantity of abstract labour objectified in it. He writes:

> [W]ith reference to use-value, the labour contained in a commodity counts only qualitatively, with reference to value it counts only quantitatively, once it has been reduced to labour pure and simple. In the former case it was a matter of the 'how' and 'what' of labour, in the latter of the 'how much', of the temporal duration of labour.[58]

Exchange value is the objectification of abstract labour quantitatively measured according to labour-time. Marx's 'labour theory of value' is inextricably bound up with the concept of objectification. He writes:

> A use-value, or useful article . . . has value only because abstract human labour is objectified [*vergegenständlicht*] or materialized in it. How, then, is the magnitude of this value to be measured? By means of the quantity of the 'value-forming substance', the labour, contained in the article. This quantity is measured by its duration, and the labour-time is itself measured on the particular scale of hours, days etc.[59]

The homogeneous, abstractly calculable, purely quantitative labour-time that is objectified in the exchange value of a commodity is the labour-time of social labour, the socially average, socially necessary labour-time of individual workers. Marx writes:

> [T]he labour that forms the substance of value is equal human labour, the expenditure of identical human labour-power. . . . [Which constitutes],

in order to produce a commodity, the labour time which is necessary on an average, or in other words is socially necessary.[60]

The social generality of labour produces the social generality of exchange value, and the socially general average amount of qualitatively empty labour-time required to produce a commodity determines that commodity's qualitatively empty exchange value.

Objectification is the overriding theme of both the early Marx of the *1844 Manuscripts* and the mature Marx of *Capital*. In both it is analysed in terms of the capitalist expropriation of labour and its products. Marx's later labour theory of value and his earlier theory of alienation are both ways of theoretically describing the capitalist expropriating objectification of labour. The term '*Vergegenständlichung*' (translated as 'objectification') is prevalent throughout his writings. This continuity belies the Althusserian thesis of a discontinuity between the early 'humanist' Marx's concern with alienation and the later 'scientific' Marx's concern with the social relations of production.

For Marx, the objectification of labour in exchange value, *via* its practical abstraction as general homogeneous labour, involves an exchange between labour and capital that forms the basis of labour's exploitation and expropriation. The limitless value-creating activity of living labour is acquired by capital, and in return labour receives a pre-measured, already objectified quantity of value. Marx writes in the *Grundrisse*:

> The worker . . . sells labour as a simple, predetermined exchange value, determined by a previous process – he sells labour itself as *objectified labour*, . . . capital buys it as living labour, as the general productive force of wealth. . . . [The worker] *divests* himself [*entäussert sich*] of labour as the force productive of wealth; capital appropriates it, as such.[61]

The commodification of labour itself involves the expropriation of wealth creating power. The wage that labour receives, the price of the labour-commodity, bears no relation to the value that labour creates. Marx writes:

> What the worker exchanges with capital is his labour itself (the capacity of disposing over it); he *divests himself of it* [*entäussert sie*]. What he obtains as price is the *value* of this divestiture [*Entäusserung*]. He exchanges value-positing activity for a pre-determined value, regardless of the result of his activity. Now how is its value determined? By the objectified labour contained in his commodity. This commodity exists in his vitality. . . . Capital

has paid him the amount of objectified labour contained in his vital forces.[62]

This objectifying alienation [*Entäußerung*] is a divestment, expropriation and commodification of the productive life activity of living labour, in return for the exchange value, or objectified labour, that is enough to maintain the subsistence, health, and thus reproducibility of to-be-objectified living labour. Thus labour creates the wealth of society, but, in return, is paid only enough to maintain itself effectively as labour. This exchange allows for the production of surplus value, which, for Marx, amounts to an extortion of value from labour. He writes in *Capital*: '[T]he valorization process is essentially the *production of surplus-value*, i.e. the *objectification of unpaid labour*.'[63] Value-creating living labour is bought with objectified labour, or money as exchange value. It is the labour-time of living labour that determines exchange value, but when that living labour is itself commodified, objectified as a unit of duration, its exchange value is equivalent to the objectified labour-time socially required to produce the commodities whose use value can maintain its mere existence as living labour. This exchange of living labour for objectified 'dead' labour both maintains and rests on the poverty and lack of property of the workers. Marx writes in the *Grundrisse*:

> Production based on exchange value . . . is at its base the exchange of *objectified labour* as exchange value for living labour as use value. . . . At the same time, the condition of exchange value is its measurement by labour time, and hence living labour – not its value – as measure of values. . . . [Labour] appears as mere labour on one side, while on the other side its product, as objectified labour, has an entirely independent existence as value opposite it. *The exchange of labour for labour . . . rests on the foundation of the worker's propertylessness.*[64]

The propertylessness of living labour, its status as 'mere labour', its constant expropriation by capital, makes possible the qualityless insubstantiality of value, the universal substitutability of exchange value and the accumulation of abstract financial wealth through the production of surplus value.

The living labour that is required to produce exchange value is thus necessarily propertyless. In its very existence as abstract homogeneous qualityless labour it is always already expropriated, pre-expropriated, or, to use Derrida's term, ex-appropriated. This non-objectified labour, a purely subjective labour devoid of objects and objectivity, a productive negativity entirely separated from its products, is the precondition of the existence of the insubstantial substitutability of exchange value, which is its spectral objectification. Marx writes:

> *Separation of property from labour* appears as the necessary law of [the] exchange between capital and labour. Labour posited as *not-capital* as such is: (1) *not-objectified labour* [*nicht-vergegenständlichte Arbeit*], *conceived negatively*. . . . This living labour, existing as . . . this complete denudation, purely subjective existence of labour, stripped of all objectivity. . . . (2) *Not-objectified labour, not-value*, conceived *positively*, or as a negativity in relation to itself, is the not-*objectified*, hence non-objective, i.e. subjective existence of labour itself. Labour not as an object, but as activity; not as itself *value*, but as the *living source* of value.[65]

This pure labour, appropriated by capital as a use value that produces exchange value, is sold to capital as an objectified exchange value, measured as limited units of labour-time. The productive nothingness of pure labour is a limitless determinability that has always already lost its determinations. Marx refers to '*labour pure and simple*, abstract labour; absolutely indifferent to its particular specificity [*Bestimmheit* (determination)], but capable of all specificities'.[66] 'All specificities' are appropriated by capital and alienated from labour.

The empty, insubstantial, indeterminacy of abstract homogeneous social labour has its limitless determinability appropriated by capital, taking the form of the limitlessly substitutable determinability of exchange value, entirely separated from the labour that makes it possible, a labour left indeterminate and propertyless. The poverty of indeterminacy is rigorously separated from the richness of determinability. The nothingness of indeterminacy is a necessary but not a sufficient condition of determinability.

As we have seen, for Marx, production on the basis of exchange value is the precondition of the existence of the 'universally developed individual', whose free determinability involves not being restricted to a specific determination. This mode of production, i.e. capitalism, simultaneously makes possible and inhibits the formation of such an individual. The free determinability is abstractly socialized, a characteristic of society as a whole entirely separated and alienated from the individual. A post-capitalist overcoming of alienation would involve an internalization of this social determinability on the part of the individual. While, in such a society, the products of labour would not be alienated and expropriated from the producers, the generality and sociality of production, itself dependent on abstract labour, would be maintained. The generality of production would not produce the generality of exchange value, of money, which is but the alienation of human generality; it would produce human generality and substitutability, not the financial liquidity of exchange value but the social flexibility of the multi-faceted individual. Marx writes:

> [I]n communist society, where nobody has one exclusive sphere of activity . . . society regulates the general production and thus makes it possible for me to do one thing today and another tomorrow, to hunt in the morning, fish in the afternoon . . . criticize after dinner . . . without ever becoming hunter, fisherman . . . or critic.[67]

It is unfortunate that Marx here uses pre-capitalist, pastoral examples whose relation to 'general production' is not entirely clear. This raises the question of whether the generality of production upon which this overcoming of the division of labour depends does not itself depend upon this same division of labour. However, the abstract labour at the basis of the generality and sociality of production does not necessarily involve a rigorous, rigid and inflexible assignment of labour-roles to individuals. Its very abstraction opens the possibility of substitutability. The point here is that the overcoming of exchange value is not an 'exorcism' of the spectrality of *différance* and the manifestation of the fullness of presence in a humanized sociality, but rather a reabsorption of *différance*, in the form of an indeterminacy productive of free infinite determinability, into the individual, from whom it had been separated and alienated in the form of exchange value or money.

Although exchange value may have the form of *différance*, it is largely experienced in the form of the fetishism of commodities, a form of consciousness which involves a fixation on the spectral embodiment of exchange value as if it is a substantial thing, fully present, and not what it really is, a social relation. The commodity fetish is an ossified presence that is nothing but an effacement of *différance*, relationality, and the temporality of its becoming. Marx's analysis of the commodity form in terms of objectified labour deconstructs that fetishistic presence. For Derrida, presence is but an effect of *différance* that hides and effaces its differential nature. To restate it with more pertinent and specific terminology, presence is an objectification and reification of the productive negativity of *différance*, of the living negativity of becoming, of 'ex-appropriated' and propertyless, objectless living labour, an objectification effaced and hidden through the fetishistic presentation of the fullness of substance. In the *Grundrisse*, Marx writes:

> [C]ommodities . . . are *objectified labour*. . . . [D]istinct from *objectified* labour is *non-objectified* labour, labour which is still objectifying itself, *labour* as

subjectivity. Or, *objectified* labour, i.e. labour which is *present in space*, can also be opposed, as *past labour*, to labour which is *present in time*. If it is to be present in time, alive, then it can be present only as the *living subject*, . . . hence as *worker*.[68]

An ossification or 'congealment' of labour in the commodity-fetish, which presents itself in the simple positivity of a thing, is 'presence' as objectification, reification and presentation, which involves the spatialization of time. However, the 'presence in time' of the non-objectified, purely subjective, productive negativity of a living, propertyless, bare singularity, is not 'presence' in the Derridian sense of the word, but what he calls 'the here and now', which, in its always otherness, is precisely *différance*.

Objectification, whether fetishized or not, is a form of consciousness. This does not mean that it is not a feature of the world of social reality, quite the contrary; consciousness is inherently social and 'objectively' effective. Marx writes:

When we speak of the commodity as a materialisation [*Materiatur*] of labour – in the sense of its exchange value – this itself is only an imaginary, that is a merely social mode of existence for the commodity which has nothing to do with its corporeal reality[.][69]

The influential distinction, promoted by Marx himself, between an *idealist* Hegelian philosophy of spirit, based on conscious contemplation, and a *materialist* Marxian philosophy of praxis, based on socio-economic reality, is thus misleading.

In the 'First Thesis on Feuerbach', Marx concedes that German Idealist 'subjectivity' is more active and practical than traditional materialist 'objectivity'. He writes:

The chief defect of all hitherto existing materialism . . . is that the thing, reality, sensuousness, is conceived only in the form of the *object* [*Objekts*] *or of contemplation,* but not as *sensuous human activity, practice,* not subjectively. Hence, in contradistinction to materialism, the *active* side was developed abstractly by idealism. . . . Feuerbach wants sensuous objects . . . but he does not conceive human activity itself as *objective* [*gegenständliche*] activity.[70]

Traditional materialism, including that of Feuerbach, is here considered by Marx to involve objects observed by a contemplative subject. Existence conceived 'in the form of the *object*' is equated with existence conceived through the contemplative consciousness rigorously separated from its objects, and is contrasted with existence conceived 'subjectively', as practical activity. The conceiving of existence in terms of objects involves its division into positive isolated determinate stases standing opposed to the merely contemplative activity of an observing subject. As, for Marx, human activity is by definition 'subjective', his claim to 'conceive human activity itself as *objective* activity' involves a redefinition of the term *gegenständliche* (translated as 'objective'). Here his use of the term '*gegenständliche*' ('objective') appears to have a similar meaning to his use of the term '*subjektiv*' ('subjective'). Marx, of course, uses the word *gegenständliche* ('objective') here to refer to activity in the world, in 'reality', nature, and society, as opposed to just in the theoretical contemplative realm of the mind, of mere ideas. This is, however, quite different to the use of the term to refer to the objectivity of objects, their petrified positive determinacy standing against the merely observing consciousness. The term 'objective [*gegenständliche*]' can mean either, 'concerning things as fixed and determinate objects of contemplation', or simply 'in the world'. Marx's own confusion of the two meanings of the term '*gegenständliche*' is the basis of his critique of Hegel's conception of the overcoming of alienation.

As we saw in the last chapter, Lukács criticizes Hegel's notion of absolute knowing for involving not only an abolition of alienation, but also an abolition of objectivity in general, claiming that it involved an ultimate internalization and thus an affirmation of subjectivity and the self. We argued that Lukács's critique depended on a spuriously individualistic interpretation of Hegel's conception of subjectivity, ignoring the professed actuality, as opposed to internality, of absolute spirit. Lukács's critique of Hegel is a repetition of Marx's own critique in his *1844 Manuscripts*, and directly derives from Lukács's reading of them when they were first posthumously published in the 1930s.

We have seen that Marx argues that there can be an alienated and an unalienated objectification, whereas for Hegel alienation and objectification are the same thing. Marx writes that Hegel's notion of consciousness 'takes offence not at estranged [*entfremdet*] objectivity, but at *objectivity* [*Gegenständlichkeit*] *as such*.'[71] For Hegel, objectivity as such is alienated objectivity, and it is objectivity as such that is overcome in the overcoming of alienation. Marx writes: '[F]or Hegel . . . it is *objectivity* [*Gegenständlichkeit*] which is to be annulled, because it is not the *determinate* character of the object [*Gegenstandes*], but rather its *objective* [*gegenständlicher*] character that is offensive and constitutes estrangement [*Entfremdung*] for self-consciousness.'[72]

According to Marx, this notion of the overcoming of objectivity means that Hegel regards 'human nature' as entirely 'spiritual', as consciousness itself. Marx writes:

Objectivity [*Gegenständlichkeit*] as such is regarded as an *estranged* human relationship which does not correspond to the *essence of man*, to self-consciousness. The *reappropriation* of the objective [*gegenständlichen*] essence of man . . . therefore denotes not only the annulment of *estrangement*, but of *objectivity* [*Gegenständlichkeit*] as well. Man . . . is regarded as a *non-objective* [*nicht-gegenständliches*] *spiritual* being.[73]

Marx regards this Hegelian non-objectivity as a purely theoretical and contemplative state of being which is inactive as regards the world. This interpretation relies on regarding 'objectivity' as activity in the world and 'subjectivity' as contemplation. However, the reverse is the case in the Hegelian usage of these terms. As we have seen, the misunderstanding stems from a slippage across two different meanings of the term *Gegenständlichkeit* ('objectivity'), i.e. 'objectivity' as observed phenomena or as involvement in the world. Spirit that knows itself as spirit is 'non-objective', because 'absolute knowing' is the self-consciousness of actuality; the world is not separated from, but is identical to, the subject that 'knows' it. This 'knowing' is not then the self-consciousness of some individual 'subject' separated from the world.

Balibar points out that in Marx's philosophy of praxis '*the subject is nothing other than practice* which has always already begun and continues indefinitely.'[74] In this regard Marx is contiguous with Hegel and German Idealism, and, according to Balibar, this notion of subjectivity means that 'Marx and his "materialism of practice" [is] the most accomplished form of the idealist tradition.'[75] While an object is a static determinacy, a subject is an active determinability, a determinability dependent on its lack of given properties. The active nature of subjectivity is an effect of its propertylessness. Marx writes in the *Grundrisse* that 'the worker . . . stands there purely without objectivity, subjectively . . .'[76] and that the 'free worker [is] object-less, purely subjective labour capacity'.[77] Objectivity is a static givenness, whereas subjectivity is a productive propertylessness. In *Capital*, Marx writes: '[L]abour constantly undergoes a transformation, from the form of unrest [*Unruhe*] into that of being [*Sein*], from the form of motion [*Bewegung*] into that of objectivity [*Gegenständlichkeit*].'[78] The givenness of objectivity involves a dead stasis independent of living human activity. Marx writes that social forces 'confront the individual workers as something *alien, objective, ready-made*, existing without their intervention'.[79] Thus, objectivity involves property, givenness and the stasis of being, whereas subjectivity involves productive nothingness and the activity of becoming.

When Marx uses the term '*gegenständliche Tätigkeit*' ('objective activity') he is referring to the activity of subjectivity in the world, and not to 'objectivity' in the sense of a positive givenness. He writes: '[H]is *objective* [*gegenständliches*] product only confirms his *objective* [*gegenständliche*] activity, his activity as the activity of an objective [*gegenständlichen*], natural being.'[80] Marx also uses the term *gegenständliches* ('objective') to refer to relationality as such, and not just to the relation between a given object and a subject of contemplation. He writes: 'A being which has no object [*Gegenstand*] outside itself is not an objective [*gegenständliches*] being. A being which is not itself an object for some third being has no being for its *object*; i.e. it is not objectively related.'[81]

The so-called 'objectivity' of both living negative activity in the world and intrinsic relationality is precisely the annulment of the 'objectivity' of the world as the dead static positivity of a reified givenness. Thus Marx's notion of an unalienated objectification, of free productive *activity* in the social world, is, to say the least, not interpretatively incompatible with the Hegelian annulment of 'objectivity' in the non-objective *actuality* of the 'subjectivity' of absolute spirit.

Humanizing Appropriation

This abolition of the reified positivity of 'objectivity' is described by Marx in terms of the humanization of nature. Marx writes in the *1844 Manuscripts*: '[W]hen the objective world becomes everywhere for man in society the world of man's essential powers . . . all *objects* become for him the *objectification* of himself . . . that is, *man himself* becomes the object.'[82] The unalienated human lives in a world in which she belongs and which belongs to her, which is an expression of her own nature, a world with which she identifies and feels at one. Marx writes: '[I]n his work upon the objective world . . . nature appears as *his* work and his reality. . . . [H]e sees himself in a world that he has created.'[83] This appropriation of the world is perverted by the institution of private property, which, in its reified externality, separates and estranges the social world from human life. Private property ironically amounts to an expropriation, an expropriation of the world from humanity. Marx writes: 'The positive transcendence of *private property* as the appropriation of *human* life, is therefore the positive transcendence of all estrangement

[*Entfremdung*].'[84] For Marx, true appropriation involves a sensual and intellectual unity with the world, and must be liberated from the mere possession which is the alienation of all the senses, of all the human relations with the world. Marx writes: '[*H*]*uman* relations to the world . . . are . . . the appropriation of the object[.] . . . [T]he sheer estrangement of *all* . . . senses . . . [is] the sense of *having.* . . . The abolition of private property is therefore the complete *emancipation* of all human senses.'[85] Genuine human appropriation is the formation of nature as human reality through free productive activity, involving a unity with the world that is free from the estranged externality of mere possession and utility.

In Derridian terms, the human who 'sees himself in a world that he has created' appears to be entangled in the narcissistic enclosure of metaphysical presence. In the *Grundrisse*, Marx writes:

> *Property* . . . originally means no more than a human being's relation to his natural conditions of production[,] . . . relations to them as *natural presuppositions* of his self, which only form . . . his extended body[,] [relating] to the earth as the individual's inorganic body[,] . . . as to a presupposition belonging to his individuality, as modes of his presence [*Dasein*].[86]

Appropriation is thus another word for the humanization of nature.

The notion of the world as a human creation is suggestive of a form of idealism. However, in *The German Ideology*, Marx claims that 'ideas' are the expressions of 'material relationships'.[87] In his early book, *Positions*, Derrida is interviewed by two Marxists, Jean-Louis Houdebine and Guy Scarpetta, who argue that Marx's assertion of the primacy of 'matter' to 'consciousness' undermines the narcissistic enclosure of consciousness in a proto-deconstructive manner. Here, Derrida expresses scepticism towards the suggestion that materialism has been a force of resistance within the history of metaphysics. He says:

> [I]f . . . *matter* . . . designates . . . radical alterity (I will specify: in relation to philosophical oppositions), then what I write can be considered 'materialist.' . . . [T]hings are not so simple. It is not always in *the* materialist text . . . that the concept of matter has been defined as absolute exterior or radical heterogeneity. . . . [T]his concept ['matter'] has been too often reinvested with 'logocentric' values, values associated with those of thing, reality, presence in general, sensible presence, for example, substantial plentitude[.][88]

Derrida suggests that it is 'rather *new*' to attribute the concept of 'alterity' to materialism.[89] By the time he wrote *Spectres of Marx*, he felt free to explicitly attribute metaphysical qualities to Marx's materialism. He writes: 'Marxist ontology was . . . struggling against the ghost in general, in the name of living presence as material actuality.'[90] For Derrida, this ontology of material presence is just as prevalent in the analysis of the commodity form in *Capital* as it is in Marx's early works. Derrida writes:

> There is a mirror, and the commodity form is also this mirror, but . . . since it does not reflect back the expected image, those who are looking for themselves can no longer find themselves in it. Men no longer recognize in it the *social* character of their *own* labor.[91]

According to Derrida, Marx's critique of the commodity form involves an advocacy of de-commodification as a narcissistic humanization in the fullness of presence of a 'material actuality', it being human expression in a material presence that is effaced by the spectrality of the commodity. Thus, alienation is a failed narcissism and de-alienation would be a narcissistic self-confirmation.

Such narcissism is the principle target of Derridian deconstruction. Derrida refers to 'the very concept of narcissism whose aporias are . . . the explicit theme of deconstruction'.[92] However, Marx's notion of a humanizing appropriation need not be interpreted in terms of the enclosure of a narcissistic self-confirmation. To understand what 'humanization' might entail, it is necessary to understand what Marx means by the word 'human'. We have already argued that Marx's understanding of the so-called human essence is of a conscious being *qua* living instantiation of an insubstantial, infinitely determinable, universality. A 'humanizing' appropriation of the world would thus bring it into the realm of the unrestricted freedom of universal consciousness, rendering the world itself as infinitely determinable. This may be read as implying a domineering conscious control over nature, a utilitarian instrumentalistic mastery of the subject over its objects, and thus a self-confirmingly narcissistic suppression of alterity. However, this is not how Marx represents it in the *1844 Manuscripts*. As we have seen, Marx regards the universality of humanity, its *Gattungswesen*, as liberating it from the immediate particularity of utilitarian concerns. Animals are trapped in the immediate particularity of need, whereas humans *qua* humans, unalienated humans, 'produce universally', free from need, for its own sake.[93] Such humans produce and consume as ends in themselves, not as mere means to other ends. Marx writes: 'For the starving man, it is not the human form of food that exists.'[94] This man is in dehumanized thrall to the immediate particularity of need; in his actualized *human* condition he is free from need, and so enjoys the activity of eating for its own sake, free from mere instrumental utility. Marx writes regarding unalienated humanity: 'The *senses* . . . relate themselves to the *thing* for the sake of the thing . . . Need or enjoyment has consequently lost its *egotistical* nature, and nature has lost its mere *utility* by use becoming *human* use.'[95] A non-egotistical, non-narcissistic humanizing appropriation would thus involve an interaction with nature not as a positive givenness to be simply utilized, but as a manifold to be experienced.

Universal An-economy

As the 'free productive activity' of the unalienated condition is inherently liberated from need and utility, it is not 'productive' at all, in the usual 'economic' sense of the term. What Derrida terms a 'restricted economy' of calculative productive appropriability, he opposes to a 'general economy' of non-appropriable non-productive activity. If something is conceived as radically being an end in itself, it ceases to circulate in any economy of calculably purposive productive meaningfulness. In his essay, '*Différance*', Derrida describes *différance* as the impossible thinking together of the restricted economy of productive reappropriation and the general economy of non-productive loss. He writes:

> How are we to think *simultaneously*, on the one hand, *différance* as the economic detour which, in the element of the same, always aims at coming back to the . . . presence . . . deferred by . . . calculation, and, on the other hand, *différance* as . . . the irreparable loss of presence, the irreversible usage of energy . . . and as the entirely other relationship that apparently interrupts every economy? . . . [T]he economical and the noneconomical, the same and the entirely other, etc., cannot be thought *together*. . . . [*D*]*ifférance* is unthinkable in this way. . . . I have attempted to indicate . . . a rigorous . . . *relating* of the 'restricted economy' that takes no part in expenditure without reserve, death, opening itself to nonmeaning, etc., to a general economy that *takes into account* the nonreserve . . . if it can be put thus.[96]

Although economy and an-economy cannot be thought together, they cannot be absolutely separated either. A deconstructive reading can always

demonstrate the inherence of the unappropriable excess of irreducible
otherness within the restricted economy of the selfsame, while it can
also demonstrate how the apprehension of the singular otherness of an
absolute outside is always already caught up in the terms of the specular
logic of the all-encompassing restricted economy of meaning, and thus
appropriated, recuperated and domesticated.

Anything imbued with value, meaning and purpose is inherently involved
in a restricted economy. The latter is a circulation of exchange, reference
and teleological relations, which is restricted in that it remains constant to
itself, not allowing itself to dissipate in non-meaning and purposelessness.
Such a dissipation would open it up to general economy, an 'economy' of
non-productive expenditure. The term 'general economy' is paradoxical,
as this type of generality is non-economic. That which is economic is part of
a circulatory system that is ultimately closed, that produces and maintains
itself in its proper limits, its *oikos.* For this reason, the term 'general economy'
is largely replaced by the term 'an-economy' in Derrida's later works.

A restricted economy of meaning means everything is a means to an end;
productive purposiveness is itself that which makes sense. What cannot be
made sense of is that which is radically an end in itself. The latter is an-
economic, unproductive, pointless and senseless. As we have seen, Marx's
'generic being', the *Gattungswesen,* is an indeterminate infinitely determinable universality which only comes into its own when freed from need. The
active expression of this unconstrained determinable universality is what
Marx calls 'free conscious activity', activity that is an end in itself, not a
means. The alienation of humanity's 'generic being' involves making its
life activity a mere means to physical subsistence. Thought radically, as
an end in itself *qua* unappropriable purposelessness, this 'free conscious
activity' is an-economic.

Despite the fact that Marx describes free activity as that which is not a
means to an end, but an end in itself,[97] he still uses the term *produktive* ('productive') in his descriptions of such free activity. For example, he writes:
'[M]an produces [*produziert*] when he is free from physical need and only
truly produces in freedom therefrom.'[98] The later Marx refers to freedom
as something separate from production, but the difference from his earlier
formulation is merely terminological, not conceptual. In the 'Results of
the Immediate Process of Production', Marx uses the term *produktive*
('productive') to refer to labour that produces capital and the term
unproduktive ('unproductive') to refer to labour that does not. He writes:

> The capitalist mode of production . . . is a process which absorbs
> unpaid labour, which makes the means of production into the means for

extorting unpaid labour. . . . [L]abour with *the same content* can be either productive or unproductive. . . . Milton, who wrote *Paradise Lost* was an unproductive worker. . . . [He] produced *Paradise Lost* . . . as an activation of *his own* nature. . . . It is possible for work of one type . . . to be performed . . . either in the service of an industrial capitalist or on behalf of the immediate consumer. . . . [The worker] is a *productive* worker in the one case and *unproductive* in the other, because in the one he produces capital and in the other not; because in the one case his work is a factor in the self-valorization process of capital and in the other it is not.[99]

In this passage the terms *Arbeit* ('labour') and *Produktion* ('production') are distinguished. 'Productive' labour is appropriable, extortable, and value creating labour. Labour that expresses and actualizes the worker's 'own nature', unalienated labour, is 'unproductive'. However, this passage refers to what is designated productive under capitalism. The terminology is used differently elsewhere in Marx's writings. A famous passage from *Capital Volume 3* rigorously separates the realm of freedom from production, while equating production and labour. Marx writes:

[T]he realm of freedom actually begins only where labour which is determined by necessity and mundane considerations ceases; thus in the very nature of things it lies beyond the sphere of actual material production. . . . Freedom in this field can only consist in socialized man, the associated producers, rationally regulating their interchange with Nature, bringing it under their common control, instead of being ruled by it. . . . But it nonetheless still remains a realm of necessity. Beyond it begins that development of human energy which is an end in itself, the true realm of freedom which, however, can blossom forth only with this realm of necessity as its basis.[100]

Here, freedom is conceived as being a liberation from both production and labour. Production may make freedom possible, but freedom itself does not involve production. Freedom is here determined as activity that is an end in itself, not a means to a further end. Marx's emphasis on production here is a recognition of the fact that the freedom of non-productive expenditure depends on the prior fulfilment of utilitarian needs.

The notion of 'an-economy' is related to ethics in *Spectres of Marx*. Derrida refers to Kant's moral philosophy, where humans are considered as ends in themselves not to be used as means to further ends, as an-economic. He mentions 'that unconditional dignity (*Würdigkeit*) that Kant placed higher, precisely [*justement*], than any economy, any compared or comparable value'.[101] Kant's utopian 'kingdom of ends' is a general an-economy. Derrida also advocates a Levinasian conception of justice as an an-economic 'relation' to alterity. He refers to 'justice as incalculability of the gift and singularity of the an-economic ex-position to others'.[102] For Derrida, the empty, insubstantial, unspecific universality of humans is precisely what makes them open to alterity and futurity, 'futurity' being the temporal equivalent of the spatial term, 'openness'. He writes regarding this human indeterminacy:

> [A]n essential lack of specificity, an indetermination that remains the ultimate mark of the future[,] . . . [m]arking any opening to the event and to the future as such, it . . . conditions the interest in and not the indifference to anything whatsoever, to all content in general.[103]

It is human empty insubstantiality and propertyless universality that provide the non-basis of a de-alienated communism to-come. Derrida speaks of an 'alliance . . . without property (the "communism" that we will later nickname the new International)'.[104]

De-alienation is not a re-establishment of the narcissistic enclosure of metaphysical presence; it is, rather, the manifestation of the free determinability of negative universality within the life of the human individual. Capitalism realizes such universality on a macro-social level, but alienates it from the individual. This alienation involves universal determinability taking the form of the 'spectrality' of money and exchange value. For Marx, humanity's 'generic being' is an insubstantial unessential universality, not tied to specificity, which is the basis of its social relationality, but which is alienated from the individual through capitalist social relations and the division of labour, which in turn tie her to specific determinacy. Exchange value and capitalist social universality in general are an objectification of general abstract homogeneous labour, labour that amounts to emptily quantitative units of labour-duration. This is an objectification separated from the life of the individual, involving an extortionate expropriation. An unalienated objectification, an actualization of an individual's free determinability, is not incompatible with the 'idealist' notion of an actualizing subjectification. This involves free activity that interacts with a nature free from merely utilitarian appropriation. Such free unalienated activity is an end in itself, not a means to an end, and is thus a liberation from the 'economic' interpretation of 'labour' and 'production'. De-alienated society is thus a general an-economy. For Marx, this involves free human 'appropriation' liberated from any economy of the proper, from private property.

Chapter 4

Heidegger's Deconstruction of Ontological Alienation

Expropriation is an intrinsic aspect of the concept of alienation; the latter depends on a prior understanding of what is 'proper'. Heidegger is the thinker for whom 'the proper' is explicitly a principal concern. He is also the thinker whose critique of metaphysics Derrida regards himself as furthering. Thus Heidegger could hardly be overlooked by an inquiry into the concept of alienation in the light of Derridian deconstruction.

The question to be investigated is the extent to which Heidegger's writings are a response to, and a deepening of the critique of, the phenomenon of alienation. Notions of objectification, technicity and finitude, will be analysed with regard to this question. There will be a discussion of Heidegger's notions of appropriation and authenticity, and the nexus of concepts summed up by Derrida's term 'the proper', involving an analysis of the relation of such concepts to the notion of singularity. The overall aim is to assess the extent to which the Heideggerian 'proper', in any of its forms, necessarily depends, as Derrida maintains, on a metaphysics of presence and suppression of difference.

The Presence of Alienation

It may be argued that it is inappropriate to speak of the concept of alienation in Heidegger's work, as alienation belongs to a paradigm alien to that of Heidegger. It inheres within the thought of Hegel and Marx, a particular configuration of the metaphysics centred on the concepts of 'subject' and 'object'. Heidegger's aim is to overcome metaphysics in general, and the post-Cartesian 'philosophy of the subject' in particular. However, a number of thinkers have regarded 'alienation' as being one of Heidegger's principal concerns. Marxist thinkers such as Lukács and Adorno regarded Heidegger as 'ontologizing', i.e. de-historicizing and de-socializing, alienation, rendering it an essential and permanent feature of the human condition. In the 1967 preface to *History and Class Consciousness* Lukács writes regarding the 1920s:

> The unmasking of alienation by philosophy was in the air. . . . In the philosophical, cultural criticism of the bourgeoisie (and we need look no further than Heidegger), it was natural . . . to convert an essentially social alienation into an eternal 'condition humaine'[.][1]

In his critique of Heidegger, *The Jargon of Authenticity*, Adorno writes: 'What Hegel and Marx in their youth condemned as alienation and reification . . . is what Heidegger interprets ontologically as well as unhistorically.'[2] Whatever their level of understanding of Heidegger, some eminent thinkers regarded alienation as being one of his principal concerns.

Heidegger explicitly refers to Marx's concept of alienation in his 'Letter on Humanism'. He writes:

> What Marx recognized in an essential and significant sense, though derived from Hegel, as the estrangement [*Entfremdung*] of man has its roots in the homelessness of modern man. This homelessness is specifically evoked from the destiny of Being in the form of metaphysics, and through metaphysics is simultaneously entrenched and covered up as such.[3]

Thus what Marx describes as the alienation of the worker under capitalist relations of production is, for Heidegger, rooted in a more fundamental predicament of modern humanity, what Heidegger calls *Heimatlosigkeit* (translated as 'homelessness').

Homelessness and its manifestation in the form of 'metaphysics' constitute a 'forgetting of Being'. The latter is a forgetting of the distinction between entities and being, the ontico-ontological difference. Such a 'forgetting' is definitive of a consciousness that is only concerned with entities and not the being of those entities. Being as such is not itself an entity, not *a* being, though 'metaphysics' traditionally treats it as such and in so doing effaces it. The human being, referred to ontologically by Heidegger as '*Dasein*' ('existence' or 'being-there'), is that entity which is 'ontically distinguished by the fact that, in its very Being, that Being is an *issue* for it'.[4] Therefore, when *Dasein* is oblivious of being, it is estranged from its 'essence', inauthentic and homeless. Heidegger writes: 'Homelessness . . . consists in the abandonment of Being by beings. Homelessness is the symptom of the oblivion of Being.'[5] In describing Marx's concept of alienation as 'rooted' in homelessness, Heidegger is suggesting that Marx's theory is too superficial, and that the overcoming of 'social alienation' would require addressing a more primordial ontological 'alienation'. He writes: '[T]he overcoming of homelessness begin[s] from Being, a homelessness in which not only man but the essence of man stumbles aimlessly about.'[6] Thus, contrary to the claims made by Lukács and Adorno, Heidegger does regard 'alienation', however 'ontologized', as surmountable.

Heidegger himself uses the term *Entfremdung* (translated as 'alienation') in *Being and Time*. It is one of the characteristics of what he calls *Verfallen* (translated as 'falling'). He writes: 'Dasein . . . drifts along towards an alienation [*Entfremdung*] in which its ownmost potentiality-for-Being is hidden from it. Falling Being-in-the-world is not only tempting and tranquillizing; it is at the same time *alienating*.'[7] Such 'falling' is a falling away from *Dasein*'s concern for its own being, for its eventual non-being, for its ownness itself, its 'authenticity [*Eigentlichkeit*]', into the social realm of 'the they [*das Man*]', a realm of inauthenticity where being is necessarily forgotten, as being is irreducibly singular, 'in each case mine'.[8] Falling is a state where *Dasein* '"lives" *away from itself*'.[9] However, the alienation involved in falling does not entail the loss of *Dasein* to an alien entity; it is an essential possibility of *Dasein* itself, *Dasein* in its inauthentic (i.e. not concerned with its own being) aspect. Heidegger writes:

This alienation [*Entfremdung*] *closes off* from Dasein its authenticity. . . . It does not, however, surrender Dasein to an entity which Dasein itself is not, but forces it into its inauthenticity – into a possible kind of Being *of itself*. The alienation [*Entfremdung*] of falling – at once tempting and tranquillizing – leads by its own movement, to Dasein's getting *entangled* [*verfängt*] in itself.[10]

In this alienation *Dasein* is not uninterested in itself, in terms of self-analysis or introspection, quite the contrary; it is, nevertheless, alienated from its own being.

In the first chapter we discussed the link between the concept of alienation and the myth of the fall. However, despite choosing to use a word with such associations, Heidegger is at pains to dissociate his concept of 'falling' from the fall. He writes:

The phenomenon of falling does not give us something like a 'night view' of Dasein . . . our existential-ontological Interpretation makes no ontical assertion about the 'corruption of human Nature' . . . [it] is *prior* to any

assertion about corruption or incorruption. Falling is conceived ontologically as a kind of motion.[11]

Falling is not a fall from an entity's originary pure essence into its impure
corrupted form; it is a fall from a concern with being into an oblivion of
being. Likewise, for Heidegger, alienation is not an alienation of an entity
from its essence, but the alienation of that entity from being as such.

In his posthumously published book, *Mindfulness* [*Besinnung*] (composed in
1938–39), Heidegger equates the alienation from being with a de-humanizing
reification. He writes: '[W]ith the help of the rational appeal to the rationally conceived and pursued beings the utmost *estrangement from be-ing*
is achieved. This is the end of man in total "dis-humanization".'[12] Such
'rationality' involves inquiring into things solely at the level of their ontical
'whatness', at the level of entities and not the being of the entities, thus
abandoning the question of being, the 'why?' of fundamental inquiry into
being as such. For Heidegger, this abandonment of being is de-humanizing,
because the human, understood in fundamental ontological terms as
Dasein, is that being for whom being as such is an issue. He writes:

> [T]he more unconstrainedly the 'dis-humanizing' of man bears itself . . .
> the more exclusively he explains himself in terms of that which is
> neutrally extant [*vorhanden*] and objectively found in him. . . . But how
> can this 'dis-humanization' of man be overcome? Only from the decision
> to ground the truth of be-ing.[13]

The 'rationalization' that involves regarding humans in the form of
objectified and present-at-hand [*vorhanden*] entities de-humanizes in that
it alienates humans from being. Heidegger's 'ontologization' of alienation
does not render the latter insurmountable, it just means that alienation
can only be overcome ontologically.

Derrida is critical of Heidegger's aim of overcoming ontological expropriation. Derrida's project of the 'deconstruction' of metaphysics derives
rhetorically from Heidegger's project of the 'destruction [*Destruktion*]' of
metaphysics. Despite this, the aims of the two projects are antithetical.
Heidegger's *Destruktion* is aimed at overcoming the forgetting of being, the
concealment of being by traditional metaphysics. Regarding traditional
ontology, or metaphysics, Heidegger writes in *Being and Time*:

> If the question of Being is to have its own history made transparent, then
> this hardened tradition must be loosened up, and the concealments

which it has brought about must be dissolved. We understand this task as one in which . . . we are to *destroy* the traditional content of ancient ontology until we arrive at those primordial experiences in which we achieved our first ways of determining the nature of Being. . . . But this destruction is . . . far from having the *negative* sense of shaking off the ontological tradition. We must, on the contrary, stake out the positive possibilities of that tradition, and this always means keeping it within its *limits*[.][14]

Thus the notion of *Destruktion* involves a kind of immanent critique of the ontological tradition. This would be proto-Derridian were it not for the fact that its ultimate aim is the reawakening of the question of being. Derrida furthers the project of deconstructing metaphysics by dismissing Heidegger's ultimate aims as themselves metaphysical. For Derrida, the arch-deconstructive notion of '*différance*' is more primordial, '"[o]lder" than Being itself'.[15] Its originary unoriginariness that 'unceasingly dislocates itself in a chain of differing and deferring substitutions'[16] must be affirmed without '*nostalgia*' or '*hope*' for a lost presence.[17] Such an affirmation involves a Nietzschean 'active forgetting of Being'.[18] Derrida dissociates his work from that of Heidegger particularly with regard to the concept of 'the proper', which involves a nexus of Heideggerian concepts, and which Derrida considers to be a form of the metaphysics of presence. Derrida says:

I have marked quite explicitly . . . a *departure* from the Heideggerean problematic. This departure is related particularly to the concepts of *origin* and *fall*. . . . This departure also . . . intervenes as concerns the value *proper* (propriety, propriate, appropriation, the entire family of *Eigentlichkeit, Eigen, Ereignis*). . . . I have also explicitly criticized this value of propriety and of original authenticity, and . . . I even, if it can be put thus, started there. . . . [T]he Heideggerean problematic is the most 'profound' and 'powerful' defense of what I attempt to put into question under the rubric of the *thought of presence*.[19]

Derrida's starting point is the furthering of the critique of metaphysics by identifying Heidegger's purportedly anti-metaphysical concepts as themselves dependent on a metaphysics of presence.

However, 'presence' is generally treated negatively in Heidegger's work. In *Being and Time*, the notion of 'falling' into the 'inauthenticity' of the 'they' involves a fixation with the present that alienates *Dasein* from being.

Heidegger writes: 'In making present [*Auch gegenwärtigend*] . . . Dasein . . .
has been alienated [*entfremdet*] from its ownmost potentiality-for-Being,
which is based primarily on the authentic future and on authentically
having been.'[20] This alienation is overcome in the 'anticipatory resoluteness' of authentic 'Being-towards-death'.[21] Concern for being involves
concern for non-being. The finite temporality of Being-towards-death constitutes authentic *Dasein*, because death, like being, is irreducibly singular,
and thus absent from the fallen, inauthentic public realm of the 'they':
'The "they" never dies because it *can*not die; for death is in each case
mine'.[22] Being-towards-death is the primordial temporality of *Dasein*'s
finitude, which Heidegger opposes to the unending temporality of the
'they', with its secondary, 'vulgar' experience of time as something that
does not end. The fallen and inauthentic fixation with the present involves
'curiosity', the need to constantly find something new, which itself involves
a forgetting of the past and future. Heidegger writes that this 'distracted
not-tarrying becomes *never-dwelling-anywhere*'.[23] Authentic temporality
'awakens' the present into an anticipatory futurity. He writes: 'Primordial
and authentic temporality . . . awakens the Present. *The primary phenomenon
of primordial and authentic temporality is the future*.'[24] This anticipatory futurity
is not a projected future present, but an infusion of finitude that 'awakens'
the tranquillized present to the projected end, eventual death. The overcoming of alienation and homeless non-dwelling is not a return to presence, but a return *from* the present *to* being, to the primordial, authentic,
finite temporality of Being-towards-death, characterized by 'anticipatory
resoluteness', not fixation with the present.

Derrida insists, however, that this reference to an authentic proximity to
being is itself a return to a form of self-presence. In his essay on Heidegger,
'*Ousia* and *Grammē*', he writes: 'The primordial, the authentic are determined as the *proper (eigentlich)*, that is, as the *near* (proper, *proprius*), the
present in the proximity of self-presence.'[25] For Derrida, the concepts
of the proper, the authentic, and the ownmost, are dependent on the
metaphysics of presence. The notion of the primordial or originary,
upon which the concepts of the authentic and the proper depend, is also
metaphysical, as it too depends on the notion of presence. Derrida writes:

Now, is not the opposition of the *primordial* to the *derivative* still metaphysical? Is not the quest for an *archia* in general, no matter with what
precautions one surrounds the concept, still the 'essential' operation of
metaphysics? . . . [I]s there not at least some Platonism in the *Verfallen*?
Why determine as *fall* the passage from one temporality to another? And

why qualify temporality as authentic or *proper (eigentlich)* – and as inauthentic – or improper – when every ethical preoccupation has been suspended?[26]

The connotations of ethical judgement surrounding the term 'authentic [*eigentlich*]' do not preclude its use in an ethically neutral, 'matter-of-fact' manner, a use that Heidegger, however unconvincingly, insists he is employing. As *Dasein* is that entity for whom being as such is an issue, authentic *Dasein* is concerned with being, inauthentic *Dasein* is oblivious of being, inauthentic *Dasein* is oblivious of its *Dasein*. As we have seen in a previous chapter, Derrida regards the metaphysical notion of origin (or *archia*) as referring to a unified fullness of presence, not yet corrupted by plurality and alterity. Yet the Heideggerian '*archia*' is an originariness (or primordiality) [*Ursprünglichkeit*] that is not a single unified plenitude, but an underivative, hence originary, multiplicity. This is demonstrated by his use of the term *gleichursprünglich* (translated as 'equiprimordial'). Heidegger writes:

> [T]he fact that something primordial is underivable does not rule out the possibility that a multiplicity of characteristics of Being may be constitutive for it. If these show themselves, then existentially they are equiprimordial [*gleichursprünglich*]. The phenomenon of the *equiprimordiality* of constitutive items has often been disregarded in ontology, because of a methodologically unrestrained tendency to derive everything and anything from some simple 'primal ground [*Urgrund*]'.[27]

Unlike the single simple unified origin of traditional ontology, Heideggerian originariness can admit a fundamental multiplicity. Moreover, Heidegger's *archia*, or origin, is not traditionally metaphysical in that it is not an originary being, or entity, but simply being itself, or being as such. An origin, or *Ursprung*, is not only not necessarily a 'primal ground', or *Urgrund*, but also it is not necessarily an originary thing, or *Ur-sache*; the latter is usually translated into English as 'cause', a primal cause being the ultimate 'metaphysical' concept.[28] Heidegger's philosophy bears a merely formal resemblance to metaphysics, in that if the central concept, 'being', is replaced by the concept of a primal entity, like 'God', 'Spirit' or '*energeia*', it would be an actual metaphysics. It is not a metaphysics, because its fundamental concept is not a primal entity, but simply being as such. Heidegger is compelled to use the language of metaphysics, he has no other language at his disposal, in order to get at something more fundamental than metaphysics.

To attack him for being metaphysical, as Derrida does, is to be guilty of formalism.

Heidegger's critique of metaphysics itself involves a critique of the notion of presence. In *Mindfulness* he writes: 'The metaphysical determination of being as beingness grasps beingness as presence and constancy.'[29] It is precisely through presence that being is concealed. He refers to the 'pre-eminence of *presencing* and the "present" and constancy . . . wherein being as (enowning) refuses itself for a very long while'.[30] Presence is a form of the oblivion of being. Thus authenticity [*Eigentlichkeit*] as proximity to being is something other than a case of the metaphysics of presence. Heidegger writes: '"Ownedness [*Eigentlichkeit*]" is a determination that overcomes metaphysics as such. Correspondingly *un-ownedness*, [*Un-eigentlichkeit*] . . . means lostness to *beings*.'[31] Inauthenticity [*Uneigentlichkeit*] involves being trapped in the ontical realm of entities, the realm of presence. In *Contributions to Philosophy* Heidegger's concept of 'echo' echoes Derrida's concepts of 'trace' and 'spectrality', in that it undermines presence. He writes: '*Echo* carries far into what has been and what is to come – hence . . . its striking power on the present.'[32] The metaphysical reign of presence is precisely what Heidegger himself is attempting to put into question.

Present in Heidegger's work is a concern with alienation. Alienation itself involves a fixation with presence. Thus de-alienation does not involve a return to the fullness of presence. Presence involves an oblivion of being and de-alienation involves a dwelling in the proximity of being.

Presence as Objectification

Heidegger's work also displays a concern with and reaction to the phenomenon of alienation in the form of objectification and reification. The latter two concepts are intrinsic aspects of the Hegelian and Marxian theories of alienation. Lucien Goldmann goes so far as to argue that Heidegger's work represents the same 'problematic'[33] as that of Lukács, the principal theorist of the Marxist notion of reification, and that *Being and Time* is partly a response to Lukács's *History and Class Consciousness*, specifically regarding the concept of reification. Goldmann claims that the fact that *Being and Time* concludes, on its final page, with a paragraph on the concept of reification indicates that it is a central concern of Heidegger's. Goldmann writes: 'The position of this text gives particular significance to the problem of reification and indicates that it is a central problem of the discussion for Heidegger.'[34]

Despite this, Heidegger is critical of the concept of reification as it is traditionally framed. As with Marx's concept of alienation, he insists on its 'ontologization', in other words, he claims that it does not go deeply enough, because it ignores the question of being. Reification [*Verdinglichung*] is explicitly discussed not only at the end, but also near the beginning of 'Part One' (the only existing part aside from the 'Introduction') of *Being and Time*. This discussion is part of an attempt by Heidegger to dissociate his 'analytic of *Dasein*' from other philosophical protests at objectifying 'de-humanization'. He mentions in this regard Dilthey's 'life-philosophy', Scheler's 'personalism', as well as Lukács's (implicitly, as here the proper name is absent) theory of 'reification'. Heidegger's aim in this brief discussion is to 'show that those investigations and formulations of the question which have been aimed at Dasein heretofore, have missed the real *philosophical* problem (notwithstanding their objective fertility)'.[35] The philosophical problem in question is the oblivion of the question of being. Heidegger claims that such oblivion is the root of reification, and hence that any genuine theory of the latter needs to address the problem of the former. He writes:

> The Thinghood itself which such reification implies must have its ontological origin demonstrated if we are to be in a position to ask what we are to understand *positively* when we think of the unreified *Being* of the subject, the soul, the consciousness, the spirit, the person.[36]

The theory of reification, though 'objectively fertile', is limited to the ontical realm of entities, a limitation that prevents it from getting to the roots of the problem it raises. Goldmann writes: 'According to Heidegger, this entire problematic of reification is valid. Yet it is situated at the level of science, pertains to the ontic, and can only be clarified by ontological investigations which are not concerned with science.'[37] Heidegger's 'analytic of *Dasein*' is an ontological deepening of the critique of reification.

Heidegger is similarly wary of the word *Objektivierung* ('objectification'), while occasionally using it in a manner which indicates that it is one of his principal concerns. The wariness stems from his concern to overcome the philosophy of the subject, with which the term 'object' is inherently bound. In *Being and Time* the term is usually qualified with quotation marks.[38] However, it is identified with his own concept of 'presence-at-hand [*Vorhandenheit*]'. He makes this identification when discussing the inherence of these concepts within the 'representational' model of positivist science, a model which deals with things in terms of 'presence'.

He writes: 'Being which Objectifies [*Das objektivierende Sein*] . . . is characterized by a *distinctive kind of making – present* [Gegenwärtigung]. This making-
present is . . . the kind of discovering which belongs to the science in
question [which] awaits solely the discoveredness of the present-at-hand.'[39]
This is echoed in *Contributions to Philosophy* when he writes that 'modern
"science"' abandons being by 'thinking of beings as re-presented ob-ject'.[40]
In fact, the 'modern' 'abandonment of being' in general involves objectification. He writes: '[T]he abandonment of being[,] . . . by its own unique
ways of uncovering beings and their "pure" objectification, . . . interpene-
trates a definite appearing which is seemingly without background and
fully groundless.'[41] The forgetting of being is manifested in the reduction
of everything to the sphere of quantitative calculability, the latter being
the primal characteristic of the paradigm of 'representation' and 'objectification'. He refers to quantitative calculability as 'what is ownmost to the
dominion of *re-presenting as such* and the *objectification* of beings'.[42] It is
clear that Heidegger regards objectification as a fundamental component
of the forgetting of being.

Heidegger only uses the term 'reification' in reference to someone
else's theory. However, he comes to use the term 'objectification' as a part
of his own critique (mainly in his posthumously published works of the
late 1930s). This is perhaps because an 'object' is something more precise
than a 'thing'. 'Object' is a type of 'thing', or rather, it is a particular way of
relating to thinghood. In his later essay, 'The Thing', Heidegger argues that
objectification does violence to thinghood. He writes: '[T]he thingly character of the thing does not consist in its being a represented object, nor
can it be defined in any way in terms of the objectness, the over-againstness,
of the object.'[43]

In *Being and Time*, Heidegger identifies two ways of relating to things,
in terms of 'presence-at-hand [*Vorhandenheit*]', their givenness to observation, and 'readiness-to-hand [*Zuhandenheit*]', their practical manipulability.
Present-at-hand entities are objects standing before the observing theoretical consciousness. An object is identical to a present-at-hand entity. In
Contributions to Philosophy he writes that in the abandonment of being
'beings are manifest . . . as object and as extant [*vorhanden*]'.[44] As the category of the 'present-at-hand' [*vorhanden*] involves an oblivion of being, it is
inappropriate to use it to refer to the kind of entity called *Dasein*. In *Being
and Time* Heidegger writes: '[A]ny entity is either a "who" (existence) or a
"what" (presence-at-hand in the broadest sense).'[45] 'The broadest sense' in
question means all ontically bound entities, entities which are not *Dasein*,
conceived prior to, and separately from, their involvement in the world of

ready-to-hand [*zuhanden*] practicality. Goldmann identifies Heidegger's notion of the 'present-at-hand' with Lukács's notion of 'reified consciousness'. He writes:

> Lukács . . . showed how this reification, bound to market production, finally led to . . . the perception of the external world as a pure object only capable of being known and modified, to what Heidegger would call *Vorhandenheit*. . . . [According to Heidegger, there is a tendency] to understand 'Being-there' (man) on the basis of the world as *Vorhanden*, which is none other than the Marxist and Lukácsian analysis which tells us that, in reification, human reality and social facts are understood as things.[46]

The present-at-hand is a product of reification *qua* objectification. The critical term 'presence-at-hand [*Vorhandenheit*]' is the principal component of Heidegger's ontologizing deepening of the critique of reification.

This terminological association only applies if 'reification [*Verdinglichung*]' is identified with 'objectification', as it is for the Lukács of *History and Class Consciousness*. In this case, both the terms 'reification' and 'presence-at-hand' refer to the abstraction of entities from the world, from their inherence in a living environment. This use of the term 'reification' is not appropriate for the later Heidegger of 'The Thing' essay (presented in 1950), who tries to rescue the 'thingly character of the thing' from the tentacles of objectifying presence-at-hand. Here 'the thing' is inherently worldly. Heidegger writes: 'The thing things world.'[47] The worldliness from which presence-at-hand is an ossifying abstraction is the pre-theoretical realm of ready-to-hand [*zuhanden*] practical 'everydayness'. This realm is the totality of pre-theoretical, unanalysed purposive activity that *Dasein* finds itself inherently bound up with. Here, 'things' are 'humanized' in that they are invested with 'usability' in reference to 'human' purposes and needs. (The term 'human' is qualified with inverted commas here, because it only refers to the human *qua Dasein*. The term without such a qualification is commonly associated with a biological species or the Aristotelian 'rational animal', both reifying debasements of *Dasein*; hence Heidegger's general avoidance of the term 'human'.)

These usably 'humanized' things are referred to by Heidegger as *das Zeug* (translated as 'equipment'). Regarding Heidegger's relating of 'world' and 'equipment', Hubert Dreyfus writes: 'To understand worldhood . . . we must begin with equipment. Now the primary point which distinguishes equipment from "mere things" is its thoroughgoing interrelatedness'.[48]

Equipmentality is basic to worldhood as purposive totality. In *Being and Time*, Heidegger writes about the equipmental use-value of 'humanized' things as they relate to the worldly purposiveness of work in the following way:

> That which our everyday dealings proximally dwell is not the tools themselves [*die Werkzeuge selbst*]. On the contrary, that which we concern ourselves primarily is the work – that which is to be produced at the time; and this is accordingly ready-to-hand too. The work bears with it that referential totality [*Verweisungsganzheit*] within which the equipment [*das Zeug*] is encountered.[49]

The world is the interrelatedness, or relationality, of 'human' purposive productive activity. This primordial and authentic worldhood is not only 'pre-theoretical', but also pre-alienated and pre-expropriated, prior to the de-totalizing dominion of the present-at-hand. Presence-at-hand, like Lukacs's 'reified consciousness', involves abstracting things from the totality of 'human' practical engagements, or praxis, into an isolated positivity. The focus on purposive praxis displays a Marxian concern with both the use-value of things (as opposed to their abstracted, or 'fetishized', exchangeability) and an unalienated relationship of the worker to her work, whether product or activity. Heidegger writes:

> The work produced refers not only to the 'towards-which' of its usability and the 'whereof' of which it consists: under simple craft conditions it also has an assignment to the person who is to use it or wear it. The work is cut to his figure; he 'is' there along with it as the work emerges.[50]

This is a William Morris-like description of the world of work prior to its de-authentication through the dominion of the present-at-hand. Heidegger does not ascribe the latter to any socio-economic system, but to 'metaphysics', 'technology' and the 'destiny of the West'.

'Readiness-to-hand' does not only refer to the 'humanized' things of equipmentality, but also to 'humanized' nature. Heidegger writes:

> [I]n the environment certain entities become accessible which are always ready-to-hand, but which, in themselves, do not need to be produced. . . . If its kind of Being as ready-to-hand is disregarded, this 'Nature' itself can be discovered and defined simply in its pure presence-at-hand. But when this happens, the Nature which 'stirs and strives', which assails us and enthralls us as landscape, remains hidden. The botanist's plants

are not the flowers of the hedgerow; the 'source' which the geographer establishes for a river is not the 'springhead in the dale'.[51]

Nature, when alienated from the 'world', the world of 'human' significance, becomes an object of 'science' and technological thinking through its objectification into the present-at-hand. Prior to its de-worlding alienation into the present-at-hand, nature is apprehended as readiness-to-hand within the world, that is to say, 'humanly', 'experientially' and 'subjectively'.

The use of the word 'subjectively' here would raise the terminological ire of Heidegger every bit as much as the word 'human'. This is partly because, for Heidegger, the term 'subject' is tainted by the post-Cartesian modification of the forgetting of being. It is also because Heidegger regards the term as referring to a present-at-hand entity, involving the ontologically inappropriate treatment of *Dasein* as an object. He writes:

> The question of the 'who' answers itself in terms of the 'I' itself, the 'subject', the 'Self'. . . . Ontologically we understand it as something which is in each case already constantly present-at-hand . . . and which lies at the basis, in a very special sense, as *subjectum*. . . . Even if one rejects . . . the Thinghood of consciousness, or denies that a person is an object, ontologically one is still positing something whose Being retains the meaning of present-at-hand, whether it does so explicitly or not. Substantiality is the ontological clue for determining which entity is to provide the answer to the question of the 'who'. Dasein is tacitly conceived in advance as something present-at-hand. . . . Yet presence-at-hand is the kind of Being which belongs to entities whose character is not that of Dasein.[52]

Strangely, for Heidegger, the 'subject' is a type of 'object'. He regards the term *Subjekt* ('subject') as referring exclusively to the subject of epistemological representation, a contemplative subject who contemplates objects. This subject–object relation is a relation between two present-at-hand entities. Contrasting it with his concept of being-in-the-world, he refers critically to the notion of a 'Being-present-at-hand-together of a subject [*Subjekts*] and an Object [*Objekts*].'[53] In *Mindfulness* he writes: '[S]ubjectivity means extantness [*Vorhandenheit*] of what is absolutely secured for representing.'[54] 'Subjectivity' refers to nothing other than the contemplative subject of knowledge. The conception of the human as a subject is a central facet of the dominion of presence-at-hand [*Vorhandenheit*]. Heidegger thus refers to 'the intensification of the extantness [*Vorhandenheit*] of man through the interpretation of man as "subject"'.[55] The critique of the reification of the subject does not go far enough in that the pre-reified subject in question is itself a present-at-hand entity, and therefore already subject to a certain reification. Derrida writes:

> [T]he thought of the subject . . . [leads] to interpreting the 'who' of *Dasein* as something which endures in a substantial identity of the type *Vorhandensein* or of the subject as *Vorhandensein*. As a result, however much one protests against . . . the reification of consciousness, or the objectivity of the person, one continues to determine the 'who' ontologically as a subject existing in the form of *Vorhandenheit*.[56]

However, as we have discussed in previous chapters, in the works of Hegel, Marx and others, the subject is something quite different from a 'substantial identity', a subject not of mere contemplation, but a subject of praxis, a subject that is itself praxis. To describe the subject as a present-at-hand entity is to ignore the use of the term in German Idealism and its legacy. The subject as praxis is closer to Heidegger's description of *Dasein* than to the Cartesian subject of representation. In *Contributions to Philosophy*, Heidegger writes: 'Da-sein is experienced – not re-presented as object, but rather as Da-*sein*, enacted.'[57] A conception of the subject as praxis could reasonably be used to describe *Dasein's* inherent being-in-the-world.

It is not only the spatiality of being-in-the-world that is objectified into the present-at-hand, but also *Dasein's* authentic temporality. As we have seen, authentic temporality is the finitude of being-towards-death, a finitude forgotten through the 'fallen' state of alienation in 'the they'. The latter involves the ordinary, 'vulgar' conception of time as an unending sequence of 'nows'. This amounts to seeing time in terms of the present-at-hand. Heidegger describes unending time as '*a course of "nows" which is present-at-hand*'.[58] Thus, in a sense, time itself is objectified into the present-at-hand. Derrida writes that what Heidegger calls vulgar time is 'a time which is . . . present after the fashion of an ob-ject'.[59]

In *Contributions to Philosophy*, Heidegger discusses the vulgar conception of time with reference to the German word '*Zeitraum*', which usually translates as 'timespan', but which literally means 'timespace'. He writes:

> Timespace [*Zeitraum*] means a span of 'time' which goes from now to then, from then to today, etc. – a 'span of time' of a hundred years. Time is represented here as spacious [*geräumig*], insofar as it is a ratio for measuring and encompassing something. . . . [T]he ordinary concept of 'time' is . . . represented in the word *timespace* [*Zeitraum*].[60]

The objectification of time is thus a spatialization of time. As we saw in the first chapter, Lukács describes mechanized, repetitive, quantitatively measured (as abstract labour-time) industrial work in terms of the transformation of qualitative time into quantitative space.[61] While Lukács only references Marx's *Capital* in this regard, the terminology used suggests the influence of Bergson's notion of the spatialization of time. In *Being and Time*, Heidegger argues against the equation of the rendering present-at-hand of time with its spatialization. He claims that the ordinary, inauthentic conception of time has its source in primordial, authentic temporality, and thus retains a temporal character. Thus he writes that ordinary vulgar time 'is not an externalization [*Veräußerlichung*] of a "qualitative time" into space, as Bergson's Interpretation of time . . . would have us believe'.[62] Heidegger argues that the ordinary conception of time as a sequence of present-at-hand 'nows' would logically be considered reversible, were it not for its origins in authentic finite temporality, with the latter's anticipatory futurity. He writes:

> In the ordinary interpretation, the stream of time is defined as an *irreversible* succession. Why cannot time be reversed? Especially if one looks exclusively at the stream of 'nows', it is incomprehensible in itself why this sequence should not present itself in the reverse direction. The impossibility of this reversal has its basis in the way public time originates in temporality, the temporalizing of which is primarily futural and 'goes' to its end ecstatically in such a way that it 'is' already towards its end.[63]

Objectified, present-at-hand, vulgar time is not spatial, because it is irreversible. However, Heidegger is here arguing that the irreversibility of vulgar time is a contradiction. Thus vulgar time could be described as a notion of spatialized time that contradicts itself. But the notion of spatialized time is supposed to refer to a contradiction, that is why it is used critically by Marx, Lukács and Bergson, to refer to the imposition of characteristics onto time that are not appropriate to it. Hence Heidegger's objection to the term 'spatialized' being used to describe vulgar time is merely a minor terminological quibble. As we have seen, Heidegger is happy to use the term 'spacious [*geräumig*]' to describe vulgar time in his later *Contributions to Philosophy*.

The finite, primordial, authentic temporality of being-towards-death, characterized by the futurity of 'anticipatory resoluteness', is also described by Heidegger in terms of *Dasein*'s 'being-a-whole'. He refers to 'Dasein's Being-at-an-end in death, and therewith its Being-a-whole'.[64] This wholeness is experienced in the form of its anticipation, as something *towards*

which *Dasein* faces. Heidegger writes: '*Temporality gets experienced in a phenomenally primordial way in Dasein's authentic Being-a-whole, in the phenomenon
of anticipatory resoluteness.*'[65] This is a paradoxical wholeness, as it only
occurs when *Dasein* ceases to be. Heidegger writes: 'As long as Dasein *is* as
an entity, it has never reached its "wholeness".'[66] However, this notion of
'wholeness' as a completed temporality is itself a spatialization of time and
reification of *Dasein*. Though it is a projected and anticipated 'wholeness',
the completed temporality is itself a span of time [*Zeitraum*], a reification of
a living temporality into a spatialized artifact, a 'whole' life. However much
this is an anticipation, a being-towards, it is still an anticipation of *Dasein*'s
eventual artifactualization. It is an anticipation of a completed life, a potential completed life that stands before *Dasein* as something present-at-hand.
'Being-towards-death' could thus be redescribed as 'being-towards-being-
eventually-rendered-present-at-hand'. This means that objectification is
overcome by the anticipation of eventually being thoroughly objectified.
The dominion of the present-at-hand is overcome by the anticipation of
eventually being rendered present-at-hand. As Adorno writes, 'Insofar as
death is absolutely alien to the subject, it is the model of all reification.'[67]

Occasionally, Heidegger uses the word 'spirit' to refer to the non-reified,
non-objectified, non-present-at-hand state that is appropriate to *Dasein*.
Dasein is not only temporal in its being-towards-death, but also spatial in its
being-in-the-world. This spatiality is not the spatiality of a three-dimensional
ordering of corporeal things; it refers to the inherent worldhood of *Dasein*.
Heidegger writes:

> To be able to say that Dasein is present-at-hand at a position in space,
> we must first *take* [*auffasen*] this entity in a way which is ontologically
> inappropriate. . . . Dasein's spatiality [may not] be interpreted as an
> imperfection which adheres to existence by reason of the fatal 'linkage of
> the spirit to a body'. On the contrary, because Dasein is 'spiritual', *and
> only because of this*, it can be spatial in a way which remains essentially
> impossible for any extended corporeal Thing.[68]

Although the word 'spiritual' is used in quotation marks, it is being used
to refer to what is not thing-like in *Dasein*. The quotation marks have
the function of dissociating *Dasein*'s 'spirituality' from the metaphysical
heritage, particularly Cartesian dualism and the notion of subjectivity as a
'thinking thing [*res cogitans*]'. The spatiality of being-in-the-world is 'spiritual' in that it does not inhere in things and animals. As we have seen, the
'world' is a context involving a living, purposive (in the sense of 'humanly

meaningful') interrelatedness. In the *Introduction to Metaphysics*, Heidegger writes: 'World is always *spiritual* world. The animal has no world.'[69]

A major claim of Derrida's *Of Spirit* is that the loss of quotation marks around the words 'spirit' and 'spiritual' in the published texts of the 1930s does not only indicate that Heidegger is appropriating the terms into his own lexicon, but also that he is deviating from his critical project of the destruction [*Destruktion*] of metaphysics. However, Derrida also argues that Heidegger already appropriates the term 'spirit' in *Being and Time* despite the quotation marks. Derrida writes: '[W]hen he undertakes to explicate . . . originary temporality . . . Heidegger finally takes up the word "spirit" as his own.'[70] Derrida is referring to the moment when Heidegger discusses Hegel's notion of a fall of spirit into time. Heidegger writes: '"Spirit" does not first fall into time, but it *exists as* the primordial *temporalizing* of temporality. . . . "Spirit" does not fall *into* time; but factical existence "falls" as falling *from* [*aus*] primordial, authentic temporality.'[71] 'Spirit' is itself the *Dasein* of primordial temporality, and in falling *Dasein* falls out of [*aus*] that temporality, externalized into vulgar objectivity. The word 'spirit' is properly Heideggerian, whether qualified with quotation marks or not, when it refers to the unalienated, un-externalized, non-present-at-hand *Dasein* in its authentic finite temporality and its worldly spatiality.

Technicity

According to Heidegger, homelessness and the forgetting of being are further entrenched by modern technological thinking. His ambivalence towards the word 'spirit' is the consequence of the tension between his wariness of its traditional metaphysical baggage and the need to resist the reduction of *Dasein* and its world to a 'spiritless' quantitative measurability. In his *Introduction to Metaphysics* he writes: 'The prevailing dimension became that of extension and number . . . until finally this quantitative temper became a quality of its own.'[72] The reduction of entities to the quantitatively measurable enables an attitude towards them of technological mastery and control. Heidegger writes: 'Being as calculable[,] . . . Being as set into calculation, makes beings into something that can be ruled in modern, mathematically structured technology.'[73]

In *Contributions to Philosophy*, Heidegger decries the dominance of the calculative and quantitative, which he regards as an outgrowth of the attitude to entities as present-at-hand, represented objects. He writes: '[M]achination [is] that interpretation of beings as re-presentable and re-presented. In one respect re-presentable means "accessible to intention and calculation"; in another respect it means "advanceable through production and execution".[74] The epoch of productivity and calculative mastery over entities is bound up with the Cartesian subject, the contemplative subject of representations. Under the dominion of technological 'machination' the merely quantitative reigns, and qualitative particularity is effaced. Heidegger describes the 'shackles' of 'machination' as '[t]he pattern of generally calculable explainability, by which everything draws nearer to everything else equally and becomes completely alien to itself – yes, totally other than just alien'.[75] The quantitativeness of the calculable involves a levelling off of everything, whereby being rendered quantitatively measurable and comparable alienates entities from their own 'alien' qualitative peculiarity. With the modern technological mentality everything is subjected to a calculative instrumentalized productivity that equalizes all particularity into a general equivalence. In *Mindfulness* Heidegger writes:

> *Machination* means the accordance of everything with producibility . . . foster[ing] in advance the completely surveyable calculability of the subjugating empowering of beings to an accessible arrangement. . . . Modern technicity releases man into the urge towards structuring his massive way of being through which every human particularity is overpowered[.][76]

The term 'massive' here refers to the condition of being a mass, wherein particularity is subsumed. Modern technology reduces the uniqueness of *Dasein* to a quantitative equivalence. As we have seen in previous chapters, the reduction of quality to quantity is an aspect of the Marxian and Lukácsian conception of reification.[77]

While Heidegger's posthumously published works of the late 1930s discuss technology in terms of objectification and present-at-hand representability, his later essay, 'The Question concerning Technology', moves subtly away from the terminology bequeathed by *Being and Time* in that it speaks of the 'objectlessness' of technological orderability. Technology involves reducing entities to a calculable and orderable 'standing-reserve', available for any utilitarian call up, a 'standing-reserve' that does not stand before consciousness or observation as an 'object'. Heidegger writes:

> Everywhere everything is ordered to stand by, to be immediately on hand, indeed to stand there just so that it may be on call for a further ordering. . . . We call it the standing-reserve [*Bestand*]. . . . Whatever stands by in the sense of standing-reserve no longer stands over against us as object [*Gegenstand*].[78]

The change of terminology from the present-at-hand objects of *Being and Time* and its wake, to the objectless standing-reserve of the 'Technology' essay, is not a significant philosophical shift, but a mere thematic shift from the present-at-hand objects of theoretical scientific observation to the practical, utilitarian, unobserved objectlessness of technological instrumentality. Heidegger writes:

> [W]hen man, investigating, observing, pursues nature as an area of his own conceiving, he has already been claimed by a way of revealing that challenges him to approach nature as an object of research, until even the object disappears into the objectlessness of standing-reserve.[79]

Technological instrumentality is not the instrumentality of the ready-to-hand, the former involving the orderability of quantitative calculability and the latter involving *Dasein*'s manipulation of entities within the purposive interrelatedness of a living 'human' world. The ordering of entities into the technological inventory of a standing-reserve is just as much a de-worlding reification as the objectification of entities into the present-at-hand. Heidegger's name for this reification is 'enframing [*Gestell*]'. He writes: 'The enframing . . . sets upon human beings . . . to order everything that comes to presence into a technical inventory.'[80] Technological enframing also captures these human orderers of orderability, rendering them a human resource, a human standing-reserve. Heidegger writes:

> As soon as what is unconcealed no longer concerns man even as object, but exclusively as standing reserve, then he comes to the very brink of a precipitous fall; that is, he comes to the point where he himself will have to be taken as standing-reserve.[81]

The calculative and mechanistic activity of technological ordering reifies the orderer herself into something calculative and mechanistic, alienated from her activity and thus from herself.

In *Of Spirit*, Derrida argues that Heidegger's critique of technology involves the desire for a pure essence uncontaminated by technicity. Derrida puts into question Heidegger's claim that the essence of technology is nothing technological. Derrida writes:

> [T]his typical and exemplary statement: the essence of technology is nothing technological[,] . . . maintains the possibility of thought that questions, which is always thought of the essence, protected from any original and essential contamination by technology. The concern

[is] . . . to analyze this desire for rigorous non-contamination and . . . to envisage . . . the fatal necessity of a *contamination* . . . of a contact originally impurifying thought or speech. Contamination, then, of the thought of essence by technology, and so contamination by technology of the thinkable essence of technology – and even of a question of technology by technology, the privilege of the question having some relation already, always, with this irreducibility of technology.[82]

The all-encompassing quantifiability of technological enframing, a manifestation of the oblivion of being, always already characterizes and contaminates any 'originary' and 'primordial' thinking of being. A principal theme of Derridian deconstruction is that of an originary irreducible technicity; the 'natural' origin is always already a prosthetic supplement. Technology is thus a form of what Derrida calls 'writing', in that it eludes presence and origin. Writing is machine-like in that, due to its essential iterability, it functions regardless of the presence of any conscious intention; and even the purported 'presence' of the latter in the voice is a mythical effacement of the mechanistic and grammatological features of speech itself.[83]

Derrida's originary technicity, another name for originary non-originariness, is not, however, an originary, reifying, calculative technological enframing. *Différance* and the trace, in their infinite undecideability, defy rational calculability and open up its restricted economy to the incalculability of irreducible alterity. The 'technicity' of *différance* is best illustrated by what we have in previous chapters termed 'determinability', its very indeterminacy being productive of a limitless malleability free from any originary fixed and 'natural' determinacy. We have demonstrated such determinability to be a central feature of traditional conceptions of de-alienation. In contrast to Derrida's interpretation, Heidegger conceives of technology not as a contamination of the pure presence of a natural determinacy, but as a particular manifestation of the reign of entities and the oblivion of being, an oblivion of precisely that which transcends all ontical determination.

Infinite Finitude

It is of *Dasein's* essence, being the being for whom being is an issue, to transcend the ontical realm of mere entities. The oblivion of being, enacted by technology, positive science and metaphysics, involves the consequence of a reified consciousness trapped in the realm of the ontical. Being itself is a transcendence of the ontical. In *Being and Time*, Heidegger writes: 'Being . . . lie[s] beyond every entity and every possible character which an entity may possess. *Being is the transcendens pure and simple.*'[84] Heidegger's name for this transcendence is *Endlichkeit* (translated as 'finitude'). Finitude is a strange name for transcendence, and indeed Heidegger has to redefine it and give it a paradoxical aporetic significance in order to appropriate it into his lexicon.

Dasein's finitude, the finitude of the finite temporality of being-towards-death, is not the mere limitedness of a span of time. It is precisely a being-towards, an anticipatory futurity, a sense of eventual non-existence infecting existence. Heidegger writes:

Dasein . . . does not have an end at which it just stops, but it *exists finitely*. . . . Its finitude does not amount primarily to a stopping, but is a characteristic of temporalization itself. The primordial and authentic future is the 'towards-oneself' (to *oneself!*), existing as the possibility of nullity[.][85]

As death is irreplaceably singular, it can only happen to the individual *Dasein*; it is what is most authentically and distinctively ownmost to *Dasein*. Heidegger writes: 'Primordial and authentic coming-towards-oneself is the meaning of existing in one's ownmost nullity.'[86] This nullity is not what merely limits *Dasein*; it is what constitutes *Dasein* in its singularity. In *Mindfulness*, Heidegger writes:

[O]ne falls . . . into the trap of the dialectic by 'considering' that whenever the 'finite' is posited, an infinite is already thought. One takes the 'finite' here generally in the sense of what is limited . . . – one thinks 'finitude' metaphysically.

However, the 'finitude' of be-ing means something entirely different: the ab-ground-dimension . . . to which the 'not-character' by no means belongs as a lack or a limit, but as a distinction. . . . The 'finitude' of be-ing . . . should guide mindfulness . . . to assert the *uniqueness of be-ing* . . . that is held unto the abground.[87]

According to Heidegger, the Hegelian critique of the Kantian finitude of knowledge, based on the claim that consciousness of a limit involves already having transcended the limit, relies on the traditional 'metaphysical' understanding of finitude as limitedness, and therefore does not apply to the Heideggerian notion of finitude. The latter refers to the essential nothingness of *Dasein*, not grounded in anything, a contentless insubstantiality that is the (non)-basis of its openness to being as such, beyond entities, as well as of its irreducible ungrounded uniqueness.

However, the Hegelian argument regarding finitude of whatever kind is that the awareness of finitude involves an awareness of infinity. Of course, when Heidegger says 'finitude', he means 'awareness of finitude', but he avoids the terms 'awareness' and 'consciousness', because they are metaphysically loaded. There is a tension in *Being and Time* between its avowedly phenomenological method and its anti-Cartesian stance. As the method is phenomenological, a term like 'finitude' means, and can only mean, 'finitude *qua* the appearance of finitude to consciousness'; yet it is precisely this observing consciousness as subject of representations that is being put into question. The problem here is that, as 'finitude' cannot be distinguished from 'appearance of finitude to consciousness', Heidegger is unable to make the thoroughly Hegelian distinction between 'finitude for consciousness' and 'finitude for us (the phenomenological observers of consciousness itself)'. Hence Heidegger is theoretically unable to theorize the effect that consciousness of a phenomenon has on that phenomenon. In Hegel's phenomenological dialectic, the consciousness of finitude involves the overcoming of finitude, and is already on the other side of its limit, on the side of infinity. A truly finite mind cannot have an awareness of its own finitude.

For Heidegger, however, it is *Dasein* that is finite, a living awareness of its finitude in the authentic anticipatory resoluteness of its existence. Its finitude does not consist in the limits of its 'mind', but in the 'limits' (or rather, the ungroundedness) of its being. Its finitude is its mortality. To be precise, its finitude consists in the awareness of its mortality. An animal does not exist 'finitely' in its awareness of its own mortality; it is not in a state of being-towards-death, and thus it is neither 'mortal' nor 'finite' in Heideggerian terms. Only *Dasein* 'dies', properly speaking; an animal merely comes to an end, or 'perishes'. Mortality and finitude are aspects of the ontological structure of *Dasein*. They are ontological, rather than merely ontico-biological, because they involve a concernful awareness, a non-oblivion, of being.

It is, however, questionable whether mortality as such is ontological rather than biological, whether it is a feature of *Dasein qua Dasein* or is merely a feature of the 'human' biological entity empirically and contingently associated with *Dasein*. In giving mortality ontological status, is not Heidegger ontologizing an empirical biological contingency? Adorno writes: '[A]n elimination of death may be highly improbable; yet it can be thought of, and according to existential ontology that should be impossible.'[88] Adorno's point may be banal, but it raises a genuine question. It is banal in that it confuses the empirical contingency of developments in medical science with questions of fundamental ontology. The genuine question it inadvertently raises is the question of whether Heidegger is falsely ontologizing the biological. Both the terms 'mortality' and 'finitude' are misleading in that they imply a limited measurable span of time, which would involve imposing a biological contingency onto what is supposed to be strictly ontological. However, the Heideggerian position is more convincing if 'finitude' is described as the openness to being deriving from the awareness of the possibility of not-being, of the nothing within being, a possibility more suggestive of ontological necessity than biological contingency.

Heidegger argues that the awareness of finitude is originary, and thus that the awareness of infinity is derivative. If this is the case it is possible to have the originary experience prior to, and thus independently of, the derivative one. But how is it possible to have an awareness of finitude without a simultaneous, or 'equiprimordial', awareness of infinity? Heidegger writes: '[T]he finitude of time does not become fully visible until we have exhibited "endless time" so that these may be contrasted.'[89] 'Not fully visible' is too vague a concept of vagueness to adequately answer objections to Heidegger's assignation of primordiality. Hence Derrida writes in *Aporias*: '[O]ne cannot think originary finitude without removing it as infinity, nor can one think being-to-death without starting from immortality.'[90]

'Finitude' *qua* 'awareness of finitude' is what gives *Dasein* a privileged access to being; it is what makes *Dasein* that entity for whom being is an issue. This is because the awareness of the non-being within being, in the form of, for example, being-towards-death, enables *Dasein* to transcend mere entities, to have access to being as such, which is that which transcends all entities, which is itself the '*transcendens*'. 'Finitude' *qua* 'awareness of finitude' overcomes, or transcends, 'finitude' *qua* 'measurable limitedness'. However, this formulation is suggestive of Hegelian infinitism. As we have said, 'finitude' is an odd choice of word; would not the word 'infinity' have been just as appropriate? Heidegger claims that he chose the metaphysically contaminated word 'finitude' provisionally as a means of dissociating himself from German Idealist infinitism, particularly that of Hegel. In *Contributions to Philosophy*, he writes:

> What does it mean to say: Be-ing 'is' infinite [or] Being is finite[?] . . . [T]he question of the essential swaying of be-ing lies beyond the dispute between those propositions; and the proposition 'Be-ing is finite' is only

meant to ward off, in crossing, any kind of 'idealism.' . . . [I]f one operates within the dispute of those propositions, then we would have to
say that, when be-ing is taken as infinite, then it is precisely *determined*.
If be-ing is set as finite, then its ab-groundness is affirmed. For what
is in-finite cannot be meant as what is endlessly in flux, . . . but as the
closed *circle*.[91]

As we have discussed in the chapter on Hegel, the infinite *qua* infinite also
cannot really be 'closed' and '*determined*'. The Hegelian infinite, whatever
its diagrammatical representation, is the infinite within the finite, the self-
transcendence of a finite determinacy that returns to itself through the
other. The supposed 'closure' of the circle of infinity is merely its actuality,
its act as the restlessness of the finite, as opposed to the unattainable beyond
of the spurious infinite. The finitude which is neither closed nor 'precisely
determined', which involves an affirmation of its ungroundedness, its transcendent openness to the nothing, its transcendence of itself as the very
affirmation of itself, is an infinite finitude.

Nevertheless, Heidegger, in his discussion of *Hegel's Phenomenology of Spirit*,
strives to dissociate himself, on the basis of finitude, from Hegelianism.
The discussion makes use of a distinction Heidegger makes between the
concepts of 'absolvence' and 'transcendence', 'absolvence' representing
Hegelian infinity and 'transcendence' representing Heideggerian finitude.
'Absolvence' is Heidegger's term for the process, in Hegel's system, of the
self-overcoming of the finite in the movement of the absolute. At one point
in the discussion Heidegger suggests that Hegelian 'absolvence' might not
be entirely dissimilar to 'transcendence'. He writes: '[I]s what Hegel represents in the *Phenomenology of Spirit* as absolvence merely transcendence in
disguise, i.e. finitude?'[92] As the 'finitude' of transcendence is an infinite
finitude, it would be pertinent to ask whether Heideggerian finitude is not
the absolute in disguise.

Owning

At the end of his study of *Hegel's Phenomenology of Spirit*, Heidegger distinguishes his own position on finitude from Hegelian infinitism in the following way: 'Can and should man as transition try to leap away from himself in
order to leave behind himself as finite? Or is his essence not abandonment
itself, in which alone what can be possessed becomes a possession?'[93] This
indicates that Heidegger regards transcendent finitude as the basis of self-
possession, of self-ownership. Ownness or authenticity can only occur in an

entity which is able to transcend its ontical limits in order to concernfully apprehend its ontological condition, its being, its possible not-being, and thus to be aware of its finitude. In *Being and Time*, Heidegger writes: '[O]nly insofar as it [*Dasein*] is essentially something which can be *authentic* – that is, something of its own – can it have lost itself and not yet won itself.'[94] Only an entity which is capable of being its 'own' can 'abandon' or lose itself. Only the entity for whom being is an issue, one that is aware of its finitude, that transcends its ontical self and apprehends its being, has the property of ownness or mineness. *Dasein*, in transcending itself, is able to own itself. Heidegger writes:

> That Being which is an *issue* for this entity in its very Being, is in each case mine. . . . Dasein has *in each case mineness* [*Jemeinigkeit*]. . . . As modes of Being, *authenticity* and *inauthenticity* . . . are both grounded in the fact that any Dasein whatsoever is characterized by mineness.[95]

Authenticity depends on mineness, which in turn depends on being being an issue of concern. The transcendence involved in Heidegger's notion of finitude is the precondition of the self-ownership of mineness and authenticity.

Authenticity is the state in which *Dasein* is genuinely itself, in its unique individuality, its finite mortality. Inauthenticity is the state in which *Dasein* has lost itself in the collective publicness of 'the They [*das Man*]', oblivious of its individual finitude. Heidegger writes:

> [T]he 'they' constantly accommodates the particular Dasein by disburdening it of its Being . . . Everyone is the other, and no one is himself. The '*they*', which supplies the answer to the question of the '*who*' of everyday Dasein, is the '*nobody*' to whom every Dasein has already surrendered itself in Being-among-one-other [Untereinandersein]. . . . In [this mode] one's way of Being is that of inauthenticity and failure to stand by one's Self.[96]

The 'disburdening' of *Dasein*'s being by 'the They' amounts to *Dasein*'s disowning of itself through its surrender to a public relationality that is ontologically oblivious in its non-finitude and non-transcendence. Authenticity involves the being-towards-death that *Dasein* returns to out of the oblivion of 'the They' through the mood of anxiety. Heidegger writes:

> [*T*]*he state-of-mind which can hold open the utter and constant threat to itself arising from Dasein's ownmost individualized Being, is anxiety. In this*

state-of-mind, Dasein finds itself *face to face* with the 'nothing' of the possible impossibility of its existence.[97]

Being-towards-death is the condition of radical authentic individuality, as it is only the individual that can die, not 'the They'.

This is a radical individuality in the sense that it is non-relational. Heidegger writes: 'The ownmost possibility is *non-relational*. . . . The non-relational character of death, as understood in anticipation, individualizes Dasein down to itself. This individualizing is a way in which the "there" is disclosed for existence.'[98] Adorno argues that this non-relationality of Heideggerian authenticity involves a reifying objectification. Adorno writes:

> Authenticity, which according to doctrine is absolutely unobjective, is made into an object. The reason for this is that authenticity is a manner of behavior that is ascribed to the being-a-subject of the subject, not to the subject as a relational factor.[99]

However, Heidegger claims that the non-relational individualization that authenticity involves enables *Dasein* to appreciate the irreducible authentic individuality of others. He writes: 'As the non-relational possibility, death individualizes – but only in such a manner that . . . it makes Dasein, as Being-with, have some understanding of the potentiality-for-Being of Others.'[100] This is, though, a brief claim that is not elaborated upon (the very next sentence involves an abrupt change of subject). The authentic non-relationality is here a paradoxical precondition of a kind of deeper relationality, that of an empathic 'understanding', a vague, untheorized (by Heidegger), ontologically unclarified, pre-Heideggerian (Diltheyan), humanistic notion that is swiftly dispensed with.

For Heidegger, the authentic, the proper and the ownmost, name a condition wherein *Dasein* is concerned with its being through an anticipatory awareness of its not-being, its 'possible impossibility'. Derrida argues that the Heideggerian proper is not the 'proper' of traditional metaphysics, of the essential attributes of something, but is rather the proper of an ontological concern, a proximity to being. In his essay, 'The Ends of Man', Derrida writes:

> The near is the proper; the proper is the nearest (*prope, proprius*). . . . Being is the proper of man . . . This proposition of the *proper*, certainly, is not to be taken in a metaphysical sense: the proper of man, here, is not

an essential attribute, the predicate of a substance, a characteristic among others, however fundamental, of a being, object or subject, called man. . . . The proper of man, his *Eigenheit*, his 'authenticity,' is to be related to the meaning of Being; he is to hear and to question (*fragen*) it in ek-sistence, to stand straight in the proximity of its light.[101]

Derrida asserts, however, that this notion of proximity 'is in consonance with the motif of presence as self-presence' and thus that the Heideggerian proper remains within the economy of a metaphysics of presence.[102] While this passage specifically comments on Heidegger's 'Letter on Humanism', the 'standing straight' in the 'light' of being is still essentially the anticipatory resoluteness in the face of possible non-being referred to in the earlier *Being and Time*, despite the shift of metaphorical nuance. In fact, the next paragraph of Derrida's essay brings up the relation between the proper and the finite, between ownmost authenticity and death. He writes: 'Man . . . is his proper end, that is, the end of his proper.'[103] The term 'end' involves the 'equivocality' of a 'play of *telos* and death'. The fact that the Heideggerian proper involves the lived finitude of the experience of the nothingness within being, that the transcendent finitude of being-towards-death is the basis of what is most authentic, the lived awareness of one's own being, means that what is most proper to *Dasein* intrinsically involves what is most radically improper, his very own non-being. This is the aporia of the Heideggerian proper. As we have seen, Adorno describes death as the ultimate alienating reification. For Derrida, the Heideggerian unreified, unalienated authenticity itself involves what is most alien, a disowning expropriation at the heart of the ownmost proper. In his later work, *Aporias*, Derrida writes:

If death, the most proper possibility of *Dasein*, is the possibility of its impossibility, death becomes the most improper possibility and the most ex-propriating, the most inauthenticating one. From the most originary inside of its possibility, the proper of *Dasein* becomes from then on contaminated, parasited, and divided by the most improper. . . . Heidegger . . . crucially needs the distinction between the authentic and the inauthentic, as well as that among the different forms of *ending*: *dying properly speaking, perishing*, and *demising*. These distinctions are threatened in their very principle, and, in truth, they remain impracticable as soon as one admits that an ultimate possibility is nothing other than the possibility of an impossibility and that the *Enteignis* always inhabited *Eigentlichkeit*[.][104]

For Derrida, the mineness [*Jemeinigkeit*] of authenticity is 'impracticable', because it depends on the awareness of and appropriation of death, the mineness of death, an aporetic inappropriate appropriation, as death is the abolition of mineness. 'My death', as the death of mineness, is not really mine.

As we have seen, Heidegger states that 'death is in each case mine', and also that '*Dasein* is in each case mine'. This ownmost mineness is dependent on transcendent finitude, the concern for being as such through the transcendence of mere entities. Of all entities, only *Dasein* has ownness and mineness, because only *Dasein* can transcend the ontical and be aware of its own being. *Dasein*'s finitude as the transcendence of entities is an ontologically fundamental description of 'consciousness', a word avoided in order to dissociate *Dasein* from the metaphysical Cartesian heritage of the thinking thing [*res cogitans*]. 'Consciousness' is a non-thing, a nothingness that goes beyond the limitedness of mere entities, going beyond the limitedness of *Dasein* qua entity itself in its ability to 'conceive' such limits, and thus 'conceive' of 'my death'. It is the 'conscious' projection of future death that is appropriable as 'mine', not death itself. Finitude is transcendence in that it is the 'consciousness' that goes beyond death in order to be aware of death. As we argued earlier, this 'conscious' finitude that transcends death as a limit by being aware of it is an 'infinite finitude', the infinite within the finite of the Hegelian infinite, of Hegelian transcendent 'absolvence'. The point here is that this 'nothingness' of a transcendent 'consciousness', as evinced in the works of, among others, Hegel, Feuerbach and Marx, and discussed in previous chapters, constitutes an infinite determinability predicated upon a substanceless universality and inherent social relationality. That is to say, 'consciousness' as transcendent finitude can only occur in a social being. Awareness of one's own finitude depends on a prior awareness of others, as in Hegel's dialectical tale of the struggle for recognition, which is the basis of the social relationality he calls 'spirit'. Only a social being can separate itself from itself, or transcend itself, in order to appropriate itself. Only a social being can be 'authentic'. The social generic being is conceived by Heidegger as the no-one in particular of 'the They', an inauthenticity that constitutes a 'fall' from a primordial and originary individuality. However, authentic individuality is hardly 'originary', as it involves a self-transcendence that depends on social generality. For Heidegger, the social qua 'the They' is neither finite nor mortal ('the They never dies'), and thus constitutes an oblivion of being. But is 'the social' reducible to 'the They' and its ontological oblivion? Not necessarily, if 'the social' is not considered as a substantial mass entity, but as the transcendence of immediate particularity. This form of the social is itself a transcendence of entities. It is thus generic consciousness and 'spirit' (in the Hegelian sense). It may itself be non-finite and non-mortal, but it is nothing more than the self-overcoming relationality of finite and mortal individuals, and finitude is inscribed within it. It is thus not a positive entity, nor is it an abstract unlimitedness; it is the self-transcendence within the finite itself, the self-overcoming of the 'limited', the 'truth' of the finite that is the Hegelian infinite. The abstract one that is no-one of 'the They' is merely one aspect of the social, its inauthentic and alienated aspect. Thus the solipsistic non-relationality of Heidegger's notion of authentic finitude is incoherent. This understanding of authenticity does not overcome the metaphysics of the Cartesian subject. On the contrary, the solipsism of Heideggerian authenticity is a consequence of the Cartesianism inherent in the phenomenological approach.

While the transcendent awareness of being and death may depend on sociality, it is still the irreducible, 'non-relational', singularity of the individual *Dasein* that ends up not-being. The notion of authenticity is an attempt at theorizing the awareness of singularity, and any such awareness will take a paradoxical or aporetic form, due to the universality and iterability inherent in 'conscious' awareness. Heideggerian finitude is the transcendent awareness of irreducible singularity, of the singularity that being 'is', but it is not identical to it. However paradoxical it is, 'authenticity' names the 'conscious' manifestation of singularity and uniterability.

Heidegger's language often equates authenticity with singularity. Although, as we have already pointed out, the self-ownership of authenticity depends on the self-separation of a 'conscious' transcendence, the phenomenological idiom discourages any distinction between 'consciousness' of being and singular being itself. As we have seen, the Heideggerian authentic proper does not refer to essential properties, to the generalized essence of traditional metaphysics, but to the singularity of being. Heidegger maintains a Stirnerian equation of ownness and uniqueness, and a concomitant Stirnerian contradistinction between ownness and essence. He writes: 'What is ownmost is not what is general. . . . All essential swaying is determined according to what is ownmost in the sense of what is originary and unique.'[105] In fact, according to Heidegger, being itself, which has traditionally been seen as what is most general, a feature belonging to all entities, is, when conceived properly, what is most singular. He writes:

Simpleness of be-ing carries within itself the mark of *uniqueness*. It does not at all need any distinguishing or differences, not even the difference from beings. For this difference is required only if being itself is branded as a kind of being and thereby never preserved as the unique but generalized into what is most general.[106]

The forgetting of the ontico-ontological difference renders being as the most general of entities, a rendering which is, for Heidegger, the principal Platonic, onto-theological, metaphysical gesture. Being *qua* being, properly thought in its distinction from entities, is nothing but radical, irreducible singularity. In *Mindfulness*, Heidegger writes: 'Be-ing's singularity and uniqueness are not qualities attributed to be-ing. . . . Rather, be-ing itself is uniqueness, is singularity.'[107] It is not so much that being is singular, but that being is singularity, the two terms being identical.

As we have seen in the introductory chapter, singularity is a major theme of the later works of Derrida. This is because he regards the movement of *différance* as enacting a dislocating disjuncture within the field of presence, within the closed system and restricted economy of the *logos*, a disjuncture that constitutes an opening onto the irreducible singularity of otherness, death and the event. This contrasts with Derrida's earlier works where the same *différance* is said to dislocate the singular itself in a chain of substitutability, and where Heidegger's assertion of the uniqueness of being is criticized on that very basis.[108]

If being is to be identified with radical singularity, it must itself involve a disjuncture within the field of presence, within the realm of present entities. While in *Being and Time*, '*Being is the transcendens pure and simple*', the transcendence of entities, this 'transcendence' could be redescribed as a 'disjuncture'. The ontico-ontological difference names the *différance* of the disjuncture within being, of being as disjuncture. 'Disjuncture' may not strictly be a Heideggerian term, but nor are terms like 'transcendence' and 'finitude'; the latter are metaphysical terms that Heidegger is turning against metaphysics. Much of Heidegger's work after *Being and Time* is concerned with finding a less metaphysically tainted idiom. The disjuncture within the present that the singularity of being 'is', this opening onto the unassimilable radical alterity of an irreducible uniqueness, is, in Derridian terms, an irruption within the logocentric enclosure of the present, an irruption of undetermined incalculable singularity, the irreducibility of the unique moment, the '"now" of the untimely',[109] the event as such. An event in this sense is not a predictable or predicable occurrence within the sphere of meaningfulness, within the present as the economy of the *logos*, but is the irruption of a unique happening. Heidegger himself uses the term *Ereignis* (usually translated as 'event') to describe the unique momentariness of being. In *Contributions to Philosophy*, he writes: '*Be-ing holds sway as enowning* [*Ereignis*]. To enowning [*Ereignis*] belongs the uniqueness and strangeness which inhere in the momentariness of the unexpectedly befalling. . . . Therefore "being" can never be made *common*, as much as the word sounds common to everything.'[110] The German word for 'event', *Ereignis*, is sugges-tive of owning and ownness [*Eigenheit*]. However, as Richard Polt points out, translating it into English as 'enowning' (or, for that matter, 'propriation' and 'appropriation') is misleading, as it does not convey the sense that the German word has of a unique happening.[111] The word '*Ereignis*' combines ownness [*Eigenheit*] *qua* uniqueness with the undetermined irruption of a fundamental momentariness.

Being as *Ereignis* is the always singular happening from which springs the irreducibly new; it is the inception, the radical beginning. Heidegger writes: 'The *beginning* is *be-ing itself* as enowning [*Ereignis*].'[112] To use Derridian terms, *Ereignis* is the uniterable beginning of any domain of iterability, the an-economic inception of any economy, the meaningless inception of any system of meaningfulness. Polt writes:

> Enowning [*Ereignis*] is marked by its uniqueness. Moments of enowning happen only once, for the first and last time. They can never be repro-duced or represented, although they may serve as 'beginnings' that *initi-ate* a domain of reproducibility and representability.[113]

These 'domains' constitute the constancy, stasis and ontical givenness of that which is present, a givenness and positivity involving a disowning [*Enteignis*] of being as enowning [*Ereignis*], replacing and effacing the fun-damental surprise of a genuine 'happening [*Ereignis*]' with the neutralizing familiarity of an everyday occurrence.

As *Ereignis* is singular alterity that takes the form of a dislocation of, and irruption of 'negative' indeterminateness within, the positive givenness of the present, it names a fundamental and radical praxis. This links it with the German Idealist tradition and its Marxian inflection, in that the dissolu-tion of given positivity constitutes a de-reification. As the givenness of the realm of presence is also called 'objectivity', Hegel chooses to use the word 'subject' to refer to the living praxis of its dissolution. As Heidegger restricts this word 'subject' to its substantialist Cartesian aspect, it is for him taboo. Whatever the shifts in vocabulary from 'Idealism' to 'the thinking of being', *Ereignis*, in its dislocation of the present, the present-at-hand, the 'objective', constitutes a de-objectification, de-reification and de-alienation. In 'The Way to Language', Heidegger asks: 'What if propriation [*Ereignis*] by its entry withdrew every present being that is subject to sheer orderability and brought that being back into its own?'[114] In *Mindfulness* he puts it more stridently: 'As en-ownment, be-ing itself destroys the pre-eminence of λόγος [*logos*]; tears away beings as such from power and thus from machination, and en-sways them unto "*ownhood*".'[115] Being as *Ereignis* is the disjuncture in the presence of logocentric alienation.

This means that *Ereignis* is, in Derridian terms, a disjuncture in the economy of the proper. Is not the happening of 'propriation' [*Ereignis*], then, the improper inception of the proper? Derrida suggests as much when in *Spurs* he writes:

> [P]ropriation is named as exactly that which is proper to nothing and no one. . . . [N]o being [*étant*], nothing, happens except *Ereignis'* unfathomable process. The proper-ty of the abyss (*das Eigentum des Ab-grundes*) is necessarily the abyss of proper-ty, the violence of an event which befalls without Being [*être*].[116]

As Heidegger identifies 'being [*Sein (être)*]' with such an 'event [*Ereignis (événement)*]', Derrida must be referring to a non-Heideggerian determination of being, presumably a metaphysical one. Likewise, 'propriation' as the non-proper is only an apparent paradox, because the Heideggerian and Derridian notions of the 'proper' have different meanings. For Derrida, the proper, including not only its metaphysical determination, but also the Heideggerian terms associated with it (*Eigentlichkeit, Ereignis*), refers to an exclusionary identity, a closed economy. For Heidegger, however, the 'proper' refers to the irreducible uniqueness and singularity of being, a singularity that, for Derrida, would constitute a rupture in the economy of the logocentric 'proper'.

The de-alienating overcoming of the structures of ontological expropriation requires a deconstructive dismantling of those structures. Derridian deconstruction is a furthering of the Heideggerian destruction [*Destruktion*] of metaphysics. However, Heidegger aims to dismantle the structures of the oblivion and disowning of being, whereas Derrida regards the ownness of being as itself metaphysical, and asserts the infinite substitutability of *différance* as a dislocating force within the structures of metaphysics, which include the economy of the proper. Heideggerian deconstruction is an ontological deepening of the critique of alienation and reification. The oblivion of being manifests itself as a falling from an authentic ownness to an uprooted 'homelessness' and 'alienation'. Alienation is characterized by a 'fixation with the present', and a consequent 'never-dwelling-anywhere'.

Presence is the principal form of the oblivion of being and the ontological uprootedness of alienation. This includes the objectification of entities, such that they are rendered 'present-at-hand [*Vorhanden*]', which involves abstracting them from the 'world' of living interrelatedness. This objectification also involves an externalization of the primordial authentic finite temporality of *Dasein* into 'vulgar' public time, an unending sequence of present-at-hand 'nows', quantifiably measurable. The loss of qualitative ownness to quantitative calculability is also a characteristic of the reign of modern technology, which involves a reduction of things and people to the orderability of a 'standing-reserve', a reification that Heidegger calls 'enframing'. For Heidegger, authentic ownness involves the lived finitude, the anticipatory futurity, of being-towards-death, the concernful awareness of the possibility of not-being. Heidegger chooses the word 'finitude' to contrast his position with Hegelian infinitism, but it names the transcendence of entities that makes possible the 'awareness' of being and eventual non-being, a transcendence that indicates that such 'awareness' has the form of the self-transcendence of finitude characterizing the Hegelian infinite. The same argument applies to the ultimately incoherent 'non-relational' radical individualism of Heideggerian authenticity – which contrasts with the post-Hegelian notion of an unalienated social 'generic-being' – because authenticity depends on the self-transcendent 'awareness' of finitude that itself depends on a 'social' and 'generic' overcoming of immediate particularity. Whatever the incoherencies of such non-relationality, Heidegger, throughout his work, identifies ownness, in all its facets, with the uniqueness and singularity of being. This is particularly the case with his concept of *Ereignis*, 'enowning' as the unique happening of being. Although Derrida misreads Heideggerian ownness as a metaphysical exclusionary identity, this always irreducibly singular event actually constitutes a disjuncture in the logocentric enclosure of the present. It is itself the singular praxis and *différance* that undermines the positive givenness of the present.

Chapter 5

Deconstructive De-alienation

The viewpoint, held by, among others, Derrida himself, that the notion of *différance* irremediably undermines the concept of a surmountable alienation, has been put under critical scrutiny. Our readings of Hegel and Marx have indicated that the overcoming of alienation is not necessarily implicated in a metaphysics of presence, while Heidegger's proto-deconstruction has been demonstrated to be an ontological inflection of the critique of alienation itself. Now Derrida's work needs to be re-engaged directly, in the light of those readings, with regard to the relationship between *différance* and de-alienation.

For a theory of de-alienation to be put forward in the light of the deconstruction of the metaphysics of presence a number of issues remain to be addressed. For one, there is the relationship between the notions of *différance* and praxis. The idea of a free, de-alienating, transformative praxis bears with it the problematic relations between the notions of subject, force, act and event, notions whose relationships to Derridian *différance* need clarifying. There is also the question of how an overcoming of alienation would avoid the narcissistic suppression of otherness, of that which is alien. This can be addressed by investigating the relationship between Derrida and Levinas, their differences and similarities and how these are relevant to the theme of alienation. Another related problem is the extent to which de-alienation has been conceived as an overcoming of the political, and thus as a reduction of the undecideability that needs to be the basis of any genuinely responsible decision. Ultimately, the form of a deconstructively de-alienated social condition will have to be expounded.

Différance and Praxis

Prior to the later Derrida's purported 'turn' to issues of an explicitly ethical and political nature, it was not uncommon for 'deconstruction' to be described as an apolitical form of playful textual exegesis. One example of this is Rorty's contention that Derrida's work constitutes an apolitical 'private ironism'. An analogous interpretation, from a very different context and perspective, can be found in Julia Kristeva's *Revolution in Poetic Language*, published in 1974, which contains a brief critique of Derrida and 'grammatology'. Kristeva argues that grammatology is politically 'neutral' and 'peaceful', because its abandonment of the 'subject' disables the dislocations and substitutions it describes from intervening in any social and signifying practice. She writes:

> [T]he grammatological deluge of meaning gives up on the subject and must remain ignorant of . . . his functioning as social practice. . . . Neutral in the face of all positions, theses, and structures, grammatology is, as a consequence, equally restrained when they break, burst, or rupture[.][1]

This is asserted despite Derrida's earlier expression of adherence to Kristeva's notion of 'signifying practice' in a 1971 interview published in *Positions.* Derrida says:

> In order to define . . . *différance* . . . I have always insisted on the value *practice.* Consequently, everywhere, from this point of view, that . . . a general theoretical-practice of the 'signifying practices' is elaborated, I have always subscribed to the task thus defined. I suppose that you are referring to the works of Julia Kristeva.[2]

This indicates that Derrida himself does not concur with an interpretation of *différance* as a non-intervening, inactive neutrality. By claiming that 'practice' is intrinsic to the very 'definition' of *différance,* Derrida is suggesting that the dislocations and disjunctions that *différance* enacts within theory constitute an opening onto practice.

In the discussion that followed Derrida's reading of the paper '*Différance*' at the Sorbonne in 1968, Lucien Goldmann goes so far as to equate *différance* with praxis. He says:

> [T]he words difference and *différance* . . . seem to me to correspond fairly closely to Marxist concepts of theory and praxis. . . . [T]o say that all theory is connected . . . to praxis and derives from it, or indeed, to say that difference presupposes *différance,* do not appear to me to be . . . entirely different claims. For Marx, all knowledge . . . derives from praxis, which is a detour, an action in time, and implicitly . . . *différance.*[3]

Constituted and established differences are an effect of the generative movement of differentiation and deferral, of *différance*. However, as no subject does the differing, this movement is a praxis without a subject, a notion that Goldmann ultimately finds incoherent.[4] It must be noted that the 'subject' that is supposed to have been abandoned by grammatology is the substantial and present-to-itself autonomous individual agent, which, as we have demonstrated in, among other places, our discussion of Hegel's notion of 'subject', is far from being the only conception of the subject in the history of philosophy. We will come back to the relationship between the notions of subject and praxis later.

Derrida himself, in his later work *The Politics of Friendship*, identifies the word 'praxis', specifically politics as praxis, with a deconstructive conceptual disjuncture. He writes:

[N]o politics has ever been adequate to its concept. . . . [T]his inadequation is not accidental, since politics is essentially a *prâxis*. . . . This inadequation of the concept to itself manifests itself pre-eminently in the order of the political or political practice, unless this order . . . would situate the very place . . . of an inadequation of any concept to itself: the concept of disjunction *qua* the conceptual being of the concept.[5]

Thus, that which is essentially praxis cannot be adequate to its own concept, and this just exemplifies conceptuality as such, which constitutes merely an effacement of the inadequation of all concepts to themselves, an effacement of praxis. Political practice is paradigmatic of the self-inadequacy of conceptuality in general. Praxis manifests itself as a deconstructive intervention and disjuncture within theory. *Différance* is this productive disjuncture.

A genuine praxis, a praxis that affects and changes things as opposed to a mere functioning within the enclosure of presence, is necessarily an intervening manifestation of the productive disjuncture of *différance*. *Différance* is both a disjuncture within the ossified positivity of a reified consciousness and the opening of praxis and history. During 'The Original Discussion of "Différance" (1968)' Derrida says:

Différance is the 'productive' movement of differences, the 'history' . . . of constituted differences. . . . From this point of view, I'm not unaware of what, in a most classical idiom, is called again today the creative or generative activity of man. . . . Translated into classical idiom . . . *différance* would . . . implicate this generative activity. Let us say that *différance* marks it.[6]

Différance refers to 'history' in the sense of the generative acts that constitute and reconstitute synchronic structures of differences, economies of presence.

Just as presence effaces its differential generation, the already constituted configuration of objectivity effaces the act of its constitution. The 'history' that is here effaced is history as *différance*, a 'constitutive history' that involves irreducibly singular acts, meaningless acts that found new configurations of meaningfulness. It is not to be confused with 'history' as a development within the restricted economy of such a configuration. In his *Introduction to Husserl's Origin of Geometry*, Derrida discusses 'constitutive history' in terms of Husserl's project of searching for the constitutive acts, or 'origins', that found particular sciences. Derrida states that the idea of such a search implies the need for a 'constitutive history, a history in which the consideration of facts themselves would become indispensable, because for the first time, as singular historical origin, the instituting fact would be irreplaceable'.[7] Here Derrida refers to Trân-Dúc-Tháo's assertion that Husserl is, in the *Origin of Geometry*, trying 'to ground geometrical truth on human *praxis*',[8] rather than on internal subjective constitutive acts. Trân-Dúc-Tháo, in his book *Phenomenology and Dialectical Materialism*, argues that phenomenology needs to be supplemented with a Marxist praxis philosophy, because subjective constitutive acts are not foundational, but derive, or are transposed, from acts in the more primordial realm of the world of material production. Husserl's *Origin of Geometry* is thus said to hint at a way out of the solipsism of earlier phenomenology.

Radical institutive and constitutive historicity involves a history of irreducibly singular events. The singular alterity of such events is futural as a disjunctive opening within the present; it is thus a precondition of any genuine historical change and therefore of history itself. In his later essay, 'Force of Law' (1989), Derrida writes: '[T]he experience of absolute alterity . . . is the chance of the event and the condition of history.'[9] The present is the effacement of history; history only really occurs as the dissolution of the identity of the present.

In the earlier *Introduction to Husserl's Origin of Geometry* (1962), Derrida similarly argues that history depends on an inherent disjuncture within presence. He writes:

[T]he Living Present . . . is only the maintenance of what indeed must be called the *dialectic* of protention and retention, despite Husserl's repugnance for that word. . . . Without this extraordinary absolute alteration of . . . an absolute Present, without this always renewed originality of an absolute primordiality . . . no history would be possible.[10]

This historical dialectic that simultaneously constitutes and deconstitutes the present is identified with *différance* on the last page of the essay. Derrida writes:

> The impossibility of resting in the simple maintenance [nowness] of a Living Present . . .; the inability to live enclosed in the innocent undividedness [*indivision*] of the primordial Absolute, because the Absolute is *present* only in being *deferred-delayed* [*différant*] without respite, this impotence and this impossibility are given in a primordial and pure consciousness of Difference.[11]

Just as the movement of *différance* generates and includes its own effacement, this dialectic of temporality is also a dialectic between the dialectical and the non-dialectical. Derrida writes:

> We have seen . . . that the movement of primordial temporalization (the ultimate ground of all constitution) was dialectical through and through; and that (as every authentic dialecticity wants) this movement was only the dialectic between the dialectical (the indefinite mutual and irreducible implication of protentions and retentions) and the nondialectical (the absolute and concrete identity of the Living Present . . .)[.][12]

Derrida will soon develop his own repugnance for the word 'dialectic', insisting that it only refer to an appropriative restricted economy, and prohibiting it from referring, as it does in the *Introduction to Husserl's Origin of Geometry*, to the relationship between a restricted economy of presence and a general economy of *différance*. This is already the case in the 1967 essay, 'From Restricted to General Economy', wherein the dialectic is the principal example of a restricted economy, and where Georges Bataille is reprimanded for explaining the transgression of the restricted economy in dialectical terms.[13]

The term 'dialectical' is used by the Derrida of the *Introduction to Husserl's Origin of Geometry* to refer to cases of a mutual dependence of irreconcilable opposites. He refers, in his reading of Husserl, to 'the unity of the noncoincidence and of the indefinite coimplication of the constituted and constituting moments *in the absolute identity* of a Living Present that dialectically projects and maintains *itself*'.[14] A concern with the paradoxical and undecideable (dis)unity ('noncoincidence' *and* 'coimplication') of the constituting act and what it constitutes is maintained throughout Derrida's *oeuvre*. An example of this is the non-legal foundation of legality discussed in 'Force of Law'. This non-legal foundation is expressed using the terms 'force' and 'violence', terms that are used in the same way, i.e. to refer to instituting acts, in Derrida's earlier works of the 1960s. In his essay, 'Force and Signification' (1963), 'force', the constituting act, founds 'form', the constituted structure. The non-coinciding co-implication of force and form are here put forward as the basis of a genuine historicity. Derrida writes:

> The divergence, the *difference* between Dionysus and Apollo, between ardor and structure, cannot be erased in history, because it is not *in* history. It . . . is an original structure: the opening of history, historicity itself. *Difference* does not simply belong either to history or to structure.[15]

The productive difference between the ardour of Dionysian force and the structure of Apollonian form is the precondition of history. The term '*difference*' is here used to refer to what will later be called *différance*, and it is this *différance* itself that does not belong to history, because it *is* historicity. In his later essay, 'Force of Law', Derrida also refers to the relationship between force and form that constitutes historicity. He writes that force, for him, is not substantial:

> [I]t is always a matter of differential force, of difference as difference of force, of force as *différance* or force of *différance* . . .; it is always a matter of the relation between force and form, between force and signification. . . . And that is the whole story, the whole of history.[16]

Différance is implicated in the force, acts and praxis that are the basis of history.

As we have mentioned, a constitutive history, a history of genuine acts and events that institute new configurations, must be distinguished from the use of the word *histoire* ('history') to refer to a description of the empirically observable immanent developments functioning teleologically within an already constituted configuration. That is why from the late 1960s onwards Derrida's use of the word is accompanied by disclaimers and quotation marks which had been absent from his use of the word hitherto. This already constituted configuration, characteristic of the reified consciousness of both ideology and theory, is what Levinas calls *totalité* ('totality'), and, for Levinas, 'history' only exists as totality. Levinas reserves the term *eschatologie* ('eschatology') for that which breaches the enclosure of totality and goes beyond 'history'. He writes: 'Eschatology institutes a relation with being *beyond the totality* or beyond history.'[17] Derrida, in his early essay on

Levinas, 'Violence and Metaphysics' (1964), makes it clear that his own use of the word *histoire* ('history'), in contradistinction to that of Levinas, itself names the breach of totality. Derrida writes that 'history' for him

> is not history in the sense given it by Levinas (totality), but is the history of the departures from totality, history as the very movement of transcendence, of the excess over the totality without which no totality would appear as such. History is not the totality transcended by eschatology, metaphysics, or speech. It is transcendence itself.[18]

This Derridian history, history as *différance*, is the condition of possibility and impossibility of totality, the movement of non-totalizable acts that both found and breach totalities. Such transcendence is history in its most authentically historical form, a radical historicity that itself breaches and goes beyond 'history' in the weak, not fundamentally historical, sense of the word. Derrida writes:

> Is not the beyond-history of eschatology the other name of the transition to a more profound history, to History itself? But to a history which, unable any longer to be *itself* in any original or final *presence*, would have to change its name?[19]

ok - but deal w/ eschatology

History, to be genuinely itself, genuinely historical, must be the differential praxis that makes it impossible for anything to be genuinely itself, a praxis without any teleological reference to an ultimate presence.

Instituting acts and events, irreducibly singular and uniterable, are characterized by 'force' and 'violence', in that they can only occur within a totality as irruptions, not yet appropriated within the totality as anything meaningful and therefore iterable. Such activity is *différance* as praxis, a praxis without teleological reference to presence, and also a praxis without a reference to presence in the form of a substantial and active subject. As we have seen, Goldmann, for one, finds the notion of praxis without a subject to be incoherent. Without a subject there can be movement and happening, but not praxis. Praxis involves some kind of agent, but the instituting acts and events of Derridian radical historicity seem to come from nowhere.

While praxis to be praxis may require a 'subject' of some kind, it is only a certain understanding of the term 'subject', i.e. a substantial, present-to-itself, conscious autonomous agent, that is precluded by the events of a Derridian historicity. We have demonstrated in an earlier chapter how

Hegel's notion of 'subject' refers to an irruption of negativity within substance. We have also mentioned Balibar's dictum that 'the subject *is* praxis', a dictum that avoids the question of what kind of subject praxis is. The Levinasian subject is itself a breach of totality. Levinas refers to it as 'a subjectivity born from the eschatological vision'.[20] Subjectivity is here identified with radical historicity, which makes it closer to *différance* than to a substantial presence. The subject is not an enclosed narcissistic identity suppressive of otherness; it is the opening within the totality and the exposure to otherness itself. Levinas writes: 'It is in order that alterity be produced *in being* that a "thought" is needed and that an I is needed. . . . "Thought" and "interiority" are the very break-up of being and the production . . . of transcendence.'[21] This subjective breach within the totality of positive objectivity and 'history', the exposure to alterity, includes the act of speech, or speech *as* act, in the radically irruptive sense of the word 'act'. Levinas writes:

> Form . . . alienates the exteriority of the other. . . . The life of expression consists in undoing the form in which the existent, exposed as a theme, is thereby dissimulated. The face speaks. The manifestation of the face is already discourse. He who manifests himself . . . at each instant undoes the form he presents.[22]

The speaking subject that breaches totality by exposing itself to the other in the face-to-face relation is alienated by its form, objectified and reified as a 'theme [*thème*]', a phenomenal and theoretical object within totality. To use the terminology of Émile Benveniste, the subject of the *act* of uttering [*énonciation*] is alienated by the subject of the uttered statement [*énoncé*]. Only the subject as an act of speech is exposed to the other and is thus able to breach totality. Levinas's emphasis on the act of speech is problematic for Derrida, because, while the 'act' constitutes an irruption in the restricted economy of totality, the 'speech' is a case of the phonocentrism of the metaphysics of presence. The relationship between Derrida and Levinas will be discussed in the next section. What is important here is that Levinas understands the term 'subject' as referring to the breach of totality and its opening onto alterity through an irreducibly singular and irruptive act.

As has been said, what Derrida calls *sujet* ('subject'), throughout his work, is strictly a self-present substantial identity, a type of object, and an object subject to deconstruction. However, this does not mean that the 'subject-less' events and acts of what we have termed Derridian radical historicity come from some fatalistic Heideggerian 'sending', in other words, from nowhere. On the contrary, in his later work, *The Politics of Friendship*, Derrida claims that behind an event there often lies a decision, albeit a radical and irreducibly singular decision. He writes: 'There is no event . . . that is not as unique, singular and irreplaceable as the decision with which it is frequently associated, notably in politics. . . . Certainly the decision makes the event.'[23] For a decision to be genuinely a decision, to be sovereign and free, it must itself be an irruption in the givenness of positive objectivity, and not merely a functional moment in the operativity of the latter. The manifestation of *différance*, the experience of the undecideability of an aporia, is the precondition of a genuine decision. Derrida writes:

> The crucial experience of the *perhaps* imposed by the undecidable – that is to say, the condition of decision – is not a moment to be . . . suppressed. It continues to constitute the decision as such; . . . it produces it *qua* decision *in and through* the undecidable; there is no other decision than this: decision in the matter and form of the undecidable. . . . [T]he instant of decision must remain heterogeneous to all knowledge as such, to all theoretical or reportive determination, even if it may and must be preceded by all possible science and conscience. The latter are unable to determine the leap of decision without transforming it into the irresponsible application of a programme, hence without depriving it of what makes it a sovereign and free decision. . . . At this point, practical performativity is irreducible to any theorem[.][24]

The decision, or at least the 'instant' of decision, cannot, by definition, be conditioned by any programmatic functionality or determined by any theoretical knowledge. The irreducibility of decision is nothing other than the irreducibility of praxis, or 'practical performativity', to theory.

This Derridian praxis does without a subject only if 'subject' is defined as a substantial decision-maker. There is nothing substantial behind a decision; a decision is itself a rupture of the closed identity of substance. As we have discussed, the 'subject' can be defined otherwise, otherwise than a substantial closed identity. Examples of this other 'subject' include Hegel's subject that is in contradistinction to substance ('spirit' is the unity of the subject and substance opposition), and Levinas's subject that is the opening of the closed totality and the exposure to the other. If the word 'subject' can be legitimately used in these senses then the word can refer to the point of an active disjuncture within totality, substance and the givenness of positive objectivity. It is 'active' because it decides. 'It' is a being that becomes 'subject' through the irruptive force of its own decision. The subject 'consists' not of substance but of differential force. The subject is inherently relational, and so is its 'force'; its force is nothing but the rupturing of the given. As Derridian praxis requires decisions, and the insubstantial but forceful decision-maker can legitimately be called a 'subject', then Lucien Goldmann need not have fretted about the incoherencies of a Derridian subjectless praxis.

Nevertheless, as Derrida insists throughout his work that the term *sujet* ('subject') can only legitimately name a substantial presence-to-itself, the word, for him, is taboo. In 'Force of Law' Derrida writes: '[A] subject can never decide anything: a subject is even that to *which* a decision cannot come or happen . . . [or] . . . affect the essential identity and the substantial presence-to-self that make a subject what it is.'[25] This is a mere terminological argument, as, for Derrida, the decision comes from a passive exposure to the other, a state that Levinas terms *subjectivité* ('subjectivity'). In *The Politics of Friendship* Derrida writes:

> [T]he subjectivity of a subject . . . never decides anything; its identity in itself and its calculable permanence make every decision an accident which leaves the subject unchanged and indifferent. *A theory of the subject is incapable of accounting for the slightest decision.* . . . [S]hould one imagine . . . a 'passive' decision . . .? . . . The passive decision, condition of the event, is always in me, structurally, another event, a rending decision as the decision of the other.[26]

A genuine decision, one that is not just a programmed functioning within the economy of the same, comes from the call of the other. It thus involves a passive receptivity. As it is the 'condition of the event', this passivity is the basis of any genuine act, of any rupture within the closure of the present. The only genuine acts are passive acts. Such 'acts' involve either a loss of the self, a suspension of the ego, a loss of the subject as the condition of its non-functional sovereignty, or a suspension of the identity of the ego and the receptive opening to the other as the condition of the subject that acts, depending on one's terminological preferences.

This passive receptivity is a condition of genuine activity. This loss of the unified subject of theoretical contemplation standing over and against the world as object is a condition of the subject as act, as praxis. It is the performativity of praxis that is at the basis of the passive, i.e. exposed to alterity, moment of decision. Derrida writes in 'Force of Law':

> The instant of decision is a madness . . . because such decision is both hyper-active and suffered [*sur-active et subie*], it preserves something

passive, even unconscious, as if the deciding one was free only by letting himself be affected by his own decision and as if it came to him from the other[,] . . . a decision . . . acting in the night of nonknowledge and nonrule. Not of the absence of rules and knowledge but of a reinstitution of rules that by definition is not preceded by any knowledge or by any guarantee as such. If one were to trust in a massive and decisive distinction between performative and constative . . . one would have to attribute this . . . inherent irreducibility of thoughtlessness and unconsciousness, however intelligent it may be, to the performative structure of 'speech acts' and acts in general[.][27]

This 'performative structure', this inherent praxis, this 'subject' of the decisive act, involves a dissolution of the 'subject' as a self-present closed identity.

Différance is praxis as the dissolution of the reified positivity of a given objectivity. It is the infinite determinability of an instituting activity that constitutes and deconstitutes configurations of objectivity, economies of the proper, preventing the latter from coagulating into the static permanence of absolute presence. It thus effects a de-alienating deconstruction of the givenness of presence, demonstrating that the latter is not a 'givenness' at all, but the effect of acts and decisions.

The Other's Other: The Alienation of Alterity

Praxis as the deconstruction of givenness involves an opening to the event of the irreducibly other. Alienation is the effacement of this instituting activity, of *différance*, through the latter's objectification into the ossified stasis of the closed totality of presence, a presence that always presents itself as given and not as instituted. This is an alienation of subjectivity insofar as subjectivity is the opening to the other. Thus alienation is a suppression of otherness, and de-alienation is then an opening to and welcoming of the other. This may seem paradoxical, as it means that alienation suppresses alienness and de-alienation welcomes the alien. This alienation refers to the alienation of alterity itself, where the always other singularity is alienated into 'the same', the realm of general equivalence. The use of the term 'alienation' here is only as paradoxical as the use of the term 'welcoming' in the phrase 'welcoming the other as other', whereby the term 'welcoming' is compelled to refer to a de-estrangement that does not involve the 'de-othering' of a domesticating appropriation.

However, Adorno, in *Negative Dialectics*, claims that de-alienation involves a suppression of otherness. He writes:

[T]he theory of alienation . . . confuses the need to approach the heteronomous and thus irrational world – 'to be at home everywhere,' as Novalis put it – with the archaic barbarism that the longing subject cannot love what is alien and different, with the craving for incorporation and persecution. If the alien were no longer ostracized, there hardly would be any more alienation.[28]

For Adorno, alienation [*Entfremdung*] is merely a symptom of an aversion to otherness and difference, and would disappear with the overcoming of this aversion. Adorno himself seems to be confusing 'the theory of alienation' with the implications of a popular 'psychological' usage of the word 'alienation', a usage that is entirely detached from the specificities of the Hegelian and Marxian 'theory'.

Levinas, in contrast, uses the word *aliénation* ('alienation') in the Hegelian sense. Levinas is the thinker who most explicitly develops the notion of a non-appropriative relation to alterity. Yet, as we have seen, he writes of the 'form' that 'alienates the exteriority of the other'. 'Form' is the reified objectification of the living, 'expressive', singularity of the other, the rendering of the latter as a 'theme', a phenomenal object of observation. It is the other that is alienated. As we have discussed in our readings of Hegel and Marx, alienation is this objectification of an always other singularity into the closed totality of a positive phenomenality. Levinas uses the term '*aliénation*' in this sense, one that is derived from Hegel's notion of '*Entäußerung*' but that Levinas, nevertheless, uses to convey his own ideas regarding the suppression of otherness.

For Levinas, theoretical knowledge involves such a reification of the other. He writes: 'Philosophy itself is identified with the substitution of ideas for persons, the theme for the interlocutor, the interiority of the logical relation for the exteriority of interpellation.'[29] Such knowledge enacts a reifying de-personalization of the other through the phenomenalizing effacement of the face-to-face relation, a relation inherent to the speech act. Thus it is the person, the other as a person, that can rupture and undermine the closed totality of the phenomenal world of objects, a world of general equivalence and typological classifications, one that suppresses irreducible singularity. Levinas writes: '[I]t is only man who could be absolutely foreign to me – refractory to every typology, to every genus, to every characterology, to every classification – and consequently the term of a "knowledge" finally penetrating beyond the object.'[30] The alienated objectivity effaces the person, who is not an object and is essentially non-phenomenal.

This non-phenomenality of the other gives it a paradoxical relationship to the notion of 'presence'. Derrida writes in 'Violence and Metaphysics' regarding Levinas's concept of the other: '[T]he other . . . must present himself as absence, and must appear as nonphenomenal.'[31] However, such a presentation remains a *present*ation, and such a non-phenomenal appearance remains an appearance. Levinas refers to this non-phenomenal actuality of the other as 'the face'. For Derrida, the Levinasian face is embroiled in the metaphysics of presence. Derrida writes: 'The face is presence, *ousia.*'[32] Certainly, Levinas puts forward his notion of the face and the speech act that opens the face-to-face relation in terms of presence. Levinas writes:

> The face is a living presence; it is expression. . . . The face speaks. . . . [T]o present oneself as other is to signify. . . . To present oneself by signifying is to speak. This presence, affirmed in the presence of the image as the focus of the gaze that is fixed on you, is said. . . . It is preeminently the presence of exteriority.[33]

The linking of presence and speech is suggestive of what Derrida calls the phonocentrism of the metaphysics of presence. However, the phrase 'presence of exteriority' indicates that this 'presence' is something other than the presence of a closed totality, of a restricted economy, something other than presence in the Derridian sense. In Derridian terms 'exteriority' and alterity constitute ruptures and openings within presence. In contrast, for Levinas, the term *présence* ('presence') itself refers to precisely those ruptures that undermine a closed totality. Levinas writes:

> The object of knowledge is always a fact, already happened and passed through. The interpellated one is called upon to speak; his speech consists . . . in being *present*. . . . The present is produced in this struggle against the past. . . . The unique actuality of speech tears it from the situation in which it appears[.][34]

'Presence', in the Levinasian sense, is the irreducibly unique act of speech which transcends the given situation, which transcends 'presence' in the Derridian sense. The reified objectivity of the already there is referred to by Levinas as 'the past', and the rupturing and transcendence of this totality is referred to as 'the present'. In Derridian terms, the former is the closed economy of 'presence', and the latter is the rupture in this 'presence' that Derrida refers to as 'futural'. Thus what Levinas calls 'the past', Derrida calls the 'present', and what Levinas calls 'the present', Derrida calls 'the future'.

The 'presence' involved in the Levinasian speech act is not a case of phonocentrism *qua* logocentrism. It is the *actuality* of the act, not the univocity of the voice. While, for Derrida, phonocentrism as the privileging of speech [*parole*] is a privileging of the voice [*voix*] as the unifying and anchoring principle of meaning, as the *logos*, for Levinas, in contrast, the privileging of speech is the privileging of the *act* that opens the relationship with alterity. The voice is not the act; the voice is that which functions within a written text to restrict the play of meaning and suppress alterity. The voice is an effacement of the act. In the later Derrida's terms, the act is the 'here-and-now' rupturing the presence of the already there. This 'here-and-now' is what Levinas calls 'presence', and the already-there of the Derridian 'present' is identical to the already-there of the Levinasian 'past'. The act of institution is effaced and repressed by the instituted economy, because this act is a force that is extraneous to such an economy and thus can only appear within the economy as a rupture or dislocation. The act is the condition of possibility and impossibility of the presence and propriety of the economy it institutes. The speech act is the condition of possibility and impossibility of the voice, of the restricted economy and closed totality of the *logos*, of the voice as *logos*. In the terms set out in Levinas's later book, *Otherwise than Being or Beyond Essence*, the 'Saying' [*le Dire*], the act of speech, makes possible and undermines the 'Said' [*le Dit*], the utterance objectified, reified, and 'thematized', into the 'past' of a given statement.[35]

The Levinasian speech act and face-to-face relation are thus not a case of the metaphysics of presence, despite Derrida suggesting as such in 'Violence and Metaphysics', but are an effect of the active *différance* of the irreducible 'here-and-now'. Nevertheless, Derrida, in 'Violence and Metaphysics', objects to Levinas's privileging of speech and the face. This is despite Derrida's voicing of adherence to Levinas's proto-deconstructive undermining of the logocentric closure of identity. Derrida writes: '[Levinas's] thought summons us to a dislocation of the Greek logos, to a dislocation of our identity, and perhaps of identity in general.'[36] Derrida argues that as the face-to-face relation of the Levinasian speech act is embroiled in a metaphysical notion of presence it cannot genuinely breach the closed totality that is itself founded on such a notion. The dislocation of identity must be approached formally, and not merely on the empirical basis of an act of face-to-face communication. Derrida writes:

> [T]he attempt to achieve an opening toward the beyond of philosophical discourse, by means of philosophical discourse, . . . cannot possibly succeed *within language* . . . except by *formally* and *thematically* posing *the question of the relations between belonging and the opening,* the *question of closure.* Formally – . . . not in a *logic* . . . but in an inscribed description, in an inscription of the relations between the philosophical and non-philosophical, in a kind of unheard of *graphics,* within which philosophical conceptuality would be no more than a *function.*[37]

Totality can be most effectively ruptured and dislocated by a grammato-logical and deconstructive 'formalism', whereby the inscribed 'form' is demonstrated to formally dislodge and overflow the univocity and closure of the form of presence.

The 'unheard of graphics' that situates philosophical conceptuality within a field it cannot master, i.e. the movement of *différance,* is a formulation and formalization, in grammatological terminology, of the Levinasian notion of the transcendence of totality through the encounter with the other, through the act that opens the relation to radical alterity. The praxis of this unassimilable act takes an aporetic and disjunctive form within that conceptuality. As the Levinasian transcendent relation to alterity is consti-tuted by the face-to-face relation of the speech act, it is a dialogical notion of transcendence. But what would the formalization of dialogism be? Would it not be dialectics? As we have seen, the Derrida of 'From Restricted to General Economy' (1967) regards dialectics as being entirely within philosophical conceptuality, whereas the Derrida of the *Introduction to Husserl's Origin of Geometry* (1962) regards true dialectics as involving the dialectic between the dialectical and the non-dialectical, between philo-sophical conceptuality and the heterology of non-conceptuality. 'Violence and Metaphysics' (1964) is a thoroughly Hegelian critique of Levinas, and formalizes Levinasian dialogical transcendence into the immanent-transcendence of a 'dialectical' disjuncture.

What Derrida objects to in Levinas is the notion of the absolutely other, the other as entirely separate from the same. Levinas writes:

> The metaphysical other is other with an alterity that is not formal, is not the simple reverse of identity, and is not formed out of resistance to the same, but is prior to every initiative, to every imperialism of the same.

It is other with an alterity constitutive of the very content of the other. Other with an alterity that does not limit the same, for in limiting the same the other would not be rigorously other: by virtue of the common frontier the other, within the system, would yet be the same.[38]

This non-formal alterity that is constitutive of its very content and rigorously independent is a substantialist notion of the other. But if the other is itself in itself, in what way is it 'other' at all? Alterity is relational, not substantial. Derrida frames this objection in explicitly Hegelian terms. He writes:

What authorizes him [Levinas] to say 'infinitely other' if the infinitely other does not appear as such in the zone he calls the same . . .? . . . The other, for me, is an ego which I know to be in relation to me as to an other. Where have these movements been better described than in *The Phenomenology of the Mind?* The movement of transcendence toward the other, as invoked by Levinas, would have no meaning if it did not bear within it, as one of its essential meanings, that in my ipseity I know myself to be other for the other. . . . [T]he other cannot be absolutely exterior to the same without ceasing to be other; . . . consequently, the same is not a totality closed in upon itself. . . . How could there be a 'play of the Same' if alterity itself was not already *in* the Same . . .? Without alterity *in* the same, how could the 'play of the Same' occur, in the sense of playful activity, or of dislocation, in a machine or organic totality which *plays* or *works?* . . . The Stranger in the *Sophist* knows that alterity can be thought only as negativity, . . . [and that] the other is always relative[.][39]

The other is the self's other and the self is the other's other, and this is the condition of both the self and the otherness of, and within, the self itself. As we have discussed in the chapter on Hegel, the appropriation of the other in the dialectic of recognition is more of an assertion of the otherness within identity than an 'imperialism of the same', which is to say, more formally, the genuine infinite is the infinite within the finite and not separate from it. The other is the condition of possibility and impossibility of the self; the self's own disjuncture.

Nevertheless, the other is not reducible to being a moment in the constitution of the same, however 'playful' and open the same may be as a result of its own othering through the other. While the encounter with the other is always an encounter of the other with its other, in both directions, a paradoxical symmetry of mutual asymmetry, the other is not reducible to this relation or to relationality as such. Levinas writes:

> [L]anguage accomplishes a relation such that the terms are not limitrophe within this relation, such that the other, despite the relationship with the same, remains transcendent to the same. The relation between the same and the other, metaphysics, is primordially enacted as conversation [*discours*], where the same, gathered up in its ipseity as an 'I,' as a particular existent unique and autochthonous, leaves itself.[40]

However, if the other 'remains transcendent to the same', and transcendent to its relationship with the same, it remains not as 'other', but as a residue of bare singularity, a singularity that is always other when exposed to any relation. It is only this singularity that makes the other genuinely other when encountering the same, but the singular only becomes an 'other' in this encounter.

There is certainly a tension in Levinas's work between substantial and relational portrayals of alterity. The following passage indicates that the other's transcendence of the same does not involve a non-relational conception of alterity:

> A relation whose terms do not form a totality can . . . be produced within the general economy of being only as proceeding from the I to the other, as a *face to face*, . . . irreducible to the distance the synthetic activity of the understanding establishes between the diverse terms, other with respect to one another, that lend themselves to its synoptic operation. The I is not a contingent formation by which the same and the other, as logical determinations of being, can in addition be reflected *within a thought*. It is in order that alterity be produced *in being* . . . that an I is needed. . . . Alterity is possible only starting from *me*.[41]

The face-to-face relation does not form a totality, because it is a non-phenomenal relation. It is not a relation between objects in an economy of objects. It is a relation that cannot be compared to a relation in the form of the 'along side of',[42] a relation between juxtaposed objects presented to an observing consciousness, a consciousness that is itself separate from that relation. For this reason Levinas would object to any formulation of the face-to-face relation as a relation between two others. The other is just as noumenal *qua* non-phenomenal as the 'I' which is the Kantian moral (practical) subject. This means that the relation between the 'I' and the other is a practical one, in the sense of the radical praxis that we have already discussed, the praxis that dissolves and transcends the givenness of an observable phenomenality. The other is alienated by its phenomenal form, and this alienation is overcome in the dissolutive and transcending praxis of the face-to-face speech act. Alterity is only possible 'starting from' the subject of praxis that dissolves phenomenality, and such a subject is only possible as a movement towards alterity. Thus alterity is only possible in a relation, albeit a practical relation that transcends totality.

A relation that rends totality is different to a relation within a relational totality. The non-phenomenal face-to-face relation is radically different to any relation within a phenomenal totality. This relation with the other is a relation with something that remains non-relational within the relation. It is thus a non-relational relation. The other retains its absolute autonomy within the face-to-face relation with the subject. Nevertheless, it is the subject, the 'I', that makes possible the production of alterity 'within being'. Thus totality would never be breached and there would be no alterity within 'being' without the event of the face-to-face encounter, and thus without the non-phenomenal 'subjectivity' that opens the relation to the other, a 'relation' and an opening that rupture the proprietary economy of the same. Hence, for Levinas, the supposed absolute autonomy of the other depends on the subject as act in the face-to-face relation.

Despite this, Derrida, at the end of 'Violence and Metaphysics', reduces the Levinasian position to an assertion of the absolute autonomy of the other in itself. Derrida writes of there being a choice between 'the form of the absolute, speculative logic of Hegel, the living logic which *reconciles* formal tautology and empirical heterology' and 'the form of infinite separation and of the unthinkable, unsayable transcendence of the other'.[43] However, the similarity between Levinas's notion of subjectivity as the condition of the production of alterity in 'being' and Hegel's notion of the reconciliation of subject and substance wherein the subject constitutes an irruption of negativity within substance that prevents substance from being a totality identical to itself indicates that Derrida overplays the distinction between Levinas and Hegel.

It is alterity that is alienated in the reified, objectified and phenomenal positivity of the closed totality of the same, and this alienation is overcome in the non-phenomenal praxis of the face-to-face communicative encounter. Such a de-alienation involves an activity wherein alterity can be produced within the totality. Derrida's reduction of this Levinasian breach of totality to the formalism of a grammatological graphics does not in itself account for the 'subjective' non-phenomenality required for a genuine

encounter with alterity. The latter is, however, not incompatible with
Derrida's notion of *différance* as the praxis of institutive *acts* that make
possible and ultimately impossible any economy of the same.

Irreducibility of the Political

Such a praxis is political insofar as the political is understood as involving
the rupture of the closed homogeneous economy of the neutral. The
absolute suppression of alterity in what Derrida calls a 'totalitarianism
of the neutral'[44] would be an absolute de-politicization. In its deconstructive, denaturalizing, undermining of objectified, positive and present
givenness, the political involves irreducible and foundationless acts and
decisions, irreducible to any programmatic functionality. The political is
polemical and is not just a functioning within the given. For there to be
alterity 'in being' there must be such a 'political' breach of the given, and
for there to be 'the political' in this sense there must be a 'relation' to unassimilable alterity that prevents the totality from ossifying into an apolitical
functionality.

Levinas does not use the word political in this sense; instead he uses the
word 'war'. He writes:

> War . . . presuppose[s] the face and the transcendence of the being
> appearing in the face. . . . Only beings capable of war can rise to peace.
> War like peace presupposes beings structured otherwise than as parts of
> a totality. . . . War presupposes the transcendence of the antagonist; it is
> waged against man.[45]

What Levinas says about 'war' can equally be said about political antagonism, or the antagonism inherent to the notion of the political. Both war
and political antagonism involve what Levinas calls a '*refus de la totalité*'
('refusal of totality').[46] The analogy between war and political antagonism
is used by Carl Schmitt, who regards the notion of the enemy as the condition of the political. Derrida discusses Schmitt's concept of the political in
The Politics of Friendship. He writes: 'Schmittian decisionism . . . is a theory of
the enemy. . . . [T]he figure of the enemy [is the] condition of the political
as such.'[47] The political rests on the irreducibility of antagonism and polemical decision, and any attempt to circumvent antagonism and decision
constitutes a de-politicization.

Derrida regards such a de-politicizing overcoming of antagonism as
undesirable and dangerous. The loss of the 'enemy' would mean the final

closure of totality in an absolute present suppressive of all alterity. He writes: '[L]osing the enemy would not necessarily be progress, reconciliation, or the opening of an era of peace and human fraternity. It would be . . . an unheard-of violence.'[48] It is the *potential* for antagonism, not necessarily antagonism itself, which must be maintained in order to prevent the final and absolute victory of the metaphysics of presence. Interpreting and appropriating Schmitt, Derrida writes:

> [H]ostility is required by method and *by definition* – the very definition of the definition. By the dialecticity or diacriticity, by the necessity of the *topic* as well, which cannot function without the possibility of war. There is no space, nor is there any place – . . . for a definition or for a distinction – without the real possibility of war.[49]

For there to be difference there must be the possibility of antagonism.

For Derrida, the apolitical neutrality of the closed totality of phenomenal objectivity amounts to a kind of reification that must be resisted. He writes:

> [The] subjection of the *who* to the *what* will call for a question on our part. . . . The question will bring with it a protestation. . . . It will signify . . . the principle of a possible resistance to the reduction of the political, even the ethical, to the ontophenomenological.[50]

The rupture of totality that the irreducibly political and ethical enact, the transcendent opening to alterity, requires a de-reifying re-subjectivization, an awakening of the *who* within the *what*. What Derrida is here asserting is not dissimilar to Levinas's notion of non-phenomenal subjectivity as the opening to the other.

The assertion of the irreducibility of antagonism involves an opposition to any political ideology that aims to overcome the political in a final teleo-logical realization of peace and consensus. Simon Critchley claims that Derrida's politically inclined later work involves an attempt to reassert the political against the de-politicizing tendencies within emancipatory politics. Critchley writes:

> [W]hat Derrida is attempting in his recent work is nothing less than a *repoliticization of Marxism*; that is . . . a repoliticization waged against both the subordination of the political to the socio-economic in classical Marxism, but most of all against the gnawing cynicism of neo-liberalism and its disempowering ideology of 'globalization'.[51]

Although this passage in itself suggests that Derrida is merely putting forward a form of Leninism, Derrida's assertion of the political is also aimed against the irenic aims of a certain form of Marxism. The latter involve the realization of peace and consensus in a communist totality of absolute presence bereft of antagonism and alterity.

As we have seen in the chapter on Marx, Derrida regards Marx's notion of the overcoming of alienation and the commodity form as indicating a desire to exorcise the spectrality of *différance* in a realization of total presence. We also discussed how Marxian de-alienation can be interpreted differently, as a freeing of the infinite determinability of 'generic-being' [*Gattungswesen*] in a general an-economy of non-appropriable ends, one which awakens rather than suppresses alterity. The de-alienated condition is not an overcoming of the political. On the contrary, alienation itself constitutes a de-politicization, involving the reification and neutralization of 'subjective' acts and decisions in the positivity and givenness of a closed phenomenal objectivity. De-alienation is a re-subjectivizing rupture of that objectivity, an assertion of the *who* in the *what*, and an opening of the non-objective relation to alterity.

Irreconcilable De-alienation

This notion of the political as inherently polemical and antagonistic is only a specific, and even non-traditional, conception of the political. As we have seen, Derrida claims to be resisting 'the reduction of the political to the ontophenomenological'. Derrida writes that this is 'a powerful reduction – powerful enough . . . to have perhaps constructed the dominant concept of the political'.[52] Levinas uses the word 'political' in this 'dominant' traditional sense. He writes:

> [T]he attention to the Other as unicity and face (which the visibleness of the political leaves invisible) . . . can be produced only in the unicity of an I. . . . It is not to purely subjective events . . . that we appeal to in insisting on the irreducibility of the personal to the universality of the State; we appeal to a dimension and perspective of transcendence as real as the dimension and perspective of the political and more true than it, because in it the apology of the ipseity does not disappear.[53]

Here the political is precisely the realm of a phenomenal totality that elides and effaces the singularity of the other and the 'I'. However, the transcendent relation to alterity is not merely 'subjective', and is as 'real' as the political, because it itself constitutes the basis of a notion of sociality where the non-phenomenal 'ipseity' of the irreducibly singular is maintained in a paradoxical polity of the non-totalizable.

Derrida, in 'Violence and Metaphysics', describes this polity as that of a 'community of nonpresence, and therefore of nonphenomenality'.[54] As with Levinas's notion of the relation to alterity wherein the related are at the same time absolved from the relation in their very otherness, a non-relational relation, this 'community' is a communality wherein the related singularities are separated and absolved from the communal relationality, a community without community. This 'community' is one where the solitary singularity of each of its members is maintained and not abstracted into being a part of a phenomenal totality of symmetrical relations and equivalences. It is a 'community' of *différance*, in that it effectuates the undecideable simultaneity of separation and relation. In the 'Original Discussion of *Différance*', Derrida says: '*Différance* marks the separation and the relation to the entirely other . . . and is never found without solitude.'[55] A community of *différance* involves a common assertion of having nothing in common. It is not a community of equals, but a community of incommensurables. In *The Politics of Friendship*, Derrida writes regarding such a non-relational relationality:

> This is . . . a social bond, a contemporaneity, but in the common affirmation of being unbonded, an untimely being-alone and, simultaneously, in joint acquiescence to disjunction. How can you be together to bear witness to secrecy, separation, singularity? . . . How can a politics of separation be founded?[56]

An answer to these questions is not expected; their function is to announce the unanswerable undecideability within which a Derridian politics must 'operate' (a praxis that 'operates' a productive inoperability). For Derrida, the undecideability demonstrated by paradoxical and contradictory statements, such as 'non-relational relation', is not an irrationalist abdication of philosophical responsibility; on the contrary, it is precisely such undecideability that demands responsible thought. Derrida writes:

> [T]o speak this community without community . . . and thereby . . . to form or to forge it. And to do so in the language of madness that we must use, forced . . . by the most profound and rigorous necessity, to say things as contradictory, insane, absurd, impossible, undecidable as 'X without

X', 'community of those without community', 'inoperative community', 'unavowable community': these untenable syntagms and arguments . . . these inconceivable concepts exposed to the disdain of philosophical good conscience, which thinks it possible to hold out in the shade of the Enlightenment; where the light of the Enlightenment is not thought, where a heritage is misappropriated. For us there is no Enlightenment other than the one to be thought.[57]

The disjuncture within totality, community, identity, relationality, necessary for singularity and alterity not to be effaced, is a disjuncture within meaning itself, hence the need for undecideable assertions.

The non-totalizable community of incommensurables is a community without unity, without any organizing principle of unity, whether that of a generic identity or that of a general equivalence of individual rights. In *The Politics of Friendship*, where the term *amitié* ('friendship') is used to refer to such a non-unified community, Derrida writes (interpreting and appropriating Montaigne's notion of friendship):

The law of friendship . . . would be hetero*geneous* to genericity, to all law – indeed, to all concepts that would not form the genus of the non-genus, the genus of the unique. The unique must be, every time, as is said of genius, a genus: in its own unique respect its own genus.[58]

What is said here about friendship can equally be said about the non-unified community. Jean-Luc Nancy addresses these issues in his book, *The Inoperative Community*. Nancy writes: '[I]t is precisely the immanence of man to man . . . that constitutes the stumbling block to a thinking of community. A community presupposed as having to be one of human beings presupposes that it effect . . . its own essence.'[59] An 'inoperative' community of incommensurable singularities by definition cannot organically 'effect' any essence, whether that essence be the human genus or any other identifying feature. It also cannot be based on the abstract 'rights' of the isolated individual. Nancy writes: 'The individual is merely the residue of the experience of the dissolution of community. . . . It is another, and symmetrical, figure of immanence: the absolutely detached for itself, taken as origin and certainty.'[60] The inoperative community cannot have the genus or the individual as its organizing principle; nor can it have any organizing principle at all.

Irreducible singularity is as indifferent to individual particularity as it is to collective generality. Derrida refers to 'anonymous and irreducible singularities, infinitely different and thereby indifferent to particular difference, to the raging quest for identity'.[61] Identity, whether individual or collective, effaces the radical singularity which is always other. The community of singularities is not a collectivity that exists beyond the sum of its parts. It is not even the sum of its parts, as irreducible singularity is non-numerical, uniterable and non-serializable. Nancy writes: '*Community does not sublate the finitude it exposes. Community itself, in sum, is nothing but this exposition.*'[62] This so-called ex-position of 'finitude' is a Derridian formalization of the Levinasian face-to-face relation that breaches and transcends totality. What Nancy is here calling 'finitude' is singularity, which is what Derrida calls 'infinite singularity' when speaking in a Levinasian rather than Heideggerian idiom. If singularity can be ex-posed this implies that it must be initially posed; but such a positing would be its objectification into a phenomenal totality, and thus the loss of singularity as such. It is not that singularity is ex-posed, but rather that singularity occurs within totality as disjunctive ex-position. The posited or posed is within the economy of phenomenality; ex-position or exposure is a disjuncture of that phenomenality. It may seem contradictory to state that exposure is non-phenomenal, but it must be recalled that, for Levinas, it is the non-phenomenal face of the other that transcends totality, a non-phenomenality that 'undoes the form it presents'. The noumenal dislodges the order of the phenomenal.

As singularity only occurs within totality as ex-position, as the disjuncture involved in a non-relational relation to alterity, singularity as ex-position can be said to be the basis of a genuine community. Community is not the unity of a phenomenal totality; the absolute atomization of an absolute non-community would still be within the unity of such a totality. Singularity does not refer to an isolated substantiality; it is radically meaningless and unidentifiable. It thus occurs as disjuncture within meaning, identity, phenomenality and totality. It occurs as the ex-pository disjuncture that is the non-relational relation to infinite and transcendent alterity. This opening to otherness within identity is thus the precondition of a genuine communality, a communality which is not abstracted from this opening to become another form of closed totality.

To this extent Nancy is right to assert that such a community is nothing other than this opening, this ex-position. However, Nancy, in his book, *Being Singular Plural*, puts forward a notion of the inherent plurality of singularity as the basis of community. He writes:

[A] singularity is indissociable from a plurality. . . . The concept of the singular implies its singularisation and, therefore, its distinction from other singularities. . . . The singular is primarily *each* one and, therefore, also *with* and *among* all the others. The singular is a plural.[63]

This argument is based on the assertion that the 'concept' of singularity is diacritical, meaning that singularity is nothing but its distinction from other singularities. Such a singularity is not the irreducible infinite singularity that Derrida and Levinas refer to. This Nancian singularity is not irreducible; it is reduced to the notion of distinction. The problem is that there is no 'concept' of singularity, unless it is the concept of that which cannot be conceptualized. Singularity is not a distinction or a determinacy; it is pure uniterable uniqueness absolved from all determinations and distinctions, determinations that can only serve to generalize, pluralize and serialize it. As we have seen, Derrida argues that singularity is indifferent to particularity and identity; it is just as indifferent to determinacy and distinction. We have also seen that, for Levinas, the singularity of alterity, far from being 'indissociable from a plurality', is absolutely dissociable from what it is related to and from its relations. The notions of distinction and determinacy belong in the realm of phenomenality and totality, and constitute an elision of singularity. This Nancian singularity is thus a phenomenal particularity and individuality that is inherently relational and plural in the sense of the 'being-with-one-another' of the restricted economy of totality. It is not the radical irreducible singularity of infinite alterity.

Levinas emphasizes the importance of absolute separation, even within the relation to alterity. He writes: 'The same and the other at the same time maintain themselves in relationship and *absolve* themselves from this relation, remain absolutely separated.'[64] Separation is essential for there to be any relation to that which transcends totality, a non-relational relation of the radically separate. He writes:

Separation, effected in the concrete as habitation and economy, makes possible the relation with the detached, absolute exteriority. . . . Separation opens up between terms that are absolute and yet in relation, that absolve themselves from the relation they maintain. . . . Thus the metaphysical relation realizes a multiple existing [un exister multiple] – a pluralism. But this relation would not realize pluralism if the formal structure of relationship exhausted the essence of relationship. . . . The dimension of height . . . indicates a sort of non-homogeneity of space, such that a radical multiplicity, distinct from numerical multiplicity, can here be produced. Numerical multiplicity remains defenseless against totalization. . . . Multiplicity . . . implies an objectivity posited in . . . the impossibility of conjoining the I and the non-I in a whole.[65]

A genuine multiplicity, an infinite non-totalizable multiplicity of uniterable non-serializable irreducible singularities, one thus radically distinct from a homogeneous numerical multiplicity, one that does not coagulate into the abstract and objective unity of a closed totality, requires the non-relational relation of the absolutely separate, a non-objective and transcendent relation that is inherently asymmetrical, where the infinite excess of the other dominates the subject. Separation makes possible the 'relation' with the other that breaches the objective observable totality, a totality characterized by the homogeneous space of symmetrical relations and general equivalence. Separation is necessary for there to be the genuine heterogeneous and qualitative multiplicity or plurality of a community of alterity.

However, Derrida expresses doubt as to whether 'community' is an appropriate term to refer to such a non-totalizable plurality. Derrida writes:

> [T]he aporia requiring the unceasing neutralization of one predicate by another (relation without relation, community without community, sharing without sharing, etc.) calls on significations altogether different from those of the part shared or held in common. . . . This desire . . . which engages me with a singular 'who', . . . this desire of the call to bridge the distance (necessarily unbridgeable) is (perhaps) no longer of the order of the common or the community.[66]

Derrida here equates community with commonality as such. But the two concepts can be rigorously differentiated. Commonality is objective whereas community is intersubjective. Intersubjective relations, radically thought, are non-phenomenal, non-objectifiable communicative acts that open up to infinite alterity. Commonality, the notion of the in common, refers to relations between phenomenally objective entities within a closed totality.

Derrida, however, wishes to drop the term 'community' and retain the term 'friendship', albeit a 'friendship' without anything being in common. Derrida writes:

> [I]f *philía* cannot function without *oikeiótēs*, then little would stand in the way of saying that the central question of this essay . . . would be that . . . of a *philía* without *oikeiótēs*. Ultimately, a friendship without presence, without resemblance, without affinity, without analogy. . . . Is an *aneco-nomic* friendship possible? Can there be any other friendship?[67]

Friendship, properly thought, must be an-economic. The same can be said of community, if community is thought of as an immanently infinitized community of singular alterity whose relationality is each time a totality-breaching praxis. Genuine community can only be intersubjective, and thus non-phenomenal, rather than an objectively phenomenal commonality. Such a non-phenomenal intersubjective community, properly thought, can only be an-economic.

Nevertheless, Derrida is suspicious of the very intersubjectivity of such a communality. Regarding his notion of a 'community' of friends, he refers to '[t]he incalculable equality of these friends of solitude, of the incommensurable subjects, of these subjects without subject and without inter-subjectivity'.[68] As Derrida always regards the subject as a substantial object, he regards intersubjectivity as a relationality among such phenomenal objects. In this passage, Derrida is referring to incommensurable subjects without phenomenal objectivity and thus without objective relationality, an incommensurability that is inherently non-totalizable.

However, intersubjectivity *qua* intersubjectivity, intersubjectivity properly thought, is non-objectifiable. Levinasian intersubjectivity is the asymmetrical relation to absolute alterity. While the term 'asymmetry' is used to convey a dominance of the other over the same in the face-to-face relation, it is actually an attempt to think through the paradoxical notion of an incommensurable relation. It refers to the active incommensurability in which infinite alterity breaches the closed totality of the commensurable. The relation between irreducible singularities is always a relation between the other and the same, which is itself a relation between the infinite and the finite, an asymmetrical and incommensurable relation.

Levinasian non-objectifiable intersubjectivity is based on the irreducibility of the face-to-face relation, a relation that is established through the speech act, through an act of communication. A theoretical 'scientific' consciousness that deals with abstract universalities can only observe phenomenal objectivity, and thus cannot accept the irreducibility of communication. Levinas writes: 'A universal thought dispenses with communication.'[69] However, it is Levinas's view that the irreducible act of communication, addressed to the other, is itself the basis of universality. He writes:

[L]anguage . . . is a primordial dispossession. . . . The generality of the word institutes a common world. The ethical event at the basis of generalization is the underlying intention of language. The relation with the Other . . . is this generalization itself. Generalization is a universalization – but universalization is not the entry of a sensible thing into a no man's land of the ideal . . . but is the offering of the world to the Other.[70]

Language is primarily an act of communication that opens or establishes the relation to alterity. It is this communicative activity that constitutes its universality, not its denotative reference to objects in their idealizable iterability. Levinas also writes:

Language is universal because it is the very passage from the individual to the general, because it offers things which are mine to the Other. To speak is to make the world common, to create commonplaces. Language does not refer to the generality of concepts, but lays the foundations for a possession in common.[71]

The generality of concepts is a reification of the communicative communist praxis inherent to language as act.

Non-objectified intersubjective communicative praxis is also fundamental to the philosophy of Habermas, and contrasting his portrayal of such praxis with that of Levinas is necessary in order to clarify the distinctiveness of a 'deconstructive' theory of de-alienation. Such praxis is put forward by Habermas as a way out of what he regards as the objectifying alienation inherent in the philosophy of the subject, the philosophy centred on a subject's observational knowledge of objects. Habermas writes:

[In] the model of action oriented to reaching understanding . . . the objectifying attitude in which the knowing subject regards itself as it would entities in the external world is no longer *privileged*. Fundamental to the paradigm of mutual understanding is, rather, the performative attitude of participants in interaction. . . . When ego carries out a speech act and alter takes up a position with regards to it, the two parties enter into an interpersonal relationship.[72]

As with Levinasian intersubjectivity, Habermas's notion of intersubjectivity is an attempt to replace the reified phenomenal objectivity of positive givenness with a non-objectifiable interpersonal communicative praxis. However, unlike the Levinasian intersubjective asymmetrical relation of transcendence whereby totality is breached by infinite alterity, Habermasian intersubjectivity is characterized by symmetry, equivalence and mutual understanding. However, it would be inaccurate to identify Habermasian intersubjectivity with an objective relationality suppressive of singularity, because the former is itself put forward as a way of avoiding the reduction of incommensurable subjects to commensurable objects.

For Habermas, the singular incommensurable subjects must mutually understand each other through an empathic substitution. Habermas writes: 'As soon as linguistically generated intersubjectivity gains primacy . . . ego stands within an interpersonal relationship that allows him to relate to himself as a participant in an interaction from the perspective of alter.'[73] Habermas's notion of intersubjective mutual understanding is based on a kind of empathic Diltheyan '*verstehen*'. The substitutability involved in the phrase 'from the perspective of alter' implies that alterity is itself a particular perspective, a mere placeholder, the shoes of the other in which anyone can stand. The formal substitutability of 'the perspective of alter' enables intersubjective relations to be symmetrically reciprocal.

Levinas, however, asserts the incomprehensibility of singular alterity. This incomprehensibility of alterity disables the symmetrical reciprocity of intersubjective relations, but it makes possible an intersubjective 'relation' that transcends and breaches the phenomenal totality in that it is a relation to infinite singular alterity, a relation that is necessarily asymmetrical. Levinasian intersubjective relations do not aim at the transparency of mutual understanding, which is the *telos* of all intersubjective communication according to Habermas. This transparency is in marked contrast to Levinasian transcendent relations, which enable infinite alterity to breach totality and which are characterized not by transparent straightforwardness, but by disjuncture and distortion. Levinas writes:

> The truth of being is not the *image* of being, the *idea* of its nature; it is the being situated in a subjective field which *deforms* vision, but precisely thus allows exteriority to state itself. . . . This curvature of the intersubjective space inflects distance into elevation. . . . One cannot 'allow for' this refraction 'produced' by the subjective field, so as to thus 'correct' it; it constitutes the very mode in which the exteriority of being is effectuated in its truth. . . . This 'curvature' of the intersubjective space in which exteriority is effectuated (we do not say 'in which it appears') as superiority must be distinguished from the arbitrariness of 'points of view' taken upon objects that appear.[74]

Habermas's symmetrical and straightforward (not 'curved') intersubjective space is entirely bound up within a phenomenal totality, with its 'perspectives' of alter and ego, which are 'points of view' on phenomenal objects. Although Habermas's theory of communicative action is an attempt to conceive of a non-objectifiable intersubjectivity, its emphasis on the transparency of mutual understanding prevents it from succeeding in this attempt, as the relating subjects relate phenomenally to each other and are thus rendered commensurable and objectifiable elements of a functional totality, a totality in which infinite alterity is effaced and thus where genuinely intersubjective relations are elided. For Habermas the aim of so-called intersubjective communication is the transparency of mutual understanding, whereas for Levinas the point is not to understand, which is merely to conceptually appropriate and domesticate, but to be affected by the otherness of the other, an otherness that is thus 'effectuated', that intervenes and disrupts the economy of the same. Transcendent effectuation, unlike transparent understanding, constitutes a relationality that maintains singular alterity.

Although, as we have discussed, Levinas argues that the transcendent relation to alterity constitutes the basis of communality and sociality, he is unconcerned with the calculatively practical issues of politics and social organization. Critchley writes:

> [M]y ethical relation to the Other is an unequal, asymmetrical relation to a height that cannot be comprehended, but which, *at the same time*, opens onto a relation to the third and to humanity as a whole – that is, to a symmetrical community of equals.[75]

The Levinasian asymmetrical relation to alterity makes possible the Habermasian symmetrical community that elides that very alterity. They supplement and complement each other heteronomously. The alterity suppressing dangers of Habermasian transparency can be circumvented by such a heteronomous complementarity.

Derrida asserts the 'democratic' necessity of the maintenance of this simultaneous complementarity of these incommensurable orders. Derrida writes:

> There is no democracy without respect for irreducible singularity or alterity, but there is no democracy without the 'community of friends' (*koína ta philōn*), without the calculation of majorities, without identifiable, stabilizable, representable subjects, all equal. These two laws are irreducible one to the other. Tragically irreconcilable and forever wounding.[76]

The maintenance of two incommensurable 'orders' can only be described as 'tragic' and 'wounding' from the standpoint of a closed totality. Derrida claims that a negotiation between these two 'orders' is essential to his politics. He says: '[A] perpetually indispensable negotiation between the singular opening to the impossible which must be safeguarded and the method, the right, the technique, the democratic calculation . . . [t]his is perhaps what politics is!'[77] As the two incommensurable 'orders' that must be maintained are 'irreconcilable', Derrida prefers to refer to a 'negotiation' rather than a 'reconciliation' between them.

However, it is here worth recalling that Hegel's notion of 'spirit' is put forward as a 'reconciliation' of 'subject' and 'substance', a reconciliation where the singular 'subjectivity' which can only manifest itself as a disjuncture within the closed totality of 'substance' is reconciled with that totality itself, a reconciliation that makes possible the living unity-in-diversity of 'spirit'. The word 'living' here refers to the non-reified state of perpetual transcendence. The living totality ('spirit') comes about through the perpetual breach of the reified closed totality ('substance') by the effectivity of subjectivity, a subjectivity which is nothing but the praxis of relating to irreducible alterity, the infinite within the finite, the infinite as the self-transcendence of the finite. This perpetual transcendence is what Derrida calls a perpetual 'negotiation' between incalculable singularity and the closed totality of calculable meaningfulness. Such a negotiation does not only describe a 'politics', it describes the 'living' itself, non-reified and unalienated life.

This perpetual transcendence involves the perpetual separation that makes it possible. It may seem odd that separation is an intrinsic aspect of such a de-alienation, as the word 'separation' ostensibly implies something closer to the word 'alienation' itself. However, for Levinas, separation makes possible not only the transcendent relation to alterity, but also 'habitation' and 'dwelling'. Levinas writes: 'To be separated is to dwell somewhere'.[78] Thus separation is an overcoming of the subject's alienation in the homelessness of the objectified totality. In *Otherwise than Being*, Levinas writes: 'Paradoxically, it is qua *alienus* – foreigner and other – that man is not alienated.'[79] As we have discussed, it is alterity itself that is alienated in the objectifying phenomenal totality. We have also mentioned that Derrida characterizes *différance* as marking separation and the relation to alterity; thus *différance* is itself de-alienation.

Alienation is the objectification of the non-phenomenal singular alterity of the subject into the realm of presence and identity, a phenomenal objectivity that presents itself as a positive givenness. De-alienation is a Derridian perpetual 'negotiation' as a political manifestation of *différance* in a 'politics of separation'. As *Versöhnung* (translated as 'reconciliation') is the Hegelian word for de-alienation, could not such a perpetual negotiation be termed a type of reconciliation? But as this is a 'negotiation' between irreconcilables, reconciliation would appear to be an inappropriate word for such a de-alienation, unless the paradox of a reconciliation of irreconcilables can be admitted, rather like the Levinasian non-relational relation. As we have discussed, Adorno objects to the term 'alienation', because the notion of its overcoming implies the suppression of alterity. However, he does not have any objection to the term *Versöhnung* ('reconciliation'), which he uses to refer to the freeing of the non-identical, the aim of his philosophy. Adorno writes:

> Reconcilement would release the nonidentical, would rid it of coercion
> . . . it would open the road to the multiplicity of different things and
> strip dialectics of its power over them. Reconcilement would be the
> thought of the many as no longer inimical[.][80]

Thus Adorno's notion of 'reconciliation' refers to a genuine qualitative pluralism based on the separation and transcendence of non-identical singular alterity, the very non-totalizable community without commonality that Levinas and Derrida are advocating. Adorno also writes:

> The reconciled condition would not be the philosophical imperialism
> of annexing the alien. Instead, its happiness would lie in the fact that the
> alien, in the proximity it is granted, remains what is distant and different,
> beyond the heterogeneous and beyond that which is one's own.[81]

If this is a 'reconciliation' at all, it is a reconciliation between incommensurables wherein their irreconcilability is maintained in their very reconciliation. What for Adorno is a reconciliation without de-alienation is for us a de-alienation without reconciliation, but the distinction between the two is merely lexical.

Rather than necessarily involving the claim that alienation is essential and insurmountable, deconstruction is itself a development of the critique of alienation and reification. The latter refer to the very givenness and positivity of what Derrida calls the metaphysics of presence, the target of deconstruction. *Différance* is then, when freed from its effacement by presence, the infinite productive determinability of the unalienated condition. *Différance* is praxis in that it enacts a dissolution of the givenness of presence; hence it involves the irruptive and constitutive force of irreducibly singular acts, events and decisions. Such praxis is de-alienating in itself, rather than being a mere means to a de-alienated end. The praxis of the encounter with alterity undoes and breaches the reified objectivity of the closed totality of presence and the same. Thus, despite the etymology, it is this alienation that suppresses alterity, whereas de-alienation makes possible the effectuation and welcoming of the other in its singular otherness. Rather than overcoming all political antagonism in a peaceful de-politicized 'reconciliation', this de-alienation involves the de-totalizing praxis of institutive acts and decisions that in dissolving the neutral positivity of the givenness of the closed totality of presence – a totality which in effacing alterity effaces the potentiality of antagonism – constitutes a re-politicization. The de-alienated social condition is a community without commonality, a community of absolvable strangers, an intersubjective field where singular alterity is maintained and effectuated in the transcendent praxis of communicative encounters. *Différance* is the praxis of perpetual othering and separation, a praxis that thus dissolves the singular-alterity suppressing realm of the same, a praxis that deconstructs the reified, objectified and alienated phenomenal totality of given presence.

Conclusion

It has been demonstrated that not only does the concept of de-alienation not depend on a 'pre-deconstructive' metaphysics of presence, but also that a certain form of this very concept lies at the heart of the ethos of deconstruction itself. Deconstruction does not constitute a debunking of the possibility of de-alienation through a demonstration of the constitutive nature of the always-already alienated. On the contrary, it is itself a critique of the phenomenon of alienation in the latter's most metaphysically fundamental insistence, and in this regard deconstruction opens up the conceptual possibility of a genuine de-alienation. This claim may run directly counter to Derrida's own assertions regarding the relationship between deconstruction and de-alienation, but it is a claim that rests on an argument that is immanently developed through critical analyses of relevant texts within the traditions of both deconstruction and the critique of alienation.

For Derrida, the notion of de-alienation indeed depends on an ontology of presence and 'myth of origins' that involve the elision of fundamental difference. Deconstruction reveals what he calls a fundamental 'ex-appropriation' or 'inalienable alienation', meaning that any 'appropriate', or authentic, unalienated condition is demonstrated to be always already expropriated and alienated. He claims that writing has been traditionally conceived as an externalization, or alienation, of the *logos* as speech, of the full presence of meaning in the voice, and that grammatology reveals the latter as the effect of a generalized and originary writing, or 'arche-writing', an assertion of the always already written nature of meaning. The notion of presence is a myth, one that effaces its nature as a trace and an effect of the movement of differentiation or *différance*. According to Derrida, presence is the basis not only of the notions of substance and identity, but also of consciousness and subjectivity. This is despite the fact that for Kant subjectivity is non-phenomenal and non-substantial. What Derrida calls 'the proper' involves all the trappings of presence, and it is identified with the notions of identity and essence. He rigorously distinguishes the proper from singularity, which he conceives on the basis of alterity and not ownness. This contrasts with Stirner and Heidegger who conceive of ownness, or the proper, on the basis of singularity. Derrida protests against the reduction of the singular 'who' to the general 'what', the latter being the form of identity and propriety. In this way the deconstruction of presence involves a critique of reification, a critique of the reification of the unpresentable non-phenomenalizable singularity of the 'who' into the identifiable form of presence.

In tracing the history of the concept of alienation, we have demonstrated that the conceptualization of de-alienation has largely involved a reference to something other than the restoration of the fullness of presence. While onto-theological and logocentric references to the latter can be discerned in Christian thought and in forms of Platonism, Derrida himself concedes that the Plotinian 'One' can be read otherwise. For Derrida, Rousseau's appropriation of the fall myth provides a paradigmatic example of a modern logocentric reference to a lost natural uncorrupted purity. However, the concept of alienation only really comes into its own, as something distinguishable from the notion of 'the fall', in post-Kantian German philosophy, and it is here that the notion of de-alienation takes on an aspect that is closer to Derridian *différance* than to presence. The non-phenomenal nature of the Kantian subject means that it is not a type of object, which is to say that its phenomenalization, its presentation, would be its objectifying reification, its alienation. Schiller's notion of an unalienated wholeness of personality is founded on the subject's infinite determinability, on not being bound to a particular determination, rather than on the determinate integration and closure of a present identity. Novalis's notion of a return to a oneness with nature and being involves the suspension of the presence and identity of the ego as a 'posited' object. Schelling's notion of the overcoming of alienation in a non-reflective 'wisdom' does not describe a oneness with being as a fullness of presence, but involves apprehending the non-objectifiable absolute subject in a state of objectless 'indifference', a state that in its very indeterminacy is itself the 'eternal freedom' of a productive determinability. Hegel's 'absolute knowing' is not the '*parousia*' of an all-encompassing closure of presence, but is rather the comprehension of the dislocation and overcoming of any positive determination. Feuerbach's unalienated 'human essence' is no unified identity, but is a generic universality as an absence of specific determination, allowing for a free determinability. Stirner regards any identifying determination as an alienation of the unique singularity of the individual. Marx's conceptualization of de-alienation does not involve the closure of a reintegrated presence, but it involves an appropriation of capitalism's openly generic and generative determinability by the individual from whom it had been alienated. Lukács's notion of the overcoming of reified consciousness includes the appropriation of the movement of time, transforming time from the passivity and givenness of presence into the praxis of becoming. In the history of the concept of alienation, contrary to what Derrida claims, presence is more often a characteristic of alienation itself than of de-alienation.

Hegel's notions of alienation and reconciliation are expressions of a system of thought that Derrida himself concedes to be infinitesimally close to his philosophy of difference and deconstruction. This proximity enables an interpretation of Hegelian de-alienation that differs from Derrida's usual reading of it as the '*parousia*' and return of the *logos* to itself in its full presence. The term alienation translates two Hegelian concepts, externalization and estrangement, the latter referring to the conscious experience of the former, while the former is in itself a purely logical concept. The details of Hegel's depictions of the experience of alienation, for example the 'unhappy consciousness' and the realm of 'self-alienated spirit', prefigure many of Derrida's portrayals of the effects of *différance*. However, Hegel's unalienated 'absolute knowing' involves accounting for the philosophical standpoint and consciousness that comprehends the ultimate dislocation and overcoming of all positive determinacies and given identities, a self-theorizing of the possibility of his own deconstructive discourse that is absent from Derrida's work. Hegelianism is a post-Kantian 'critical' philosophy and is thus not the philosophy of origins and expressive organicism that Derrida, his contemporaries, and some of Hegel's commentators largely regard it as. It does not involve the notion of the loss of the immediacy of a plenitude of presence that is regained at a higher level through the immanence of a necessary teleological development, because the 'originary' immediacy is demonstrated to be itself an alienated abstraction, and the dialectical process of the reconfigurations of forms of consciousness takes on the aspect of teleological necessity retroactively, interpreted in this way from the philosophical standpoint that is brought about when the mind overcomes the limits of figuration. The de-alienated condition of spirit occurs when substance becomes at the same time 'subject'. The subject acts as the non-identity-of-substance-with-itself, as negativity. This makes possible the unity-in-diversity of spirit, its 'community of negativity', to use Nancy's term. The Hegelian appropriation of the negativity of otherness is not a violent assimilation, but the othering of the self through its own exposure to alterity. Hegel's system is not the exclusionary totality that Derrida claims it to be, because it itself already involves an understanding of the actuality of infinity whereby any excluded remainder immanently affects any closed configuration. The Hegelian infinite is not the *parousia* of an all-inclusive presence, but is the self-overcoming of the finite, the infinite within the finite, which is the opening of identity to infinite alterity. Hegel's system theorizes itself as the unalienated mind in the form of the actuality of infinity, the consciousness of the immanent overcoming of all finite determination, which is absolute spirit that knows itself as absolute spirit throughout all its manifestations. If Hegel's insistence on the infinite is taken seriously, his conceptualization of de-alienation cannot be interpreted as involving the plenitude of presence as an exclusionary enclosure, for the act of infinity produces the freedom that is the opening to otherness.

Derrida characterizes Marx's conception of de-alienation as involving the desire to 'exorcise' the 'spectral' *différance* of capitalism, of exchange value and the commodity form, and to re-establish the narcissistic enclosure of a real presence. We have demonstrated that, in contrast to Derrida's view, Marx's notion of de-alienation is actually the generation of free determinability within the life of the individual. Universal determinability is realized by capitalism at the general societal level, but this universality is alienated from the individual. In this alienation the universal determinability becomes exchange value and money. Marx's notion of 'generic-being [*Gattungswesen*]' is not a metaphysical essence, but an unessential determinability, unbounded by any specificity. Capitalist social relations and the division of labour alienate the individual from this universal 'generic-being' and restrict her to specific determinacy. Exchange value and capitalist social generality are an objectification of the generality of abstract homogeneous labour, labour as quantitatively measurable labour-time. If this objectification were reappropriated by labour, it would make possible the generation of the unrestricted substitutability and determinability of the individual. Marx's conception of an unalienated form of objectification as the actualization of the individual's free determinability is compatible with the Hegelian notion of the actualizing subjectification of absolute spirit. Marx's conception of de-alienation as involving a 'humanization of nature' does not necessarily entail a narcissistic anthropomorphism. On the contrary, it can be interpreted as involving a freeing of nature from the restricted economy of a utilitarian instrumentality. Unalienated free activity is a liberation from the 'economic' interpretation of labour and production, because it is an end in itself and not a mere means to an end. Thus the Marxian de-alienated condition does not involve, as Derrida claims, a narcissistically enclosed restricted economy, but rather involves, to use Derrida's own term, a general an-economy.

Derridian deconstruction derives from the Heideggerian deconstruction [*Destruktion*] of metaphysics, which itself takes the critique of alienation and reification to an ontological level. Heidegger's deconstruction involves the notion of dismantling the metaphysical structures of thought that effectively formulate the abandonment and oblivion of being. The oblivion of being manifests itself phenomenologically in what Heidegger refers to as 'homelessness', 'inauthenticity' and 'alienation'. Presence is put forward as a principal characteristic of alienation and the oblivion of being. 'Alienation [*Entfremdung*]' involves a 'fixation with the present' that causes a 'never-dwelling-anywhere'. The oblivion of being also takes the form of a reifying objectification of entities, which Heidegger refers to as making entities 'present-at-hand [*Vorhanden*]'. This objectification involves abstracting entities from the totality of living interrelatedness that Heidegger calls 'the world'. It also involves the externalization of *Dasein*'s finite primordial temporality into 'vulgar' public time, a quantifiably measurable endless sequence of present-at-hand moments. For Heidegger, modern technological thinking also manifests the reduction of qualitative uniqueness to quantitative calculability, a reduction of people and things to the orderability of a 'standing-reserve', involving a form of reification that he calls 'enframing'. The authentic relationship to being, for Heidegger, involves a conscious and lived 'finitude', which is the anticipatory futurity of 'being-towards-death'. However, for Heidegger, 'finitude' refers to *Dasein*'s transcendence of entities that makes possible its consciousness of being and non-being, a consciousness that thus takes the form of the self transcendence of finitude, a self-transcendence that Hegel refers to as 'infinite'. Heidegger's individualistic notion of an unalienated 'authenticity' depends on that same transcendent consciousness of finitude, a consciousness that can be demonstrated to depend on a non-individualistic generic and social overcoming of particular immediacy, an overcoming that is most clearly conceptualized by the post-Hegelian notion of 'generic-being'. The 'non-relational' individualism of Heideggerian authenticity is thus ultimately incoherent. Heidegger identifies 'ownness' (what Derrida calls 'the proper') with the singularity of being, and his concept of *Ereignis* refers to an appropriation that is the singular event of being. Derrida interprets all forms of Heideggerian 'ownness' as involving an exclusionary identity, yet the irreducibly singular event of being really amounts to, in its very singularity, a disjuncture of the present in its logocentric enclosure. Thus Heideggerian ownness, freed from the various forms of its objectification and alienation, is closer to Derridian *différance* than Derrida envisaged.

Contrary to Derrida's claim that alienation is essential and insurmountable, deconstruction, in its Derridian and Heideggerian forms, is itself a development of the critique of reification and alienation. The target of deconstruction, the metaphysics of presence, is itself the alienated condition of givenness and positivity. The unalienated condition, in its generative determinability, is itself *différance, différance* freed from the presence that is its own effacement. *Différance* involves the constitutive and irruptive force of singular acts, decisions and events. In this way it is the de-alienating praxis that dissolves the givenness of presence. This dissolution of phenomenal givenness is the basis of Levinas's theorization of the 'intersubjective' encounter with the other. Derridian deconstruction involves a formalization of Levinasian ethics, one that is largely due to Derrida's rejection of the concept of 'subject', a rejection that derives from his Heideggerian misunderstanding of the 'subject' as a kind of object. The encounter with alterity is a praxis that undoes the reified objectivity of the closed phenomenal totality of presence. Thus, as it is the other that is alienated, in that alienation *qua* phenomenalizing objectification suppresses alterity, de-alienation involves an opening to otherness. As de-alienation involves the dissolution of the closed phenomenal totality, a 'neutral' totality which suppresses alterity and thus the possibility of antagonism, it effectively re-politicizes. Thus it does not constitute a de-politicizing reconciliation that neutralizes all antagonism. A deconstructively de-alienated social condition would be a paradoxical 'community' without commonality wherein singularity and alterity would be maintained in an intersubjective praxis characterized by a perpetual transcendence of phenomenality. This de-alienating praxis of perpetual othering and separation that deconstructs the homogeneous enclosure of presence is *différance*.

The Hegelian and Marxian theory of alienation is a post-Kantian philosophical conception that has been misread by many, including Derrida, as if it were the bearer of a pre-critical metaphysics. The latter is the metaphysical odyssey of the departure of the *logos* from its originary identity and plenitude into the fallenness of a world of difference and division, followed by its eventual redemptive return to that originary unity through a teleological and eschatological movement. The German Idealist conception of alienation (from which the Marxian one derives), while employing some of the rhetoric of the fall–redemption model, contains a conceptual content that derives from Kant's notion of practical subjectivity, one which bears no reference to plenitude or identity. The subject of practical reason, in its freedom from mechanistic causality, is noumenal and non-phenomenal, meaning not only that it is unknowable, but also that it is unrepresentable and unidentifiable. It ceases to be what it is, a subject, a free practical agent, if it is phenomenalized, objectified or presented in any way. 'Alienation' is Hegel's term for such a phenomenalizing objectification.

Levinas also uses the term 'alienates' to refer to the realm of phenomenality when he claims that 'form . . . alienates the exteriority of the other'. Thus 'alienation' is when non-phenomenal alterity is 'thematized' and formalized into the phenomenal objectivity that Levinas calls 'totality'. Singular alterity ceases to be singular alterity when it is presented as something with a phenomenal form. It is 'thematized' and objectified. Alterity is only encountered through 'intersubjective' communicative praxis where the 'face . . . undoes the form he presents', a non-objective, non-phenomenal 'relation' that transcends the alienated phenomenal totality.

The rejection of the concept of alienation by Derrida and his contemporaries is an aspect of their critique of the philosophy of the subject, the latter constituting a paradigm that they regard themselves as overcoming. However, their critique of the 'subject' involves a misunderstanding of the use of this term in post-Kantian German philosophy. As we have seen, for Kant and his 'Idealist' successors, the subject is not phenomenal, is not an object. Yet Derrida regards the subject as a substantial and present entity, as a type of object. This mistake stems from Heidegger's understanding of the philosophy of the subject as treating *Dasein* inappropriately as a present-at-hand entity. Thus for Heidegger, *Dasein*'s subjectification is the same as its objectification. But the non-objectifiable and non-phenomenal subject of German Idealism is neither substantial nor present-at-hand. For example, for Hegel, the subject resists figuration and acts as negativity within the totality of 'substance', preventing the latter from ossifying into a fully present-to-itself identity.

Levinas uses the term 'subjectivity' to refer to the exposure to alterity, an exposure that enacts an 'intersubjective' encounter that breaches and transcends the phenomenal totality. This usage ultimately derives from the non-phenomenality of the Kantian practical subject. The subject is every bit as transcendent as Heideggerian *Dasein*.

The non-phenomenal subject is the subject of practical activity, of praxis. Marx, in his 'First Thesis on Feuerbach', identifies praxis with the notion of subjectivity as developed by the German Idealists. The subject is the singular act that breaches the positive givenness of the determined totality of presence. In this way, to use Derridian terms, the subject as praxis is the singular irruption of *différance* within the present. De-alienation is a re-subjectification, a de-objectification that brings the subject back to its non-phenomenal, non-present, undetermined basis.

The subject as praxis is not present and determined; it is futural and determinable. For Heidegger, *Dasein* is 'futural' and the 'present' is the form of its 'alienation'. The presence of the subject's determined objectification constitutes an alienation of its freely determinable becoming. The notion of free determinability is a recurrent feature of traditional characterizations of the unalienated condition, from Schiller to Marx. For example, Marx's notion of generic-being involves a freedom from specific determinacy that makes possible both the universality of consciousness and a limitless determinability where the subject can freely adopt a form, all determinations being provisional and substitutable.

The undetermined determinability of the subject is the condition of its conscious universality. This is a negative and contentless universality, the overcoming of all specific determinacy; thus it is not the universalization of any determination. The overcoming of the isolated immediacy of particular determination is also the condition of the subject's sociality and relationality, a sociality that is itself this self-overcoming and not an overarching identification. The generic awareness of the limits of determination is already their overcoming. The negative universality of consciousness involves sociality and *vice versa*. The alienation of the subject's generic determinability reduces the subject to a rigidly determined specificity while that very determinability becomes a feature of an alien realm of commodities, exchange values and money. In this way the subject's inherent negative universality and sociality is separated from it and projected onto a fetishized phenomenality.

The indetermination of the subject is not only the condition of its universality, but also of its singularity. The irreducible and unconceptualizable uniqueness is alienated by being identified through generally applicable attributes and determinations. As Derrida himself asserts, the singular alterity of the 'who' becomes, when identified and determined, the generality of the 'what'. This reification is a fundamental expropriating alienation, provided that the 'proper' in question is irreducible singularity and not the 'properties' and determinations of an identifiable phenomenality.

The overcoming of all alienated forms, the forms of phenomenal figuration and finite determination, is what Hegel terms the genuine infinite. The latter is the 'form' of the absolute, a non-phenomenalizable non-objectifiable absolute which cannot be represented in any finite figuration, which acts as negativity within all limited conceptions, revealing them to be self-contradictory, and preventing any of them from being absolutized. The genuine infinite is not opposed to and separated from the finite, but is the infinite within the finite, the self-transcendence of finitude. Heidegger uses the term 'finitude' itself to refer to the transcendence of entities in the 'awareness' of being and eventual death, but it is precisely such transcendence, conceived in terms of effectively being the consciousness of finitude, that Hegel terms the 'infinite', the infinite whereby consciousness of a limit is already its transcendence. Levinas uses the term 'infinity' to refer to the transcendence of finite identity in the opening to irreducible alterity. The Hegelian infinite is not an all-encompassing totality that suppresses and excludes alterity, as it is itself the overcoming of finite identity through the exposure to the other, the absolute manifesting itself only as the self-dissolution of 'the same', as always other. De-alienation is the actuality of infinity as the manifestation of a universal 'social' relationality and determinability through the self-transcendence of phenomenal identity.

For such a 'sociality' to avoid itself becoming the alienation of singular alterity in an overarching identification it needs to be conceived in terms of an intersubjective communality without the commonality and unity of an objective and phenomenal totality. Hegel's notion of absolute spirit as a unity-in-diversity which is both substance and subject can be read radically as such a 'community of negativity', but the latter can be clarified through a recourse to certain Levinasian conceptions. Such a community without objective commonality would be an intersubjective field of transcendent communicative 'relations' wherein the subjects are absolvable, communications that transcend the forms of phenomenal objectivity in a non-transparent 'curvature of social space' wherein the singular 'who' of alterity is not reduced to the identifiable 'what' of phenomenality. This 'curvature' is to be contrasted with the Habermasian transparency of intersubjective communicativity, which, while similarly emphasizing intersubjective rather than objective relations, fails to conceive of intersubjectivity radically, in terms of noumenal non-phenomenal and therefore non-transparent subjects.

Instead of 'totality' and 'infinity', Derrida uses the Bataillean terms 'restricted economy' and 'general economy' to refer to the closure of presence and its transcendence respectively. In his later writings the term 'general economy' is replaced by the term 'an-economy'. The system of objects of the phenomenal totality of the present is an economy where meaningfulness and productive purposefulness are maintained through a calculable circulation of references, and thus where everything is a means to an end. That which is an end-in-itself is meaningless and unproductive and thus an-economic. That which is conceived radically as an end-in-itself is a transcendence and breach of the restricted economy and finite totality of presence. For Marx, the subject manifests its unalienated universal and infinitely determinable 'generic being' through 'free conscious activity',

activity done for its own sake. Generic being is alienated by being determined as a means to an end. For Derrida, irreducibly singular acts, decisions and events, transcend the given economy of means and meaning.
The overcoming of the alienated economy of the present makes possible
the exposure to the incomparable singularity of the other, whereby the
other can be treated as an irreducibly unique end-in-itself. Derrida himself
identifies his notion of an-economy with the utopian 'kingdom of ends'
in Kant's moral philosophy.

Interpreting traditional theories of alienation in the light of Derrida's
deconstruction of the metaphysics of presence has led us to the conclusion
that de-alienation is closer to *différance* than to presence. This discovery
has enabled an interpretation of deconstruction itself as a process of
de-alienation.

Notes

Introduction

1 Althusser, L., *For Marx*, trans. Brewster, B. (London: Verso, 1996), p.199.
2 Foucault, M., *The Order of Things: An Archaeology of the Human Sciences*, trans. Sheridan, A. (London: Routledge, 1990), p.327.
3 Ibid., pp.328–330.
4 Derrida, J., *Monolingualism of the Other; or, the Prosthesis of Origin*, trans. Mensah, P. (Stanford: Stanford University Press, 1998), p.25.
5 Derrida, J., *Of Grammatology*, trans. Spivak, G. C. (Baltimore: Johns Hopkins University Press, 1976), p.37.
6 Ibid., p.24.
7 Ibid., p.97.
8 Derrida, J., *Margins of Philosophy*, trans. Bass, A. (Hemel Hempstead: Harvester Wheatsheaf, 1982), p.65.
9 Ibid., p.33.
10 Derrida, J., *Of Grammatology*, p.71.
11 Ibid., p.40.
12 Ibid., p.8.
13 Derrida, J., *Margins of Philosophy*, p.66.
14 Ibid., p.38.
15 Derrida, J., *Of Grammatology*, p.67.
16 Ibid., p.66.
17 Ibid., p.69.
18 Ibid., p.78.
19 Ibid., p.93.
20 Ibid., p.66.
21 Ibid., p.12.
22 Derrida, J., *Margins of Philosophy*, pp.25–26.
23 Ibid., p.40.
24 Derrida, J., *Of Grammatology*, p.26.
25 Ibid., p.68.
26 Ibid.
27 Ibid., p.12.
28 Ibid., p.16.
29 Ibid., pp.68–69.
30 Descartes, R., *Discourse on Method and the Meditations*, trans. Sutcliffe, F. E. (London: Penguin, 1968), p.106.
31 Derrida, J., *Of Grammatology*, p.98.

32 Ibid.
33 Ibid., p.71.
34 Ibid., p.70.
35 Ibid., p.71.
36 Derrida, J., *Specters of Marx: The State of the Debt, the Work of Mourning, and the New International*, trans. Kamuf, P. (London: Routledge, 1994), p.175.
37 Derrida, J., *Of Grammatology*, p.57.
38 Ibid., p.12.
39 Derrida, J., *Margins of Philosophy*, p.158.
40 Ibid., p.172.
41 Derrida, J., *Specters of Marx*, p.90.
42 Ibid., p.73.
43 Derrida, J., *Margins of Philosophy*, p.60.
44 Derrida, J., *Of Grammatology*, p.87.
45 Ibid., p.85.
46 Ibid., p.69.
47 Ibid., p.70.
48 Derrida, J., *Margins of Philosophy*, p.24.
49 Derrida, J., *Of Grammatology*, p.327.
50 Derrida, J., *Specters of Marx*, p.126.
51 Derrida, J., *Writing and Difference*, trans. Bass, A. (London: Routledge, 2001), p.228.
52 Ibid., p.225.
53 Ibid., p.234.
54 Ibid., p.230.
55 Ibid.
56 Ibid.
57 Ibid., p.243.
58 Ibid., p.228.
59 Ibid., p.230.
60 Derrida, J., *Specters of Marx*, p.42.
61 Ibid., p.128.
62 Derrida, J., *Of Grammatology*, p.91.
63 Derrida, J., *Writing and Difference*, p.217.
64 Ibid., p.218.
65 Derrida, J., 'I Have a Taste for the Secret', trans. Donis, G., in Derrida, J. and Ferraris, M., *A Taste for the Secret* (Cambridge: Polity, 2001), p.76.
66 Ibid., pp.76–77.
67 Derrida, J., *Margins of Philosophy*, p.19.
68 Derrida, J., *Specters of Marx*, p.33.
69 Ibid., p.31.
70 Ibid., p.23.
71 Derrida, J., 'I Have a Taste for the Secret', p.21.
72 Derrida, J., *Specters of Marx*, p.169.
73 Derrida, J., 'I Have a Taste for the Secret', p.41.
74 Derrida, J., *Specters of Marx*, p.23.
75 Ibid., p.74.

76 Derrida, J., *Margins of Philosophy*, p.134.

Chapter 1

1 Derrida, J., *Of Grammatology*, trans. Spivak, G. C. (Baltimore: Johns Hopkins University Press, 1976), pp.12–13.
2 Saint Paul, 'Galations 5:4', in The New Testament: Revised Standard Edition (New York: Collins, 1971), p.176.
3 Saint Paul, 'Ephesians 4:18', in The New Testament: Revised Standard Edition, p.182.
4 Saint Paul, 'Ephesians 2:12-16', in The New Testament: Revised Standard Edition, p.181.
5 Saint Paul, 'Philippians 2:5-7', in The New Testament: Revised Standard Edition, p.185.
6 Saint Paul (Sankt Paulus), 'Die Epistel Pauli an die Philipper 2:7' , in Die Bibel: Das Neue Testament, trans. Luther, M. (Frankfurt am Main: J. C. Hermannsche Bibelanstalt, 1824), p.237.
7 Derrida, J., 'A time for farewells: Heidegger (read by) Hegel (read by) Malabou', trans. During, L., preface to Malabou, C., *The Future of Hegel: Plasticity, Temporality and Dialectic* (London: Routledge, 2005), p.xliv.
8 Derrida, J., *Of Grammatology*, p.71.
9 Plotinus, *The Enneads*, trans. MacKenna, S. (London: Penguin, 1991), p.348.
10 Saint Augustine, *The Confessions*, trans. Pine-Coffin, R. S. (London: Penguin, 1961) pp.144–150.
11 Saint Augustine, *The City of God*, trans. Dyson, R. W. (Cambridge: Cambridge University Press, 1998), p.266.
12 Derrida, J., *Of Grammatology*, p.71.
13 Derrida, J., *Margins of Philosophy*, trans. Bass, A. (Hemel Hempstead: Harvester Wheatsheaf, 1982), p.157.
14 Plotinus, *The Enneads*, p.502. (Translation adapted. (MacKenna translates the phrase as 'Shape is an impress from the unshaped'.))
15 Derrida, J., *Margins of Philosophy*, p.66.
16 Ibid., p.172.
17 Steuart, J., *An Inquiry into the Principles of Political Oeconomy* (Edinburgh: Oliver & Boyd, 1966), p.59.
18 Rousseau, J-J., *The Social Contract and Discourses*, trans. Cole, G. D. H. (London: Everyman, 1993), p.185.
19 Ibid., p.196.
20 Rousseau, J-J., *Rousseau, Judge of Jean-Jacques, Dialogues*, trans. Masters, R. D., Kelly, C. and Bush, J. R. (Hanover: University Press of New England, 1990), p.213.
21 Rousseau, J-J., *The Social Contract and Discourses*, p.82.
22 Ibid., p.84.
23 Derrida, J., *Of Grammatology*, pp.97–99.
24 Ibid., p.159.
25 Goethe, J. W., *The Auto-biography of Goethe: Truth and Poetry: From My Own Life*, trans. Oxenford, J. (London: Bell and Daldy, 1867), pp.446–447.

26 Schiller, F., 'Letters on the Aesthetic Education of Man', trans. Wilkinson, E. M. and Willoughby, L. A., in Hinderer, W. and Dahlstrom, D. O. (eds), *Friedrich Schiller: Essays* (New York: Continuum, 1993), p.97.

27 Schiller, F., 'On Naive and Sentimental Poetry', trans. Dahlstrom, D. O., in *Friedrich Schiller: Essays*, p.181.

28 Schiller, F., 'Letters on the Aesthetic Education of Man', p.98.

29 Ibid., pp.99–100.

30 Ibid., p.100.

31 Ibid., p.101.

32 Ibid., p.104.

33 Ibid., p.119.

34 Ibid.

35 Ibid., pp.120–121.

36 Ibid., p.131.

37 Ibid., p.146.

38 Ibid., pp.145–147.

39 Derrida, J., 'I Have a Taste for the Secret', trans. Donis, G., in Derrida, J. and Ferraris, M., *A Taste for the Secret* (Cambridge: Polity, 2001), p.28.

40 Derrida, J., *Monolingualism of the Other; or, The Prosthesis of Origin*, trans. Mensah, P. (Stanford: Stanford University Press), 1998, p.28.

41 Schiller, F., 'Letters on the Aesthetic Education of Man', pp. 162–163.

42 Ibid., p.168.

43 Derrida, J., *Writing and Difference*, trans. Bass, A. (London: Routledge, 2001), p.369.

44 Schiller, F., 'Letters on the Aesthetic Education of Man', p.173.

45 Derrida, J., *Writing and Difference*, p.369.

46 Hölderlin, F., 'Hölderlin and Novalis', quoted and trans. Larmore, C., in Ameriks, K. (ed.), *The Cambridge Companion to German Idealism* (Cambridge: Cambridge University Press, 2000), p.146.

47 Hölderlin, F., 'The Significance of Tragedy', trans. Bird-Pollan, S., in Bernstein, J. M. (ed.), *Classic and Romantic German Aesthetics* (Cambridge: Cambridge University Press, 2003), p.193.

48 Hölderlin, F., 'Being Judgement Possibility', trans. Bird-Pollan, S., in Bernstein, J. M. (ed.), *Classic and Romantic German Aesthetics*, pp.191–192.

49 Hölderlin, F., 'On the Difference of Poetic Modes', trans. Pfau, T., in Pfau, T. (ed.), *Friedrich Hölderlin: Essays and Letters on Theory* (Albany: SUNY Press, 1988), p.84.

50 Novalis, 'Fragments from the Notebooks', trans. Beiser, F. C., in Beiser, F. C. (ed.), *The Early Political Writings of the German Romantics* (Cambridge: Cambridge University Press, 1996), p.90.

51 Novalis, 'Pollen', trans. Beiser, F. C., in Beiser, F. C. (ed.), *The Early Political Writings of the German Romantics*, p.28.

52 Novalis, 'Fragments from the Notebooks', pp.85–86.

53 Novalis, 'Miscellaneous Remarks', trans. Crick, J. P., in Bernstein, J. M. (ed.), *Classic and Romantic German Aesthetics* (Cambridge: Cambridge University Press, 1996), p.205.

54 Novalis, *Fichte Studies*, trans. Kneller, J. (Cambridge: Cambridge University Press, 2003), p.93. (Translation adapted. (Kneller translates '*aufhebe*' as 'sublate'.))

55 Schlegel, F., 'On Incomprehensibility', in Bernstein, J. M. (ed.), *Classic and Romantic German Aesthetics*, p.304.

56 Schlegel, F., 'Ideas', in Bernstein, J. M. (ed.), *Classic and Romantic German Aesthetics*, p.264.

57 Derrida, J., *Of Grammatology*, p.36.

58 Schelling, F. W. J., *The Ages of the World*, trans. Wirth, J. M. (Albany: SUNY Press, 2000), p.7.

59 Schelling, F. W. J., *Ideas for a Philosophy of Nature*, trans. Harris, E. E. and Heath, P. (Cambridge: Cambridge University Press, 1988), p.11.

60 Ibid., p.36.

61 Ibid., p.35.

62 Schelling, F. W. J., *System of Transcendental Idealism*, trans. Heath, P. (Charlottesville: University of Virginia Press, 1993), p.14.

63 Schelling, F. W. J., 'On the Nature of Philosophy as Science', trans. Weigelt, M., in Bubner, R. (ed.), *German Idealist Philosophy* (London: Penguin, 1997), p.234.

64 Ibid., pp.222–223.

65 Ibid., p.220.

66 Ibid.

67 Ibid., p.222.

68 Ibid., p.228.

69 Ibid., p.240.

70 Hegel, G. W. F., *Philosophy of Right*, trans. Dyde, S. W. (Amherst: Prometheus Books, 1996), p.12.

71 Hegel, G. W. F., *Phenomenology of Spirit*, trans. Miller, A. V. (Oxford: Oxford University Press, 1977), p.11.

72 Hegel, G. W. F., *System of Ethical Life and First Philosophy of Spirit*, trans. Harris, H. S. and Knox, T. M. (Albany: SUNY Press, 1979), p.117.

73 Hegel, G. W. F., *Phenomenology of Spirit*, p.10.

74 Derrida, J., *Positions*, trans. Bass, A. (London: The Athlone Press, 1987), p.40.

75 Derrida, J., *Margins of Philosophy*, p.27.

76 Feuerbach, L., *The Essence of Christianity*, trans. Evans, M. (New York: Calvin Blanchard, 1855), p.56.

77 Ibid., p.300.

78 Ibid., p.28.

79 Feuerbach, L., 'Provisional Theses for the Reformation of Philosophy', trans. Dahlstrom, D. O., in Stepelevich, L. S. (ed.) *The Young Hegelians: An Anthology* (New Jersey: Humanities Press International, 1997), p.159.

80 Ibid., p.164.

81 Derrida, J., *Margins of Philosophy*, pp.25–26.

82 Feuerbach, L., 'Provisional Theses for the Reformation of Philosophy', p.168.

83 Feuerbach, L., *The Essence of Christianity*, p.20.

84 Feuerbach, L., 'Provisional Theses for the Reformation of Philosophy', p.168.

85 Stirner, M., *The Ego and Its Own*, trans. Byington, S. (Cambridge: Cambridge University Press, 1995), p.38.

86 Ibid., p.143.

87 Ibid., p.153.

88 Ibid., p.157.

[89] Ibid., p.74.

[90] Ibid., p.81.

[91] Ibid., p.7.

[92] Ibid., pp.147–148.

[93] Ibid., p.148.

[94] Marx, K., *Economic and Philosophic Manuscripts of 1844*, trans. Milligan, M. (Moscow: Progress, 1977), p.90.

[95] Ibid., pp.65–66.

[96] Ibid., p.68.

[97] Marx, K., *Capital: A Critique of Political Economy: Volume 1*, trans. Fowkes, B. (London: Penguin, 1990), p.166.

[98] Ibid., p.165.

[99] Derrida, J., *Specters of Marx: The State of the Debt, the Work of Mourning, and the New International*, trans. Kamuf, P. (London: Routledge, 1994), p.170.

[100] Lukács, G., *History and Class Consciousness*, trans. Livinstone, R. (London: Merlin, 1971), p.87.

[101] Ibid., p.90.

[102] Ibid., p.92.

[103] Ibid., p.163.

[104] Ibid., p.197.

[105] Ibid., p.203.

[106] Ibid., p.204.

[107] Ibid.

[108] Derrida, J., *Of Grammatology*, p.67.

[109] Ibid., p.66.

[110] Marx, K., *Economic and Philosophic Manuscripts of 1844*, p.68.

[111] Mészáros, I., *Marx's Theory of Alienation* (London: Merlin, 1975), p.79.

[112] Marx, K., *Economic and Philosophic Manuscripts of 1844*, p.69.

Chapter 2

[1] Derrida, J., *Margins of Philosophy*, trans. Bass, A. (London: Harvester Wheatsheaf, 1982), p.14.

[2] Derrida, J., *Of Grammatology*, trans. Spivak, G. C. (Baltimore: Johns Hopkins University Press, 1976), p.26.

[3] Derrida, J., *Margins of Philosophy*, p.14.

[4] Derrida, J., *Positions*, trans. Bass, A. (London: The Athlone Press, 1987), p.43.

[5] Ibid., p.40.

[6] Ibid., p.44.

[7] Ibid., p.41.

[8] Hegel, G. W. F., *Phenomenology of Spirit*, trans. Miller, A. V. (Oxford: Oxford University Press, 1977), p.21.

[9] Ibid., p.124.

[10] Ibid., p.125.

[11] Ibid., p.124.

[12] Ibid., p.127.

13 Derrida, J., *Margins of Philosophy*, p.27.
14 Hegel, G. W. F., *Phenomenology of Spirit*, p.317.
15 Ibid., p.314.
16 Ibid., p.317.
17 Lukács, G., *The Young Hegel: Studies in the Relations between Dialectics and Economics*, trans. Livingstone, R. (London: Merlin Press, 1975), pp.18–19.
18 Ibid., p.22.
19 Ibid., p.314.
20 Hegel, G. W. F., *Phenomenology of Spirit*, p.294.
21 Lukács, G., *The Young Hegel*, p.538.
22 Rosen, S., *G .W. F. Hegel: An Introduction to the Science of Wisdom* (South Bend: St. Augustine's Press, 2000), p.173.
23 Ibid., p.223.
24 Ibid., p.281.
25 Rose, G., *Hegel: Contra Sociology* (London: The Athlone Press, 1981), p.164.
26 Ibid., p.219.
27 Hegel, G. W. F., *Phenomenology of Spirit*, p.493.
28 Lukács, G., *The Young Hegel*, p.494.
29 Ibid., p.487.
30 Hegel, G. W. F., *Phenomenology of Spirit*, p.21.
31 Sussman, H., 'Hegel, *Glas*, and the Broader Modernity', in Barnett, S. (ed.), *Hegel After Derrida* (London: Routledge, 1998), p.261.
32 Lukács, G., *The Young Hegel*, p.538.
33 Ibid., p.527.
34 Hegel, G. W. F., 'The Difference between Fichte's and Schelling's System of Philosophy', trans. Cerf, W. and Harris, H. S., in Bubner, R. (ed.), *German Idealist Philosophy* (London: Penguin, 1997), p.266.
35 Ibid., p.264.
36 Hegel, G. W. F., *Phenomenology of Spirit*, p.2.
37 Ibid., pp.18–19.
38 Ibid., p.20.
39 Derrida, J., *Glas*, trans. Leavey Jr., J. P. and Rand, R. (Lincoln: University of Nebraska Press, 1986), p.28.
40 Hegel, G. W. F., *Lectures on the Philosophy of Religion: Volume III: The Consummate Religion*, trans. Brown, R. F., Hodgson, P. C. and Stewart, J. M. (Berkeley: University of California Press, 1985), p.100.
41 Taylor, C., *Hegel and Modern Society* (Cambridge: Cambridge University Press, 1979), p.67.
42 Ibid., p.69.
43 Hegel, G. W. F., *Phenomenology of Spirit*, p.10.
44 Gasché, R., *Inventions of Difference: On Jacques Derrida* (Cambridge, MA: Harvard University Press, 1994), p.203.
45 Lukács, G., *The Young Hegel*, p.546.
46 Žižek, S., *For They Know Not What They Do: Enjoyment as a Political Factor* (London: Verso, 1991), p.129.
47 Ibid., p.130.

48 Hegel, G. W. F., *Philosophy of Right*, trans. Dyde, S. W. (Amherst: Prometheus Books, 1996), p.xxx.
49 Žižek, S., *For They Know Not What They Do*, p.214.
50 Derrida, J., *Glas*, p.84.
51 Ibid.
52 Ibid.
53 Taylor, C., *Hegel and Modern Society*, p.31.
54 Nancy, J-L., *Hegel: The Restlessness of the Negative*, trans. Smith, J. and Miller, S. (Minneapolis: University of Minnesota Press, 2002), p.9.
55 Hegel, G. W. F., *The Encyclopaedia Logic: Part I of the Encyclopaedia of Philosophical Sciences*, trans. Geraets, T. F., Suchting, W. A. and Harris, H. S. (Indianapolis: Hackett Publishing Company, 1991), p.41.
56 Hegel, G. W. F., *Phenomenology of Spirit*, pp.54–55.
57 Ibid., p.55.
58 Žižek, S., *For They Know Not What They Do*, p.168.
59 Ibid., p.78.
60 Hegel, G. W. F., *The Encyclopaedia Logic*, p.306.
61 Hegel, G. W. F., *Science of Logic*, trans. Miller, A. V. (New Jersey: Humanities Press International, 1989), p.841.
62 Hegel, G. W. F., *Phenomenology of Spirit*, pp.60–61.
63 Hegel, G. W. F., *Lectures on the Philosophy of Religion: Volume III*, pp.92–93.
64 Ibid., pp.95–96.
65 Hegel, G. W. F., *Phenomenology of Spirit*, p.19.
66 Ibid., p.110.
67 Hegel, G. W. F., *Science of Logic*, pp.835–836.
68 Rosen, S., *G. W. F. Hegel*, pp.220–221.
69 Hegel, G. W. F., *Phenomenology of Spirit*, p.476.
70 Ibid., p.488.
71 Ibid., p.111.
72 Ibid., p.488.
73 Lukács, G., *The Young Hegel*, p.85.
74 Ibid., p.491.
75 Ibid., p.185.
76 Ibid., p.514.
77 Hegel, G. W. F., *Phenomenology of Spirit*, p.10.
78 Ibid., p.493.
79 Lukács, G., *The Young Hegel*, p.515.
80 Hegel, G. W. F., *Phenomenology of Spirit*, p.465.
81 Nancy, J-L., *Hegel: The Restlessness of the Negative*, p.5.
82 Hegel, G. W. F., *Phenomenology of Spirit*, p.21.
83 Žižek, S., *For They Know Not What They Do*, p.131.
84 Nancy, J-L., *Hegel: The Restlessness of the Negative*, pp.42–43.
85 Derrida, J., *Of Grammatology*, pp.68–69.
86 Hegel, G. W. F., *Science of Logic*, p.583.
87 Žižek, S., *For They Know Not What They Do*, p.47.
88 Hegel, G. W. F., *Phenomenology of Spirit*, p.105.

89 Derrida, J., *Margins of Philosophy*, pp.19–20.
90 Derrida, J., *Glas*, p.136.
91 Hegel, G. W. F., *Phenomenology of Spirit*, p.110.
92 Ibid., p.114.
93 Ibid., p.146.
94 Nancy, J-L., *Hegel: The Restlessness of the Negative*, p.62.
95 Derrida, J., *Glas*, p.167.
96 Hegel, G. W. F., *Science of Logic*, p.835.
97 Nancy, J-L., *Hegel: The Restlessness of the Negative*, p.58.
98 Ibid.
99 Derrida, J., *Glas*, p.83.
100 Ibid., p.162.
101 Hegel, G. W. F., *The Encyclopaedia Logic*, pp.105–106.
102 Gasché, R., *The Tain of the Mirror: Derrida and the Philosophy of Reflection* (Cambridge, MA: Harvard University Press, 1986), p.221.
103 Gasché, R., *Inventions of Difference*, p.221.
104 Ibid., p.222.
105 Hegel, G. W. F., *Phenomenology of Spirit*, p.420.
106 Derrida, J., *Glas*, p.240.
107 Ibid., p.241.
108 Hegel, G. W. F., *Phenomenology of Spirit*, p.420.
109 Gasché, R., *Inventions of Difference*, p.194.
110 Hegel, G. W. F., *Phenomenology of Spirit*, p.274.
111 Derrida, J., *Glas*, p.150.
112 Hegel, G. W. F., *Phenomenology of Spirit*, p.278.
113 Hegel, G. W. F., *Philosophy of Right*, pp.291–293.
114 Žižek, S., *For They Know Not What They Do*, p.83.
115 Ibid., p.85.
116 Hegel, G. W. F., *Philosophy of Right*, p.291.
117 Hegel, G. W. F., *Phenomenology of Spirit*, p.11.
118 Nancy, J-L., *Hegel: The Restlessness of the Negative*, p.28.
119 Hegel, G. W. F., *Science of Logic*, p.142.
120 Ibid.
121 Ibid., p.149.
122 Ibid., p.150.
123 Ibid., p.152.
124 Ibid., p.138.
125 Hegel, G. W. F., *Phenomenology of Spirit*, p.106.
126 Hegel, G. W. F., *The Encyclopaedia Logic*, p.149.
127 Ibid., p.151
128 Derrida, J., *Glas*, p.137.
129 Ibid., p.212.
130 Derrida, J., *Margins of Philosophy*, pp.52–53.
131 Hegel, G. W. F., *Science of Logic*, p.149.
132 Nancy, J-L., *Hegel: The Restlessness of the Negative*, p.17–18.
133 Ibid., p.9.

[134] Schlegel, F., *Lucinda and the Fragments*, trans. Firchow, P. (Minnesota: University of Minnesota Press, 1971), p.175.

[135] Derrida, J., *Of Grammatology*, p.36.

[136] Ibid., p.163.

[137] Ibid.

[138] Gasché, R., *Inventions of Difference*, p.141.

[139] Ibid., p.148.

[140] Derrida, J., *Margins of Philosophy*, p.65.

[141] Derrida, J., *Glas*, p.80.

[142] Hegel, G. W. F., 'On the Scientific Ways of Treating Natural Law, on its Place in Practical Philosophy, and its Relation to the Positive Sciences of Right', trans. Nisbet, H. B., in Dickey, L. and Nisbet, H. B. (eds), *Hegel: Political Writings* (Cambridge: Cambridge University Press, 1999), p.137.

[143] Derrida, J., *Glas*, p.215.

[144] Hegel, G. W. F., 'On the Scientific Ways of Treating Natural Law', p.162.

[145] Hegel, G. W. F., *Lectures on the Philosophy of Religion: Vol.III*, p.126.

[146] Hegel, G. W. F., *Philosophy of Mind*, trans. Wallace, W. (Oxford: Oxford University Press, 1971), pp.301–302.

[147] Hegel, G. W. F., *Science of Logic*, p.825.

[148] Hegel, G. W. F., *The Encyclopaedia Logic*, p.303.

[149] Žižek, S., *For They Know Not What They Do*, p.100.

[150] Hegel, G. W. F., *Philosophy of Mind*, p.302.

[151] Hegel, G. W. F., *Phenomenology of Spirit*, p.487.

[152] Lukács, G. *The Young Hegel*, p.509.

[153] Hegel, G. W. F., *Philosophy of Right*, p.xxx.

[154] Žižek, S., *For They Know Not What They Do*, pp.217–218.

[155] Nancy, J-L., *Hegel: The Restlessness of the Negative*, p.27.

[156] Hegel, G. W. F., *Phenomenology of Spirit*, p.491.

[157] Ibid., p.486.

Chapter 3

[1] Marx, K., *Economic and Philosophic Manuscripts of 1844*, trans. Milligan, M. (Moscow: Progress Publishers, 1977), p.90.

[2] Derrida, J., *Specters of Marx: The State of the Debt, the Work of Mourning, and the New International*, trans. Kamuf, P. (London: Routledge, 1994), p.22.

[3] Ibid., p.126.

[4] Ibid., p.170.

[5] Ibid., p.161.

[6] Marx, K., *Grundrisse: Foundations of the Critique of Political Economy (Rough Draft)*, trans. Nicolaus, M. (London: Penguin, 1993), p.456.

[7] Ibid., p.638.

[8] Derrida, J., *Specters of Marx*, p.151.

[9] Ibid., p.160.

[10] Ryan, M., *Marxism and Deconstruction: A Critical Articulation* (Baltimore: Johns Hopkins University Press, 1982), p.91.

[11] Marx, K., *Economic and Philosophic Manuscripts of 1844*, pp.123–124.

[12] Derrida, J., *Given Time: I. Counterfeit Money*, trans. Kamuf, P. (Chicago: University of Chicago Press, 1992), p.158.

[13] Critchley, S., *Ethics-Politics-Subjectivity: Essays on Derrida, Levinas and Contemporary French Thought* (London: Verso, 1999), p.169.

[14] Marx, K., *Economic and Philosophic Manuscripts of 1844*, p.123.

[15] Derrida, J., *Specters of Marx*, p.154.

[16] Marx, K., *Economic and Philosophic Manuscripts of 1844*, p.67.

[17] Ibid., p.68.

[18] Feuerbach, L., *The Essence of Christianity*, trans. Evans, M. (New York: Calvin Blanchard, 1855), pp.19–20.

[19] Ibid., p.20.

[20] Ibid., p.21.

[21] Ibid., p.45.

[22] Ibid., p.26.

[23] Hegel, G. W. F., *Phenomenology of Spirit*, trans. Miller, A. V. (Oxford: Oxford University Press, 1977), pp.108–110.

[24] Marx, K., *Economic and Philosophic Manuscripts of 1844*, p.68.

[25] Wood, A. W., *Karl Marx* (London: Routledge, 2004), p.17.

[26] Ibid., p.19.

[27] Marx, K., *Economic and Philosophic Manuscripts of 1844*, p.68.

[28] Ibid., p.69.

[29] Ibid., p.114.

[30] Ibid., p.118.

[31] Marx, K., *Capital: A Critique of Political Economy: Volume 1*, trans. Fowkes, B. (London: Penguin, 1990), p.618.

[32] Marx, K., *Grundrisse*, p.162.

[33] Ibid., p.542.

[34] Ibid., p.488.

[35] Derrida, J., *Specters of Marx*, p.74.

[36] Marx, K., *Economic and Philosophic Manuscripts of 1844*, pp.92–93.

[37] Marx, K., 'Concerning Feuerbach', trans. Livingstone, R. and Benton, G., in Colleti, L. (ed.), *Early Writings* (London: Penguin, 1992), p.423.

[38] Balibar, É., *The Philosophy of Marx*, trans. Turner, C. (London: Verso, 1995), p.29.

[39] Ibid., pp.29–30.

[40] Ibid., pp.30–32.

[41] Wood, A. W., *Karl Marx*, p.17.

[42] Ryan, M., *Marxism and Deconstruction*, p.48.

[43] Ibid., p.51.

[44] Marx, K., *Economic and Philosophic Manuscripts of 1844*, p.63.

[45] Wood, A. W., *Karl Marx*, p.39.

[46] Marx, K., *Grundrisse*, p.613.

[47] Marx, K., *Economic and Philosophic Manuscripts of 1844*, p.95.

[48] Marx, K., *Grundrisse*, p.611.

49 Marx, K., *Economic and Philosophic Manuscripts of 1844*, pp.63–64.
50 Marx, K., *Grundrisse*, p.831.
51 Ibid., pp.221–222.
52 Ibid., p.226.
53 Ibid., p.832.
54 Marx, K., *Capital: Volume 1*, p.993.
55 Ibid., p.128.
56 Ibid., p.1003.
57 Ibid., pp.164–165.
58 Ibid., p.136.
59 Ibid., p.129.
60 Ibid.
61 Marx, K., *Grundrisse*, p.307.
62 Ibid., pp.322–323.
63 Marx, K., *Capital: Volume 1*, p.991.
64 Marx, K., *Grundrisse*, pp.514–515.
65 Ibid., pp.295–296.
66 Ibid., p.296.
67 Marx, K. and Engels, F., *The German Ideology: Parts I and III*, trans. Lough, W. and Magill, C. P. (New York: International Publishers, 1947), p.22.
68 Marx, K., *Grundrisse*, p.272.
69 Marx, K., *Theories of Surplus Value*, trans. Bonner, G. A. and Burns, E. (London: Lawrence and Wishart, 1951), p.168.
70 Marx, K., 'Concerning Feuerbach', p.421.
71 Marx, K., *Economic and Philosophic Manuscripts of 1844*, p.139.
72 Ibid., p.138.
73 Ibid., p.133.
74 Balibar, E., *The Philosophy of Marx*, p.25.
75 Ibid., p.27.
76 Marx, K., *Grundrisse*, p.496.
77 Ibid., p.498.
78 Marx, K., *Capital: Vol. 1*, p.296.
79 Ibid., p.1054.
80 Marx, K., *Economic and Philosophic Manuscripts of 1844*, p.136.
81 Ibid., p.137.
82 Ibid., p.95.
83 Ibid., p.69.
84 Ibid., p.91.
85 Ibid., pp.94–95.
86 Marx, K., *Grundrisse*, pp.491–492.
87 Marx, K. and Engels, F., *The German Ideology*, p.39.
88 Derrida, J., *Positions*, trans. Bass, A. (London: Athlone, 1987), p.64.
89 Ibid., p.94.
90 Derrida, J., *Specters of Marx*, p.105.
91 Ibid., p.155.
92 Ibid., p.98.
93 Marx, K., *Economic and Philosophic Manuscripts of 1844*, p.68.

94 Ibid., p.96.
95 Ibid., p.95.
96 Derrida, J., *Margins of Philosophy*, trans. Bass, A. (Hemel Hempstead: Harvester Wheatsheaf, 1982), p.19.
97 Marx, K., *Economic and Philosophic Manuscripts of 1844*, p.69.
98 Ibid., p.68.
99 Marx, K., *Capital: Volume 1*, pp.1044–1045.
100 Marx, K., *Capital: A Critique of Political Economy: Volume 3*, trans. Fernbach, D. (New York: Random House, 1981), pp.799–800.
101 Derrida, J., *Specters of Marx*, p.xx.
102 Ibid., p.23.
103 Ibid., p.73.
104 Ibid., p.29.

Chapter 4

1   Lukács, G., *History and Class Consciousness*, trans. Livingstone, R. (London: Merlin Press, 1971), p.xxiv.
2   Adorno, T. W., *The Jargon of Authenticity*, trans. Tarnowski, K. and Will, F. (London: Routledge, 2003), p.88.
3   Heidegger, M., 'Letter on Humanism', trans. Capuzzi, F. A., in Krell, D. F. (ed.), *Basic Writings: Martin Heidegger* (London: Routledge, 1993), p.243.
4   Heidegger, M., *Being and Time*, trans. Macquarrie, J. and Robinson, E. (Oxford: Blackwell, 1978), p.32.
5   Heidegger, M., 'Letter on Humanism', p.242.
6   Ibid.
7   Heidegger, M., *Being and Time*, p.222.
8   Ibid., p.67.
9   Ibid., p.223.
10 Ibid., pp.222–223.
11 Ibid., p.224.
12 Heidegger, M., *Mindfulness*, trans. Emad, P. and Kalary, T. (London: Continuum, 2006), p.240.
13 Ibid., p.132.
14 Heidegger, M., *Being and Time*, p.44.
15 Derrida, J., *Margins of Philosophy*, trans. Bass, A. (Hemel Hempstead: Harvester Wheatsheaf, 1982), p.26.
16 Ibid.
17 Ibid., p.27.
18 Ibid., p.136.
19 Derrida, J., *Positions*, trans. Bass, A. (London: The Athlone Press, 1987), pp.54–55.
20 Heidegger, M., *Being and Time*, p.399.
21 Ibid., p.351.
22 Ibid., p.477.
23 Ibid., p.398.

24 Ibid., p.378.
25 Derrida, J., *Margins of Philosophy*, p.64.
26 Ibid., p.63.
27 Heidegger, M., *Being and Time*, p.170.
28 Pizer, J., *Toward a Theory of Radical Origin: Essays on Modern German Thought* (Lincoln: University of Nebraska Press, 1995), p.157.
29 Heidegger, M., *Mindfulness*, p.108.
30 Ibid., p.69.
31 Ibid., p.124.
32 Heidegger, M., *Contributions to Philosophy (from Enowning)*, trans. Emad, P. and Maly, K. (Bloomington: Indiana University Press, 1999), p.57.
33 Goldmann, L., *Lukács and Heidegger: Towards a New Philosophy*, trans. Boelhower, W. Q. (London: Routledge and Kegan Paul), 1977, p.1.
34 Ibid., p.28.
35 Heidegger, M., *Being and Time*, p.71.
36 Ibid., p.72.
37 Goldmann, L., *Lukács and Heidegger*, p.29.
38 Heidegger, M., *Being and Time*, p.472.
39 Ibid., pp.414–415.
40 Heidegger, M., *Contributions to Philosophy (from Enowning)*, p.98.
41 Ibid., p.93.
42 Ibid., p.95.
43 Heidegger, M., 'The Thing', trans. Hofstadter, A., in Heidegger, M., *Poetry, Language, Thought* (New York: Perennial, 2001), p.165.
44 Heidegger, M., *Contributions to Philosophy (from Enowning)*, pp.80–81.
45 Heidegger, M., *Being and Time*, p.71.
46 Goldmann, L., *Lukács and Heidegger*, pp.12–13.
47 Heidegger, M., 'The Thing', p.178.
48 Dreyfus, H., 'Heidegger's History of the Being of Equipment', in Dreyfus, H. and Hall, H. (eds), *Heidegger: A Critical Reader* (Oxford: Blackwell, 1992), p.180.
49 Heidegger, M., *Being and Time*, p.99.
50 Ibid., p.100.
51 Ibid.
52 Ibid., p.150.
53 Ibid., p.221.
54 Heidegger, M., *Mindfulness*, p.98.
55 Ibid., p.141.
56 Derrida, J., *Of Spirit: Heidegger and the Question*, trans. Bennington, G. and Bowlby, R. (Chicago: University of Chicago Press, 1989), p.20.
57 Heidegger, M., *Contributions to Philosophy (from Enowning)*, p.217.
58 Heidegger, M., *Being and Time*, p.476.
59 Derrida, J., *Of Spirit: Heidegger and the Question*, p.27.
60 Heidegger, M., *Contributions to Philosophy (from Enowning)*, p.264.
61 Lukács, G., *History and Class Consciousness*, p.90.
62 Heidegger, M., *Being and Time*, p.382.
63 Ibid., p.478.
64 Ibid., p.277.

65 Ibid., p.351.
66 Ibid., p.280.
67 Adorno, T. W., *The Jargon of Authenticity*, p.125.
68 Heidegger, M., *Being and Time*, p.419.
69 Heidegger, M., *Introduction to Metaphysics*, trans. Fried, G. and Polt, R. (New Haven: Yale University Press, 2000), p.47.
70 Derrida, J., *Of Spirit: Heidegger and the Question*, p.27.
71 Heidegger, M., *Being and Time*, p.486.
72 Heidegger, M., *Introduction to Metaphysics*, p.48.
73 Ibid., p.207.
74 Heidegger, M., *Contributions to Philosophy (from Enowning)*, p.76.
75 Ibid., p.92.
76 Heidegger, M., *Mindfulness*, pp.12–13.
77 Lukács, G., *History and Class Consciousness*, pp.89–90.
78 Heidegger, M., 'The Question concerning Technology', trans. Lovitt, W., in Krell, D. F. (ed.), *Basic Writings: Martin Heidegger* (London: Routledge, 1993), p.322.
79 Ibid., p.324.
80 Heidegger, M., 'The Way to Language', trans. Krell, D. F., in Krell, D. F. (ed.), *Basic Writings: Martin Heidegger*, p.420.
81 Heidegger, M., 'The Question concerning Technology', p.332.
82 Derrida, J., *Of Spirit: Heidegger and the Question*, p.10.
83 Derrida, J., *Margins of Philosophy*, p.316.
84 Heidegger, M., *Being and Time*, p.62.
85 Ibid., pp.378–379.
86 Ibid., p.379.
87 Heidegger, M., *Mindfulness*, p.73.
88 Adorno, T. W., *The Jargon of Authenticity*, p.129.
89 Heidegger, M., *Being and Time*, p.379.
90 Derrida, J., *Aporias: Dying – Awaiting (One Another at) the "Limits of Truth"*, trans. Dutoit, T. (Stanford: Stanford University Press, 1993), p.55.
91 Heidegger, M., *Contributions to Philosophy (from Enowning)*, p.189.
92 Heidegger, M., *Hegel's Phenomenology of Spirit*, trans. Emad, P. and Maly, K. (Bloomington: Indiana University Press, 1994), p.65.
93 Ibid., p.149.
94 Heidegger, M., *Being and Time*, p.68.
95 Ibid., pp.67–68.
96 Ibid., pp.165–166.
97 Ibid., p.310.
98 Ibid., p.308.
99 Adorno, T. W., *The Jargon of Authenticity*, pp.103–104.
100 Heidegger, M., *Being and Time*, p.309.
101 Derrida, J., *Margins of Philosophy*, p.133.
102 Ibid., pp.131–132.
103 Ibid., p.134.
104 Derrida, J., *Aporias*, p.77.
105 Heidegger, M., *Contributions to Philosophy (from Enowning)*, p.46.

[106] Ibid., pp.331–332.
[107] Heidegger, M., *Mindfulness*, p.108.
[108] Derrida, J., *Margins of Philosophy*, p.27.
[109] Derrida, J., 'I Have a Taste for the Secret', trans. Donis, G., in Derrida, J. and Ferraris, M., *A Taste for the Secret* (Cambridge: Polity Press, 2001), p.12.
[110] Heidegger, M., *Contributions to Philosophy (from Enowning)*, p.183.
[111] Polt, R., 'The Event of Enthinking the Event', in Scott, C. E., Schoenbohm, S. M., Vallega-Neu, D. and Vallega, A. (eds), *Companion to Heidegger's* Contributions to Philosophy (Bloomington: Indiana University Press, 2001), p.101.
[112] Heidegger, M., *Contributions to Philosophy (from Enowning)*, p.41.
[113] Polt, R., 'The Event of Enthinking the Event', p.94.
[114] Heidegger, M., 'The Way to Language', p.422.
[115] Heidegger, M., *Mindfulness*, p.274.
[116] Derrida, J., *Spurs: Nietzsche's Styles*, trans. Harlow, B. (Chicago: University of Chicago Press, 1979), p.119.

Chapter 5

[1] Kristeva, J., *Revolution in Poetic Language*, trans. Waller, M. (New York: Columbia University Press, 1984), p.142.
[2] Derrida, J., *Positions*, trans. Bass, A. (London: The Athlone Press, 1987), pp.89–90.
[3] Goldmann, L. in Derrida, J. et al., 'The Original Discussion of "Différance" (1968)', trans Wood, D., Richmond, S. and Bernard, M., in Wood, D. and Bernasconi, R. (eds), *Derrida and* Différance (Evanston: Northwestern University Press, 1988), p.90.
[4] Ibid., pp.91–92.
[5] Derrida, J., *The Politics of Friendship*, trans. Collins, G. (London: Verso, 2005), pp.114–115.
[6] Derrida, J. et al., 'The Original Discussion of "Différance" (1968)', p.85.
[7] Derrida, J., *Edmund Husserl's* Origin of Geometry: *An Introduction*, trans. Leavey Jr., J. P. (Lincoln: University of Nebraska Press, 1989), p.46.
[8] Trân-Dúc-Tháo, *Phenomenology and Dialectical Materialism*, trans. Herman, D. J. and Morano, D. V. (Boston: Reidel, 1986), p.125.
[9] Derrida, J., 'Force of Law: The "Mystical Foundation of Authority"', trans. Quaintance, M., in Derrida, J., *Acts of Religion* (London: Routledge, 2002), p.257.
[10] Derrida, J., *Edmund Husserl's* Origin of Geometry: *An Introduction*, p.58.
[11] Ibid., p.153.
[12] Ibid., p.143.
[13] Derrida, J., *Writing and Difference*, trans. Bass, A. (London: Routledge, 2001), pp.348–349.
[14] Derrida, J., *Edmund Husserl's* Origin of Geometry: *An Introduction*, p.144.
[15] Derrida, J., *Writing and Difference*, p.34.
[16] Derrida, J., 'Force of Law', pp.234–235.

[17] Levinas, E., *Totality and Infinity: An Essay on Exteriority*, trans. Lingis, A. (Pittsburgh: Duquesne University Press, 1969), p.22.

[18] Derrida, J., *Writing and Difference*, p.146.

[19] Ibid., p.187.

[20] Levinas, E., *Totality and Infinity*, p.25.

[21] Ibid., pp.39–40.

[22] Ibid., p.66.

[23] Derrida, J., *The Politics of Friendship*, p.68.

[24] Ibid., p.219.

[25] Derrida, J., 'Force of Law', p.253.

[26] Derrida, J., *The Politics of Friendship*, p.68.

[27] Derrida, J., 'Force of Law', p.255.

[28] Adorno, T. W., *Negative Dialectics*, trans. Ashton, E. B. (London: Routledge, 1990), p.172.

[29] Levinas, E., *Totality and Infinity*, p.88.

[30] Ibid., p.73.

[31] Derrida, J., *Writing and Difference*, p.128.

[32] Ibid., p.125.

[33] Levinas, E., *Totality and Infinity*, p.66.

[34] Ibid., p.69.

[35] Levinas, E., *Otherwise than Being or* Beyond *Essence*, trans. Lingis, A. (The Hague: Martinus Nijhoff, 1981), pp.6–7.

[36] Derrida, J., *Writing and Difference*, p.102.

[37] Ibid., p.138.

[38] Levinas, E., *Totality and Infinity*, pp.38–39.

[39] Derrida, J., *Writing and Difference*, pp.156–158.

[40] Levinas, E., *Totality and Infinity*, p.39.

[41] Ibid., pp.39–40.

[42] Ibid., p.80.

[43] Derrida, J., *Writing and Difference*, p.192.

[44] Ibid., p.165.

[45] Levinas, E., *Totality and Infinity*, p.222.

[46] Ibid., p.223.

[47] Derrida, J., *The Politics of Friendship*, p.67.

[48] Ibid., p.83.

[49] Ibid., pp.152–153.

[50] Ibid., p.6.

[51] Critchley, S., *Ethics-Politics-Subjectivity: Essays on Derrida, Levinas and Contemporary French Thought* (London: Verso, 1999), p.283.

[52] Derrida, J., *The Politics of Friendship*, p.6.

[53] Levinas, E., *Totality and Infinity*, pp.300–301.

[54] Derrida, J., *Writing and Difference*, p.112.

[55] Derrida, J. et al., 'The Original Discussion of "*Différance*" (1968)', p.85.

[56] Derrida, J., *The Politics of Friendship*, p.55.

[57] Ibid., p.42.

[58] Ibid., pp.182–183.

[59] Nancy, J-L., *The Inoperative Community*, trans. Connor, P., Garbus, L., Holland, M. and Sawhney, S. (Minneapolis: Minnesota University Press, 1991), p.3.
[60] Ibid.
[61] Derrida, J., *The Politics of Friendship*, p.106.
[62] Nancy, J-L., *The Inoperative Community*, p.26.
[63] Nancy, J-L., *Being Singular Plural*, trans. Richardson, R. D. and O'Byrne, A. E. (Stanford: Stanford University Press, 2000), p.32.
[64] Levinas, E., *Totality and Infinity*, p.102.
[65] Ibid., pp.220–221.
[66] Derrida, J., *The Politics of Friendship*, p.298.
[67] Ibid., pp.154–155.
[68] Ibid., p.43.
[69] Levinas, E., *Totality and Infinity*, p.72.
[70] Ibid., pp.173–174.
[71] Ibid., p.76.
[72] Habermas, J., *The Philosophical Discourse of Modernity*, trans. Lawrence, F. (Cambridge: Polity Press, 1987), p.296.
[73] Ibid., p.297.
[74] Levinas, E., *Totality and Infinity*, p.291.
[75] Critchley, S., *The Ethics of Deconstruction: Derrida and Levinas* (Edinburgh: Edinburgh University Press, 1999), p.226.
[76] Derrida, J., *The Politics of Friendship*, p.22.
[77] Derrida, J., 'Politics and Friendship: An Interview with Jacques Derrida', in Kaplin, E. A. and Sprinker, M. (eds), *The Althusserian Legacy* (London: Verso, 1993), p.228.
[78] Levinas, E., *Totality and Infinity*, p.168.
[79] Levinas, E., *Otherwise than Being or Beyond Essence*, p.59.
[80] Adorno, T. W., *Negative Dialectics*, p.6.
[81] Ibid., p.191.

Bibliography

Adorno, T. W., *The Jargon of Authenticity*, trans. Tarnowski, K. and Will, F. (London: Routledge, 2003).

—*Negative Dialectics*, trans. Ashton, E. B. (London: Routledge, 1990).

Althusser, L., *For Marx*, trans. Brewster, B. (London: Verso, 1996).

Augustine, St., *The City of God*, trans. Dyson, R. W. (Cambridge: Cambridge University Press, 1998).

—*The Confessions*, trans. Pine-Coffin, R. S. (London: Penguin, 1961).

—*De Civitate Dei* (Leipzig: Caroli Tavchnitii, 1825).

Balibar, É., *The Philosophy of Marx*, trans. Turner, C. (London. Verso, 1995).

Bataille, G., 'The Notion of Expenditure', trans. Stoekl, A., in Stoekl, A. (ed.), *Visions of Excess: Selected Writings, 1927–1939* (Minneapolis: University of Minnesota Press, 1985), pp.116–129.

Critchley, S., *The Ethics of Deconstruction: Derrida and Levinas* (Edinburgh: Edinburgh University Press, 1999).

—*Ethics-Politics-Subjectivity: Essays on Derrida, Levinas and Contemporary French Thought* (London: Verso, 1999).

Derrida, J., *Aporias: Dying – Awaiting (One Another at) the 'Limits of Truth'*, trans. Dutoit, T. (Stanford: Stanford University Press, 1993).

—*Edmund Husserl's* Origin of Geometry: *An Introduction*, trans. Leavey Jr., J. P. (Lincoln: University of Nebraska Press, 1989).

—'Force of Law: The "Mystical Foundations of Authority"', trans. Quaintance, M., in Derrida, J., *Acts of Religion* (London: Routledge, 2002), pp.228–298.

—*Given Time: I. Counterfeit Money*, trans. Kamuf, P. (Chicago: University of Chicago Press, 1992).

—*Glas*, trans. Leavey Jr., J. P. and Rand, R. (Lincoln: University of Nebraska Press, 1986).

—'I Have a Taste for the Secret', trans. Donis, G., in Derrida, J. and Ferraris, M., *A Taste for the Secret* (Cambridge: Polity Press, 2001), pp.1–92.

—*Margins of Philosophy*, trans. Bass, A. (Hemel Hempstead: Harvester Wheatsheaf, 1982).

—*Monolingualism of the Other; or, The Prosthesis of Origin*, trans. Mensah, P. (Stanford: Stanford University Press, 1998).

—*Of Grammatology*, trans. Spivak, G. C. (Baltimore: Johns Hopkins University Press, 1976).

—*Of Spirit: Heidegger and the Question*, trans. Bennington, G. and Bowlby, R. (Chicago: University of Chicago Press, 1989).

—'Politics and Friendship: An Interview with Jacques Derrida', in Kaplin, E. A. and Sprinker, M. (eds), *The Althusserian Legacy* (London: Verso, 1993), p.228.

—*The Politics of Friendship*, trans. Collins, G. (London: Verso, 2005).

—*Positions*, trans. Bass, A. (London: The Athlone Press, 1987).

—*Specters of Marx: The State of the Debt, the Work of Mourning, and the New International*, trans. Kamuf, P. (London: Routledge, 1994).

—*Spurs: Nietzsche's Styles*, trans. Harlow, B. (Chicago: University of Chicago Press, 1979).

—'A time for farewells: Heidegger (read by) Hegel (read by) Malabou', trans. During, L., preface to Malabou, C., *The Future of Hegel: Plasticity, Temporality and Dialectic* (London: Routledge, 2005), pp.vii–xlvii.

—*Writing and Difference*, trans. Bass, A. (London: Routledge, 2001).

Derrida, J., Wahl, J., Parain, B., Comtesse, G., Hersche, J., Goldmann, L., Philonenko and Kaufmann, W., 'The Original Discussion of "Différance" (1968)', trans Wood, D., Richmond, S. and Bernard, M., in Wood, D. and Bernasconi, R. (eds), *Derrida and* Différance (Evanston: Northwestern University Press, 1988), pp.83–95.

Descartes, R., *Discourse on Method and the Meditations*, trans. Sutcliffe, F. E. (London: Penguin, 1968).

Dreyfus, H., 'Heidegger's History of the Being of Equipment', in Dreyfus, H. and Hall, H. (eds), *Heidegger: A Critical Reader* (Oxford: Blackwell, 1992), pp.173–185.

Feuerbach, L., *Das Wesen des Christentums* (Stuttgart: Reclam, 1971).

—*The Essence of Christianity*, trans. Evans, M. (New York: Calvin Blanchard, 1855).

—'Provisional Theses for the Reformation of Philosophy', trans. Dahlstrom, D. O., in Stepelevich, L. S. (ed.), *The Young Hegelians: An Anthology* (New Jersey: Humanities Press International, 1997), pp.156–171.

Foucault, M., *The Order of Things: An Archaeology of the Human Sciences*, trans. Sheridan, A. (London: Routledge, 1990).

Frank, M., 'Philosophical Foundations of Early Romanticism', trans. Zöller, G., in Ameriks, A. and Sturma, D. (eds), *The Modern Subject: Conceptions of the Self in Classical German Philosophy* (Albany: SUNY Press, 1995), pp.65–85.

Gasché, R., *Inventions of Difference: On Jacques Derrida* (Cambridge, MA: Harvard University Press, 1994).

—*The Tain of the Mirror: Derrida and the Philosophy of Reflection* (Cambridge, MA: Harvard University Press, 1986).

Goethe, J. W., *The Auto-biography of Goethe: Truth and Poetry: From My Own Life*, trans. Oxenford, J. (London: Bell and Daldy, 1867).

Goldmann, L., *Lukács and Heidegger: Towards a New Philosophy*, trans. Boelhower, W. Q. (London: Routledge and Kegan Paul, 1977).

Habermas, J., *The Philosophical Discourse of Modernity*, trans. Lawrence, F. (Cambridge: Polity Press, 1987).

Hegel, G. W. F., 'The Difference between Fichte's and Schelling's System of Philosophy', trans. Cerf, W. and Harris, H. S., in Bubner, R. (ed.), *German Idealist Philosophy* (London: Penguin, 1997), pp.254–288.

—*The Encyclopaedia Logic: Part I of the Encyclopaedia of Philosophical Sciences*, trans. Geraets, T. F., Suchting, W. A., and Harris, H. S. (Indianapolis: Hackett Publishing Company, 1991).

—*Lectures on the Philosophy of Religion: Volume III: The Consummate Religion*, trans. Brown, R. F., Hodgson, P. C., and Stewart, J. M. (Berkeley: University of California Press, 1985).

—'On the Scientific Ways of Treating Natural Law, on its Place in Practical Philosophy, and its Relation to the Positive Sciences of Right', trans. Nisbet, H. B., in Dickey, L. and Nisbet, H. B. (eds), *Hegel: Political Writings* (Cambridge: Cambridge University Press, 1999), pp.102–180.

—*Phänomenologie des Geistes* (Hamburg: Meiner Verlag, 1988).

—*Phenomenology of Spirit*, trans. Miller, A. V. (Oxford: Oxford University Press, 1977).

—*Philosophy of Mind*, trans. Wallace, W. (Oxford: Oxford University Press, 1971).

—*Philosophy of Right*, trans. Dyde, S. W. (Amherst: Prometheus Books, 1996).

—*Science of Logic*, trans. Miller, A. V. (New Jersey: Humanities Press International, 1989).

—*System of Ethical Life and First Philosophy of Spirit*, trans. Harris, H. S. and Knox, T. M. (Albany: SUNY Press, 1979).

—*Wissenschaft der Logik: Die Objektive Logik. Die Lehre vom Seyn* (Berlin: Duncker und Humblot, 1841).

—*Wissenschaft der Logik: Die Subjektive Logik. Die Lehre vom Begriff* (Hamburg: Meiner Verlag, 2003).

Heidegger, M., *Being and Time*, trans. Macquarrie, J. and Robinson, E. (Oxford: Blackwell, 1978).

—*Contributions to Philosophy (from Enowning)*, trans. Emad, P. and Maly, K. (Bloomington: Indiana University Press, 1999).

—*Hegel's Phenomenology of Spirit*, trans. Emad, P. and Maly, K. (Bloomington: Indiana University Press, 1994).

—*Introduction to Metaphysics*, trans. Fried, G. and Polt, R. (New Haven: Yale University Press, 2000).

—'Letter on Humanism', trans. Capuzzi, F. A., in Krell, D. F. (ed.), *Basic Writings: Martin Heidegger* (London: Routledge, 1993).

—*Mindfulness*, trans. Emad, P. and Kalary, T. (London: Continuum, 2006).

—'The Question concerning Technology', trans. Lovitt, W., in Krell, D. F. (ed.), *Basic Writings: Martin Heidegger* (London: Routledge, 1993), pp.307–341.

—*Sein und Zeit* (Tübingen: Max Niemeyer, 1967).

—'The Thing', trans. Hofstadter, A., in Heidegger, M., *Poetry, Language, Thought* (New York: Perennial, 2001), pp.161–184.

—'The Way to Language', trans. Krell, D. F., in Krell, D. F. (ed.), *Basic Writings: Martin Heidegger* (London: Routledge, 1993), pp.393–426.

—*Wegmarken* (Frankfurt: Vittorio Klostermann, 2004).

Hölderlin, F., 'Being Judgement Possibility', trans. Bird-Pollan, S., in Bernstein, J. M. (ed.), *Classic and Romantic German Aesthetics* (Cambridge: Cambridge University Press, 2003), pp.191–192.

—'Hölderlin and Novalis', quoted and trans. Larmore, C., in Ameriks, K. (ed.), *The Cambridge Companion to German Idealism* (Cambridge: Cambridge University Press, 2000), p.146.

—'On the Difference of Poetic Modes', trans. Pfau, T., in Pfau, T. (ed.), *Friedrich Hölderlin: Essays and Letters on Theory* (Albany: SUNY Press, 1988), pp.83–88.

—'The Significance of Tragedy', trans. Bird-Pollan, S., in Bernstein, J. M. (ed.), *Classic and Romantic German Aesthetics* (Cambridge: Cambridge University Press, 2003), p.193.

Kant, I., *Critique of Practical Reason*, trans. Abbot, T. K. (Mineola, NY: Dover Publications, 2004).

—*Critique of Pure Reason*, trans. Meiklejohn, J. M. D. and Politis, V. (London: Everyman, 1993).

—*Groundwork of the Metaphysics of Morals*, trans. Gregor, M. J. (Cambridge: Cambridge University Press, 1998).

Kristeva, J., *Revolution in Poetic Language*, trans. Walter, M. (New York: Columbia University Press, 1984).

Levinas, E., *Otherwise than Being or Beyond Essence*, trans. Lingis, A. (The Hague: Martinus Nijhoff, 1981).

—*Totality and Infinity: An Essay on Exteriority*, trans. Lingis, A. (Pittsburgh: Duquesne University Press, 1969).

Lukács, G., *History and Class Consciousness*, trans. Livingstone, R. (London: Merlin Press, 1971).

—*The Young Hegel: Studies in the Relations between Dialectics and Economics*, trans. Livingstone, R. (London: Merlin Press, 1975).

Marx, K., *Capital: A Critique of Political Economy: Volume 1*, trans. Fowkes, B. (London: Penguin, 1990).

—*Capital: A Critique of Political Economy: Volume 3*, trans. Fernbach, D. (New York: Random House, 1981).

—'Concerning Feuerbach', trans. Livingstone, R. and Benton, G., in Colleti, L. (ed.), *Early Writings* (London: Penguin, 1992), pp.421–423.

—*Economic and Philosophic Manuscripts of 1844*, trans. Milligan, M. (Moscow: Progress Publishers, 1977).

—*Grundrisse: Foundations of the Critique of Political Economy (Rough Draft)*, trans. Nicolaus, M. (London: Penguin, 1993).

—'Ökonomisch-philosophische Manuskripte aus dem Jahre 1844', in *Marx-Engels Werke: Ergänzungsband, Erster Teil* (Berlin: Dietz Verlag, 1968), pp.465–588.

—*Resultate des Unmittelbaren Produktionsprozesses* (Frankfurt: Neue Kritik,1969).

—*Theories of Surplus Value*, trans. Bonner, G. A. and Burns, E. (London: Lawrence and Wishart, 1951).

—'Thesen über Feuerbach', in Marx, K. and Engels, F., *Werke: Band 3* (Berlin: Dietz Verlag, 1978), pp.5–7.

Marx, K. and Engels, F., *The German Ideology: Parts I and III*, trans. Lough, W. and Magill, C. P. (New York: International Publishers, 1947).

Mészáros, I., *Marx's Theory of Alienation* (London: Merlin, 1975).

Nancy, J-L., *Being Singular Plural*, trans. Richardson, R. D. and O'Byrne, A. E. (Stanford: Stanford University Press, 2000).

—*Hegel: The Restlessness of the Negative*, trans. Smith, J. and Miller, S. (Minneapolis: University of Minnesota Press, 2002).

—*The Inoperative Community*, trans. Connor, P., Garbus, L., Holland, M., and Sawhney, S. (Minneapolis: Minnesota University Press, 1991).

Novalis, *Fichte Studies*, trans. Kneller, J. (Cambridge: Cambridge University Press, 2003).

—'Fragments from the Notebooks', trans. Beiser, F. C., in Beiser, F. C. (ed.), *The Early Political Writings of the German Romantics* (Cambridge: Cambridge University Press, 1996), pp.81–92.

—'Miscellaneous Remarks', trans. Crick, J. P., in Bernstein, J. M. (ed.), *Classic and Romantic German Aesthetics* (Cambridge: Cambridge University Press, 1996), pp.203–213.

—*Novalis Schriften: Zweiter Band* (Leipzig: Bibliographisches Institut, 1929).

—'Pollen', trans. Beiser, F. C., in Beiser, F. C. (ed.), *The Early Political Writings of the German Romantics* (Cambridge: Cambridge University Press, 1996), pp.7–31.

Paul, St., 'Die Epistel Pauli an die Philipper' in Die Bibel: Das Neue Testament, trans. Luther, M. (Frankfurt am Main: J. C. Hermannsche Bibelanstalt, 1824), pp.236–239.

—'Galations', 'Ephesians' and 'Philippians', in The New Testament: Revised Standard Edition (New York: Collins,1971), pp.176–187.

—'Προς Γαλάτας', 'Προς Εφεσίους' and 'Προς Φιλιππησίους', in Scrivener, F. H. A. (ed.), The New Testament in the Original Greek (Cambridge: Cambridge University Press, 1894), pp.448–477.

Pizer, J., *Toward a Theory of Radical Origin: Essays on Modern German Thought* (Lincoln: University of Nebraska Press, 1995).

Plōtinos, *Enneades* (Paris: Editore A. Firmin Didot, 1855).

Plotinus, *The Enneads,* trans. MacKenna, S. (London: Penguin, 1991).

Polt, R., 'The Event of Enthinking the Event', in Scott, C. E., Schoenbohm, S. M., Vallega-Neu, D. and Vallega, A. (eds), *Companion to Heidegger's* Contributions to Philosophy (Bloomington: Indiana University Press, 2001), pp.81–104.

Rockmore, T., *Marx After Marxism* (Oxford: Blackwell, 2002).

Rorty, R., *Contingency, Irony, and Solidarity* (Cambridge: Cambridge University Press, 1989).

Rose, G., *Hegel: Contra Sociology* (London: The Athlone Press, 1981).

Rosen, S., *G. W. F. Hegel: An Introduction to the Science of Wisdom* (South Bend: St. Augustine's Press, 2000).

Rousseau, J-J., *Du Contrat Social; ou Principes du Droit Politique* (Amsterdam: Marc Michel Rey, 1762).

—*Rousseau, Judge of Jean-Jacques, Dialogues,* trans. Masters, R. D., Kelly, C., and Bush, J. R. (Hanover: University Press of New England, 1990).

—*The Social Contract and Discourses,* trans. Cole, G. D. H. (London: Everyman, 1993).

Ryan, M., *Marxism and Deconstruction: A Critical Articulation* (Baltimore: Johns Hopkins University Press, 1982).

Schelling, F. W. J., *The Ages of the World,* trans. Wirth, J. M. (Albany: SUNY Press, 2000).

—*Ideas for a Philosophy of Nature,* trans. Harris, E. E. and Heath, P. (Cambridge: Cambridge University Press, 1988).

—'On the Nature of Philosophy as Science', trans. Weigelt, M., in Bubner, R. (ed.), *German Idealist Philosophy* (London: Penguin, 1997).

—*Schellings Sämmtliche Werke: Neunter Band* (Stuttgart: J. G. Gotta, 1861).

—*System of Transcendental Idealism,* trans. Heath, P. (Charlottesville: University of Virginia Press, 1993).

Schiller, F., 'Letters on the Aesthetic Education of Man', trans. Wilkinson, E. M. and Willoughby, L. A., in Hinderer, W. and Dahlstrom, D. O. (eds), *Friedrich Schiller: Essays* (New York: Continuum, 1993), pp.86–178.

—'On Naive and Sentimental Poetry', trans. Dahlstrom, D. O., in *Friedrich Schiller: Essays* (New York: Continuum, 1993), pp.179–260.

—*Schillers Sämmtliche Werke: Zwölfter Band* (Stuttgart: J. G. Gotta, 1833).

Schlegel, F., 'Ideas', trans. Firchow, P., in Bernstein, J. M. (ed.), *Classic and Romantic German Aesthetics* (Cambridge: Cambridge University Press, 1996), pp.261–268.

—*Lucinda and the Fragments*, trans. Firchow, P. (Minnesota: University of Minnesota Press, 1971), p.175.

—'On Incomprehensibility', trans. Firchow, P., in Bernstein, J. M. (ed.), *Classic and Romantic German Aesthetics* (Cambridge: Cambridge University Press, 1996), pp.297–307.

Steuart, J., *An Inquiry into the Principles of Political Oeconomy* (Edinburgh: Oliver & Boyd, 1966).

Stirner, M., *Der Einzige und Sein Eigentum* (Munich: Hanser, 1968).

—*The Ego and Its Own*, trans. Byington, S. (Cambridge: Cambridge University Press, 1995).

Sussman, H., 'Hegel, *Glas*, and the Broader Modernity', in Barnett, S. (ed.), *Hegel After Derrida* (London: Routledge, 1998), pp.260–292.

Taylor, C., *Hegel and Modern Society* (Cambridge: Cambridge University Press, 1979).

Trân-Dúc-Tháo, *Phenomenology and Dialectical Materialism*, trans. Herman, D. J. and Morano, D. V. (Boston: Reidel, 1986).

Wood, A. W., *Karl Marx* (London: Routledge, 2004).

Žižek, S., *For They Know Not What They Do: Enjoyment as a Politcal Factor* (London: Verso, 1991).

Index